1989

A PROSPECT OF ASHRIDGE

Frontispiece: Ashridge in snow.

A Prospect of ASHRIDGE

by

Douglas Coult

PHILLIMORE

1980

Published by
PHILLIMORE & CO. LTD.
London and Chichester

Head Office: Shopwyke Hall,
Chichester, Sussex, England

ISBN 0 85033 360 1

Printed in Great Britain by
UNWIN BROTHERS LIMITED
at the Gresham Press, Old Woking, Surrey

and bound by
THE NEWDIGATE PRESS, LTD.
at Book House, Dorking, Surrey

CONTENTS

LIST OF PLATES

LIST OF TEXT FIGURES

ACKNOWLEDGMENTS

Colour Plates: Plate 1 is reproduced by gracious permission of Her Majesty the Queen; plates 2, 3, 5-8 by kind permission of Lord Brownlow. Mr. John Dyble photographed the frontispiece and plate 9.

Half-tones: Nos. 7, 11, 13 and 14, Lord Brownlow; No. 5, Herts. Records Office; No. 10, Mrs. K. N. Sanecki; No. 12, Illustrated London News; Nos. 16-19, Mr. Eric de Maré; Nos. 1-4, 6 and 9 are taken from Todd's *History*.

Text figures: Nos. 3-9 are reproduced by courtesy of Lord Brownlow.

INTRODUCTION

The approaching seventh centenary of the foundation of Ashridge offers an opportunity to look again not only at its origins, but also at the many changes that have occurred in its fortunes through the years, particularly in the last two centuries.

More than a hundred and fifty years have passed since the publication of the primary source book, *The History of the College of Bonhommes at Ashridge,* by H. J. Todd. While it might seem ungracious to criticise a book so rich in its treatment of the monastic period and so elegant in its presentation of the glories of the 7th Earl of Bridgewater's new mansion, there are undoubted disadvantages in it for the 20th-century reader. One is its scarcity—only 200 copies were printed, mostly as gifts to persons of eminence at the time; the very size of the large paper edition hardly makes for easy armchair reading; and, except for the scholar, the medieval Latin of the Charter and the Statutes of the College of Bonhommes, reproduced without translation, is an obvious impediment to a full appreciation.

In offering a more popular account, the aim has been to preserve the known main structure of past history, and also to assemble some of the more diffuse but relevant facts and events, not previously collected together, which may make for a more complete account of our past. The monastic period is assessed in a rather wider context: the brief use of Ashridge as a residence of the children of Henry VIII provides a backcloth to the uncertainties and unhappiness of their youthful upbringing. The extended occupation of Ashridge as a family residence of several generations of Egertons until the Bridgewater line died out, followed by the much shorter but important period of ownership by the Brownlows, covers more than three hundred years, and necessarily dwells more on personalities than on bricks and mortar. Finally, the reversion of Ashridge in the 20th century to the role of a college might be seen as bringing the wheel back full circle.

Plutarch aptly observed, 'So very difficult a matter is it to trace and find out the truth of anything by history'. This book pretends to be no more than one such attempt.

DOUGLAS COULT

Wimborne, Dorset
August, 1979

ACKNOWLEDGMENTS

MANY PEOPLE have given me help in the preparation of this book. I have very much valued the facilities accorded to me by Mr. P. J. Sadler, Principal of Ashridge Management College, which enabled me to pursue my researches, wherever these led me; also the encouragement and assistance of several of my former colleagues there, especially Mr. W. R. Calvert. I am grateful to Mr. Alan Johnson and to Canon Howard Senar for reading the draft and for their helpful comments.

My particular thanks go to Edward John Peregrine Cust, the 7th Baron Brownlow, and to Lady Brownlow, not only for many personal kindnesses, but for generously allowing me the freedom of the library at Belton, which revealed unsuspected and illuminating riches among long-concealed archives relating to the Egerton family and Lord Brownlow's own family's ownership of Ashridge. Miss Pearl Wheatley, a cousin of the 5th Baron Brownlow, and whose father was agent to the 3rd Earl, has given me invaluable and enthusiastic help by reason of her quite remarkable memory of events at Ashridge during a long period spanning the turn of the century until the early 1920s. Sir Arthur Bryant, C.H., the eminent historian, kindly read the chapter on the former Bonar Law College. Others whom I should mention are: Mr. C. Munn, librarian at Belton; Mr. G. G. Buckingham; Mrs. K. N. Sanecki; Mr. P. Walne, County Archivist, and his staff at Hertford; and the staff of the Dorset County Libraries at Wimborne.

Many publishers have given permission for the reproduction of extracts from their publications, which are noted in the references.

Chapter One

A MODERN COLLEGE

A ROAD WINDING northwards from Berkhamsted rises steadily along its four-mile journey towards Ashridge, running up past the moated ruins of Berkhamsted Castle, scene in 1066 of William the Conqueror's acceptance of the throne of England, to reach a height of some six hundred feet above sea level at Ashridge. The road traverses part of Berkhamsted Common, with glimpses of a golf course, and continues through to Frithsden Beeches, an area of woodland unsurpassed by any in the Chiltern Hills, towards Berkhamsted Lodge. The road begins to take a wide loop, continuing to rise, shaded from the sun by the majestic trees of Harding's Rookery, until it makes an eastern turn. It is only then that the view opens out to disclose with a sense of surprise the lawned front and great length of the grey-white stone facade of James Wyatt's mansion, with its high square tower and graceful chapel spire, and the tiled roofs and brickwork of the more recent extensions. The entrance gates at the western end suggest, but do not properly reveal, the gardens behind, and it is not until the far end is reached that the eye is allowed its first sight of the beautiful lawns and shrubs and trees of what was formerly known as the Pleasure Garden, to distinguish these private grounds from the more extensive park which surrounds the house.

This is now the home of Ashridge Management College, a mid 20th-century foundation occupying an early 19th-century mansion, built upon the site of a 13th-century monastery, the College of Bonhommes. Seven hundred years of continuous habitation is not in itself unique. It is rather the varied nature of the occupancy through such a long span of history that stimulates interest: it invites study and description and affords the principal purpose of this book. Convention would suggest that any account of the chief events and characters who have passed across the threshold of Ashridge in the course of seven centuries should begin at the beginning. In this instance, however, a good case exists for departing from custom and starting from a more recent period before returning in subsequent chapters to look at its origins.

The acquisition of Ashridge for a modern educational foundation goes back only about fifty years, and it starts with the death of the 3rd Earl Brownlow in 1921. Lord Brownlow was among the largest landowners in the country, with estates widely spread, though the major part of his 58,000 acres was established in three main areas of Shropshire, Lincolnshire and the region around Ashridge, where the counties of Buckingham, Hertford and Bedford meet. He had felt for many years that so large a holding posed too many problems of management, and soon after the end of the 1914–18 War he disposed of the Shropshire estates; in his will directed his Trustees to sell the Ashridge estate. The protracted course of the sale of Ashridge, when its future lay under threat, is described in chapter fourteen. The fortunate outcome of all the negotiations was the purchase with a generous gift from Mr. Urban Broughton in 1928 of the mansion and 80 acres of land, later extended to 235 acres, for the use of the Conservative Party as a college for the study of politics, economics, civics and related subjects. Ashridge was to maintain this political affiliation for almost twenty-five years. It was terminated in 1954, since which date no party influence of any kind has been allowed to determine the affairs of the college.

The Bonar Law Memorial College (College of Citizenship)

The new college, named in memory of Andrew Bonar Law, Prime Minister from 1922–1923, commenced its working life in 1929. The huge building, largely empty since 1923, was modernised by the installation of electricity, central heating, new plumbing, new kitchens, and a laundry. Study bedrooms were made by partitioning larger ones and by constructing 'cabins' in various corners and in former staff quarters; bathrooms, of which the former private house had but two, were added. On the ground floor the principal rooms, though adapted to new purposes, remained unchanged. The long conservatory was converted to a dining room, thus allowing the former dining room, with its unrivalled outlook on to the beautiful gardens, to become the common room. The formal opening ceremony was performed by the Prime Minister, Stanley Baldwin, on 1 July in the presence of 1,000 guests, and the college admitted its first students on 3 August.

A Bonar Law Memorial Trust was set up to bring the college into being, with a distinguished body of Governors, who included Mr. Stanley Baldwin (later Earl Baldwin) as Chairman, Viscount Astor, Viscountess Bridgeman, Lord Fairhaven, Lord Hailsham, Mr. Neville Chamberlain, Mr. J. C. C. Davidson, and Lady Greenwood, together with Mr. J. W. Beaumont-Pease (later Lord Wardington), Chairman of Lloyd's Bank, and John Buchan, M.P., as Chairman of the Finance and Education Committees respectively. A key figure in starting the college was J. C. C. Davidson, then M.P. for Hemel Hempstead, who had been private secretary to Bonar Law before the latter became Prime Minister. The role he played in the acquisition of Ashridge and in raising for it an endowment fund of £200,000 is told in chapter fourteen. His vision of the college's potential as a generating station for the educational activities of the Conservative Party extended also to the conception of a field organisation to be set up in all constituencies for the holding of classes, although an idea of having area education officers was fairly quickly dropped. His confidence in Ashridge never wavered even when it was facing difficulties, and when Lord Baldwin retired from the chairmanship of the Trust in 1947 it was entirely appropriate that Lord Davidson (as he by then was) should succeed him.

The first Principal was Sir Reginald Hoskins, a retired Major-General, who had headed the Philip Stott College, that other Conservative training centre which Ashridge was to replace. He established high standards, and both he and Lady Hoskins worked hard to create the right atmosphere for adult part-time students to enjoy what was for many of them their first experience of residential study. L. H. Sutton joined as resident tutor. From the outset the plan was to rely on employing speakers of a high standard from universities or experts in other fields and to have only a small tutorial staff to guide discussions. Courses were held in such subjects as political history, current affairs, the growth of parties, agriculture, local government, public speaking, and were interspersed with courses for party agents, for candidates, women organisers, and occasionally for M.P.s and their wives.

At an early date Arthur Bryant, the historian (later Sir Arthur) became associated with the college and wrote the introductory booklet, a warm evocation of the historical atmosphere pervading Ashridge, which expressed the aims of the College of Citizenship as offering a great opportunity for adults of every age and both sexes for learning and inspiration, the better to fit themselves for the duties of citizenship. In 1936 he became a Governor, as the Educational Adviser of the college, and he played a leading part in shaping the policy of courses, notably in the resumption of the work of the college after the war.

It quickly became evident that the seemingly large initial endowment fund would be insufficient. One of the problems was the fluctuation in the numbers attending courses. Week-end courses were popular and tended to be over-subscribed, but mid-week or longer courses were more difficult to fill and were often poorly supported. As time went on it was also clear that party workers formed only about thirty per cent. of the student complement and that the idea of residential study was making an appeal to a very much wider public. The numbers rose gradually from about 2,000 members in the first year to 3,300 by the end of 1938, and enthusiasm was very high, many students returning annually; but never very far from anyone's mind was the fear of an inadequate income, the burden of maintaining the roofs and fabric of a large old building, and a diminishing endowment fund.

Towards the end of 1937 ill health forced the resignation of General Hoskins, and he was followed in the office of Principal by E. J. Patterson, who came with a very fine reputation from Exeter University College. New teaching and tutorial methods were introduced, and a widening of the curriculum began. The threat of coming war, however, led the Governors to offer Ashridge to the Ministry of Health as an emergency hospital, and this was accepted. Permission was given for the erection of huts on the large area of land on the north front of the college and Ashridge set about adjusting to a new role for the duration. Mr. Patterson departed to join the Advisory Council for Education in H.M. forces, and tutorial staff were released. Key administrative staff, such as Henry Gordon, the college secretary, and Herbert Reasbeck, the accountant for nearly forty years, remained watching college interests and fitting into supporting roles for the hospital. Mrs. Florence Jarvis, the housekeeper, now had a very much larger 'family' of medical staff to care and cater for, since these were accommodated in the main portions of the house, and in due course she was joined by Eric, her son, to assist with stores and catering, and his wife, Marjorie, who helped in the general domestic administration. Out of such a timely arrangement was to emerge a family succession, and when Mrs. Jarvis senior retired in 1949, Eric and Marjorie Jarvis became caterer and housekeeper respectively. (By an irrelevant but happy coincidence the first housekeeper to Lady Marion Alford, the mother of Lord Brownlow, who first came to Ashridge in 1853, was also a Mrs. Jarvis.) Other staff of that period who had joined at or almost at the beginning of the college, and were to remain to give a life's service to it were R. A. Bond (Reg), who became clerk of works; Arthur Kibby, who helped Herbert Reasbeck in the accounts office, and was the college organist for over fifty years; and Jimmy Gibbling, the then head porter.

Ashridge was fortunate to escape direct damage from bombing, though it suffered some damage from nearby blast, and its vast roof area was a perpetual headache for the fire-watchers. Casualties from Dunkirk and victims of early London bombing made up most of the first patients, but when mercifully it seemed that civilian casualties were less than had been anticipated, Ashridge hospital switched roles and became a large general hospital, including maternity wards, under the aegis of the Charing Cross and University College hospitals. Over two thousand babies could later claim to have been born on this historic site.

A Standing Committee of the Trust was formed under Lord Wardington, a Founder Governor, to watch the Trust's interests. Although education had ceased, there was financial business to consider, and negotiations about the lease to the Ministry of Health had still not been satisfactorily resolved by May 1944.

When peace was declared the Ministry was asked to release the buildings and property as soon as possible in order to allow the Trust to resume its work, and it was agreed that these would be vacated by the end of March 1947. The Committee began to turn its attention towards a major consideration of policy which, if adopted, would enable the college to widen its activities. Under the Constitution provision had been made for direct representation of the Conservative Party on the Governing Body. It was now felt that this imposed an undesirable restriction which prevented the college from developing with the freedom of action that an educational establishment required. Such a change of policy would entail an alteration to the Trust Deed which could only be achieved by promoting a Private Bill in parliament. Discussions also took place with the Ministry of Education to examine in what way Ashridge might play a part in popular civic education, thereby securing recognition as an educational establishment, and allowing some exemption from the burden of taxation. The Ministry requested the Trust to allow the huts of the hospital to be converted to a temporary college for the training of teachers, men and women returning from the services. This was eventually agreed to, and the Gaddesden Training College for Teachers came into being in 1947, under the supervision of the Hertfordshire Education Authority, and remained as a neighbour for three years.[1]

In rethinking the future educational policy Sir Arthur Bryant was strongly in favour of a non party-political approach: he felt that Ashridge had a part to play in the work of popular education which had been successfully developed in the Forces during the war. Sir Winston Churchill (not then a Governor) was consulted and was opposed to the idea on the ground that Ashridge was a considerable party asset. As the discussion continued through 1946 Lord Davidson took the view that industry was now becoming seriously concerned about adult education, but R. A. Butler (later Lord Butler) was not enthusiastic. In the end the proponents of the policy of disencumbrance from a party-political bias prevailed. A new body, the Ashridge Educational Council, was formed, consisting of four Governors and 20 other persons eminent in education, such as Sir Philip Morris, Vice-Chancellor of Bristol University and lately Director-General of Army Education, Professor T. E. Jessup, S. C. Roberts of the Cambridge University Press, Brigadier T. S. J. Anderson of London University and a former Chief Education Officer of Middle East Land Forces. The Governors were Lords Davidson and Fairhaven. Sir Geoffrey Ellis, and Sir Arthur Bryant, who became Chairman of the Council, to which post was delegated supervision of all the day-to-day affairs of the college, the courses, the housekeeping and expenditure within certain limits. A new directing staff had to be formed and General Sir Bernard Paget was appointed Principal. This distinguished soldier had been successively Commander-in-Chief of the Home Forces, of 21st Army Group in 1943, and then of the Middle East Land Forces. He brought with him Colonel J. J. Harper, who had conducted the very successful Middle East army college, as the new Director of Studies. Lawrence Sutton rejoined as a resident tutor, and Henry Gordon was now designated as bursar. The college reopened its doors to students on 3 January 1947. Lord Davidson became Chairman of the Trust in succession to Lord Baldwin, who had presided over its affairs since its inception in 1929.

With now almost double the amount of student accommodation available, thanks to wartime additions, a vigorous new start was made, with fresh courses and a high standard of lecturing, and with an improved library. The climate was right, the goodwill was enormous, and there was patently a desire and need for the type of residential courses which Ashridge had pioneered. Enrolments rose encouragingly to about 5,500 in 1948 (3,000 in 1938). Indeed, where else was it possible to enjoy the advantages of hearing first-rate speakers, discussing a varied range of subjects, in good company and such beautiful surroundings? 'Spend your holidays at Ashridge', 'An ideal week in a country house', ran the advertisements, and a week-end course from Friday (dinner) to Monday (after breakfast) cost only three guineas.

One of the strengths of Ashridge has always been the loyalty of its past student members. Early in 1930 the first journal, *The Ashridge Quarterly*, was published, and the Ashridge Fellowship was formed which served to keep old students in touch with each other and with the staff, and to keep them abreast of new developments at the college. Gradually regional and local societies, known as Ashridge Circles, came into being in various parts of the country, where the aims of Ashridge were successfully kept alive by programmes of lectures and discussions. These Circles were specially valuable during the war. They were not restricted only to members of the Fellowship, and they provided a praiseworthy means of intellectual stimulus in those dark days. At least two, in London and Eastbourne, are known to be in existence today. *The Ashridge Quarterly* was not published during the war, but its place was taken temporarily by a four-page *Ashridge Journal,* published monthly in London by T. N. Graham, the secretary of the Trust. In 1947 the *Quarterly* resumed publication under the editorship first of Leslie Paul, and, later, of Ludovic Kennedy, both of whom had joined the staff as tutors.

The new educational policy permitted a much wider view to be taken of politics and economics and this was reflected in the speakers. Whereas before the war speakers were more often eminent politicians (Harold Macmillan, Stanley Baldwin, Duncan Sandys, and R. A. Butler, for example) or historians such as G. M. Trevelyan and A. L. Rowse, the range could now be broadened, irrespective of party allegiance. New topics were introduced, such as Society and the Arts, Town and Country Planning, and there was frequently an interesting pairing of subjects, such as Commonwealth and Literature, Education and Great Ages of England, the Cinema, Music, and once a year, Christianity and Education. A number of closed courses were held for particular groups. Courses in aspects of industry began to feature more frequently, such as The Structure of Industry, Industrial Leadership, and Problems of Training for Industry, in a serious attempt to provide a new focus of attention. In opening the first course of the resumed programme in 1947 Lord Davidson affirmed his faith that in trying to solve some of the problems of industry there was a need to introduce into technical education some instruction in the rights and duties of citizens and some teaching of the importance of moral values. 'I want to see Ashridge become the place, where, free from all polemical politics, young and old partners in industry, drawn from all its branches, can discuss how they can make their industries better . . .'.[2] If the country was slow to respond, at least the seeds had been sown. The list of speakers was impressive: prime ministers, foreign secretaries of both parties, editors, writers, broadcasters, poets, artists, scientists, industrialists, sportsmen—the lists are too long for names to be reproduced, but they are ample evidence of the broader outlook of a revitalised college.

If all was set fair on the educational front, the same could not be said of the financial position, which was frankly worrying. The college income from courses, lettings and property had never been sufficient to maintain all its necessary outgoings. Before the war short-term crises had usually been surmounted, often by timely generous donations, sometimes anonymous, but there had always been a need for some degree of subsidy from the Trust income. After the war there were fewer wealthy donors, the income of the Trust had been diminished by lower returns on investments, and the requirements of the college had increased. In 1947 the rate of subsidy from the Trust stood at £25,000 per year, and there was the growing danger that the Trust funds might soon be exhausted if it was necessary to maintain this rate. Appeals to industry brought a rather reluctant and limited response, as industry at that time was more concerned with its own immediate problems than with the longer-term benefits that Ashridge might bring. By 1949 there was a serious fear that the college might have to close down, and provisional notice was given in confidence to the senior staff. The Governors then considered another proposition which, when it became known, provoked the most serious controversy. Discussions took place with Miss Dorothy Neville-Rolfe about setting up at Ashridge a House of Citizenship for Girls, which aimed to provide a finishing education for girls from 17 to 25, that is, those not too long out of sixth forms, or who wanted to extend their education. The training was to consist of a general course in civics and a choice of either secretarial training or the study of French, history, literature and art. A decision was taken to proceed on these lines, the attraction being that suitable accommodation existed, and a nucleus of full-time students would provide a regular income which would help to stabilise the college finances against the fluctuations of attendance on normal mid-week courses. Unfortunately, the Principal was not consulted about the plan, but merely informed of its adoption. General Paget was totally opposed to this new development and made his position very clear. In September the argument became public through press conferences and statements. Sir Arthur Bryant resigned from the Governing Body in protest, and General Paget relinquished his command in November: the Director of Studies, J. J. Harper, and Ludovic Kennedy also retired at their own request. Here, as W. S. Gilbert might have said, was a pretty 'How d'ye do', with the 'top brass' in rebellion. It was perhaps a measure of firm governorship that the institution was not to be allowed to founder through what was no doubt seen as prejudice, but which the opposition saw as undermining the whole educational structure which they were creating. The loss of Sir Arthur Bryant from the Educational Council was a serious one.[3] His wise counsel and liberal thinking had guided Ashridge for many years and had been an inspiration to the staff in particular. The Council was forthwith disbanded and its work was allotted to three committees. The new Principal was Admiral Sir Denis Boyd, who had been captain of the aircraft-carrier *Illustrious* in 1940, and had just retired from being Commander-in-Chief of the British Pacific Fleet. It was characteristic of him that one of his first acts on appointment was to join a week-end course in order to experience for himself how Ashridge appeared to the student. The promotion of Lawrence Sutton to be Director of Studies ensured that some continuity could be preserved. The new term of January 1950 opened with the first intake of young ladies on a long course, and so the Governors' objective of securing a long future for the college had been achieved. The advantage to the girls was that of sharing in a mixed society and the opportunity to attend specialist lectures that could help to extend the horizon of their own courses of study.

For the time being, then, the corner had been turned. The first of the new industrial courses started later in the year, and when the response to the latest appeal for funds began to show some improvement there was confidence that the position had been stablilised for the next two or three years. A Steering Committee was formed to handle the business of having a Private Bill presented to parliament in order to amend the Trust Deed. The negotiations, drafting, taking of counsel's opinion all took up time, and it was not until 4 June 1954 that the Act received Royal Assent.[4] The main provisions of the Act were:

(a) to alter the name of the Trust to the Ashridge (Bonar Law Memorial) Trust
(b) to give it the status of a charitable trust
(c) the governing body was incorporated in law with succession and a common seal, with a limitation of numbers to a maximum of fifteen governors and a minimum of nine. Viscount Davidson and Lord Fairhaven were to be founder governors during their lives in addition to these
(d) the objects of the Trust were restated as being to carry on a college in which the education provided was to exclude teaching calculated to support the policies of any particular party
(e) Ashridge was to be preserved for the nation
(f) Prayers were to continue to be said in the Chapel as part of the collegiate life
(g) the powers and responsibilities of governors were delineated.

Towards the end of November 1954 was celebrated the Silver Jubilee of the College, and at a Jubilee Dinner the guest of honour, Lord Davidson, replying to tributes to his own part in bringing the college through the past 25 years, remarked 'We started in faith and it is in faith that we are going on now'. All his calm optimism was going to be required in the three or four years that were to follow. Although the new constitution had officially laid the ghost of party political affiliation, the greyer spectre of threatened insolvency would not go away. Many leading industrialists were sympathetic to Ashridge's aims for the future, but there existed an understandable reluctance to become too closely involved with an institution whose large and rambling mansion home was a liability and where the absence of a properly constituted pension scheme for staff was a distinct disadvantage. In July 1956 the Governors were reaching the point when they doubted their ability to carry on unless representatives of industry would take over the college as a going concern. A group of industrialists, led by Sir Hugh Beaver, of Arthur Guinness and Co., Ltd., who were anxious for Ashridge to be given a chance to continue, undertook to guarantee any working deficit up to the end of 1957. Miss Neville-Rolfe was informed of the position and, having the opportunity to acquire alternative accommodation, moved out with her House of Citizenship, by mutual and amicable agreement, and took up residence at Hartwell House, near Aylesbury, in April 1957.

Sir Hugh Beaver was deeply concerned about a national need for the proper training of managers in industry. His study of the facilities that existed made clear that these were very few, and he was convinced that there was a vast field of managers who needed and would benefit from training courses. By the middle of 1957 he was ready to suggest a plan for Ashridge and he set out his views, which proposed courses of three to four weeks' duration, which would give students time for real thought about management problems in conditions of comfort, conducive to study. Using accommodation in the main house only, the numbers would have to be limited to about seventy. Facilities would need to be improved and fees raised, but the market was there if it could be tapped. He and his colleagues were prepared to extend their guarantee of the deficit until April 1958 if the Governors would accept the scheme in principle, which would mean an act of faith on both sides. The Governors accepted these proposals because, quite simply, there were no practical alternatives. It was, however, their duty as Trustees to observe the terms of the Trust and maintain the house and college in being. If this could only be achieved by a change of direction, so be it. A realistic appreciation of the situation could admit of no other reasonable solution, and so a brave venture in adult education had to end. The College of Citizenship had filled a great need with conspicuous success and had set standards which could be envied. Men and women, old and young, had enjoyed the stimulation of hearing first-class lectures and taking part in discussions in friendly and inspiring surroundings. Enthusiasms were generated or regenerated and friendships formed, and many found, even within the brief duration of a week-end course, that unsuspected interests or talents had been awakened. People of widely-differing backgrounds had come together—people from the professions, from commerce or industry, from the arts; from the armed forces, who made considerable use of the post-war courses; women, whose principal occupation had been the home; and the retired—all these and others had made their contribution to the success of Ashridge, and the aims of the foundation had surely not been disappointed.

That this phase of Ashridge had to end may have been inevitable. Perhaps a little of the steam was running out, but the obstacles to further progress were proving insuperable. Moreover, as England was picking herself up after the burden and disruption of a long war, so the public provision of better adult education facilities was improving rapidly. Many authorities were experimenting with similar short residential courses, and would-be students were often able to find their needs satisfied much nearer home. From now onwards, the role of Ashridge was to lie in the more specialised field of education for management.

Ashridge Management College

The first Governors of the reorganised college were widely representative of industrial interests: Sir Hugh Beaver (Chairman), Sir Frederick Hooper (Schweppes), Viscount Caldecote (English Electric), Sir Arthur Carr-Saunders, F. C. Bagnall (British Nylon Spinners), E. W. Senior (Ransom and Marles), S. C. Roberts (Hoover), Willoughby R. Norman (Boots Chemists), Sir W. Benton-Jones (United Steel), C. M. Vignoles (Shell-Mex and B.P.), T. Roffey (Distillers Co.), H. G. Lazell (Beecham Group), K. Adams (Allied Schools), together with Viscount Davidson and Lord Fairhaven as Founder Governors.

Admiral Sir Denis Boyd retired at the end of 1957, and the new Principal, Major-General E. N. K. Estcourt, came to Ashridge direct from the N.A.T.O. Defence College in Paris, where he had been Commandant. Lawrence Sutton and Henry Gordon had also retired, and Norman Rimmer, already familiar with Ashridge from having lectured on the industrial courses since 1951, was appointed Director of Studies. B. L. H. Alder, coming from a similar post at Shrewsbury School, became the bursar. A considerable programme of refurbishing and re-equipment was set in hand in order to raise the standard of both residential and teaching accommodation to serve the needs of a different kind of student. Such obvious but essential services as central heating, plumbing, catering and laundry all needed bringing up to the standard required of a good hotel. New furnishings and lighting contributed to a general air of relaxed comfort, and sufficient progress was made to enable the college to reopen its doors in April 1959 with a capacity for 70 course members, all in the main building. A small number of tutors was appointed in general subjects, including John Lloyd and D. S. Williams, while in the more specialised areas of marketing and accounting valuable help was given by experts temporarily seconded from their firms. One of these was Mark Vardy, from the Beecham Group, who took over marketing courses and later became a member of the permanent staff. D. W. Langridge, a professional librarian, was recruited to develop the information and library facilities.

The annual prospectus was built round six executive (general management) courses of four weeks' duration, with shorter courses in marketing and accounting to supplement them. Courses had to be devised, tried out, discussed and adapted until it could be shown that they represented what was required. The initial response from companies was fairly slow. In many ways industry was not yet ready or convinced of the need for this kind of residential training. There was no tradition in the country for training comparable with that offered by the Harvard Business School, and apart from the Administrative Staff College, established in 1950, which provided courses lasting three months for senior managers and administrators, there were no other independent management colleges such as Ashridge at this time. There had been, or were being formed, departments of management studies within some universities and polytechnics, and these were developing close liaison with firms in their areas, while a few companies had set up residential training centres of their own. Ashridge enjoyed the confidence of a number of influential firms, who not only sent their managers for training, but also gave generous financial support. During the formation period some of these also gave valued practical advice, lent their expert technical services, or or contributed gifts in kind, such as furnishings, at a time when every penny had to be counted with care. The goodwill was there, but the pressing need was to promote successfully the idea and the potential of the Ashridge kind of training. Many training officers were inclined to be sceptical, and, at a time when the economy was still unsteady, any hint of a recession meant that training budgets were often the first to feel the axe. Moreover, there was an understandable desire to try to evaluate what was on offer in the training market before committing company funds.

In 1961 the first changes among the initial staff took place. Norman Rimmer left, and John Boyes was appointed Acting Director of Studies. In the following year the Governors felt that the time had come to bring in someone whose experience and thinking were closer to that of the other management centres that had come into being in the main areas of industry. General Estcourt retired, having successfully steered the college through the many problems of its formation, and leaving a sound administrative base on which to build. The new Principal, Dr. Christopher Macrae, after a distinguished career at the head of the Scottish Council for Development and Industry for 10 years after the war, had held the chair of Professor of Industrial Administration at the Royal College of Science, Glasgow, and was then head of the Chesters Residential Management Centre, Glasgow, from 1956–62. He came with a reputation that was a reassurance to many doubters that Ashridge really did mean business. As new courses were evolved, or the content of earlier ones was adapted in the light of experience of the expectations of both students and tutors, so gradually the demand for places grew and an expansion of tutorial staff was possible. Among those who joined in the period 1963–5 were a number who are either still in the service of the college or who were to give upwards of ten years' service, and who were to provide the stabilising influence without which no organisation can either develop successfully or maintain its best traditions. Mark Vardy, who had played such a large part in the promotional and publicity drives in the early years, retired as Executive Director at the end of 1969. Alan Robson resigned in 1978 to become Professor of Management Accounting at Cranfield School of Management; Leonard Wensley and Fred Keay retired in 1975 and 1977 respectively. Alan Johnson, Douglas Smallbone, Ronald Dow, Robert Whitelaw are still serving, and W. A. G.

Braddick is the present Deputy Principal. The tradition of long and loyal service is also exemplified among the administrative staff by Charles Griffiths (head porter), Bernard Winter (chief engineer), Mrs. Mary Putnam and Mrs. Betty Oakins (from the catering section), Mrs. Rose Griffiths (laundry), Jack Aylott (Driver), Paddy Keating (gardens), and Miss Jennifer Amos (domestic bursar), all of whom have served for at least fifteen years, and most for over twenty.

The year 1963 saw the resignation of Sir Hugh Beaver as Chairman of the Governors. Amid the latter-day successes of Ashridge, with its international reputation, the enormously important role played by Sir Hugh has often been overlooked. Without his guidance and his faith and conviction that there was a pressing need within industry and commerce for a training centre for managers which Ashridge was well placed to fill, and without the support he was able to inspire from like-minded leaders of industry, it is doubtful whether the new college could have even started, and Ashridge today might have been merely another stately museum. He was succeeded by Mr. H. G. Lazell, chairman of the Beecham Group, who was to pilot the course of the college during the following eight years. His vast experience of business affairs and his realistic and practical outlook on the requirements of training for effective management succession were material factors in charting the direction the college has followed. Bernard Alder left in 1964 to become bursar of Eastbourne College, and Douglas Coult moved across from the library to succeed him. Shortly afterwards John Boyes resigned, and after an interval of some months a new appointment of Deputy Principal was made. The growing use of the college meant that tutorial resources were fairly stretched, and loads had to be balanced. An increasing amount of time had to be devoted to meeting visitors and maintaining contacts with company chairmen, managing directors and training officers, that resulted as promotional efforts were beginning to bear fruit.

The philosophy of Ashridge had now crystallised firmly and the greater part of Dr. Macrae's work was devoted to expounding the conviction that the purpose of management training in a post-experience college was to help a person, by means of short courses, to build on his or her own experience to date, to compare it with that of others from often widely-differing organisations, and with the aid of new ideas and new techniques, assist him to become a better manager. The corollary to this reasoning was that a manager, faced with continuously having to adapt to changing factors, needed the stimulus of fresh courses at various stages of his career. Ashridge therefore developed a series of courses graded for all stages from junior management up to the level of director. The major contribution of Christopher Macrae was his success in the crucial role of presenting this view to regular and potential users of the college's services. His reflective and persuasive manner commanded respect among his many visitors, and if at times the profundity of his addresses to courses was tinged with doom-laden prophecies about the future state of the world it was not for nothing that he earned for himself the nickname of 'the sage of Ashridge'. The general recognition today among industrialists and educationalists that a career in management calls for a more or less continous process of education and training is sufficient vindication of the rightness of this policy. Although all members of the staff were encouraged to develop outside contacts, the burden of responsibility for external relations fell on the Principal, for herein lay both the continuance of present support and the hope for an assurance of its future development. The arrival on the scene of Dr. Stephen Manstead as Deputy Principal occurred just when his business experience, his drive and his ebullient personality were most needed. He was able to concentrate on the co-ordination and development of courses, and on strengthening the college's financial position, particularly by maximising the utilisation of space. It was a challenge which he thoroughly enjoyed.

In 1964 a small research department had been set up under Philip Sadler as director. As this developed it had to be located away in one of the huts of the former hospital for lack of space elsewhere. A policy of devising courses specially tailored to the needs of particular companies and organisations had been very well received, and new courses in the behavioural sciences were gradually introduced, employing the expertise of members of the research staff. The provisions of the Industrial Training Act of 1964 were also beginning to take effect. The combination of these and other such factors were leading to a marked increase in the demand for places, which Ashridge could respond to on the tutorial side, but suddenly there loomed the problem of insufficient accommodation, and it became urgent to search out every remote corner of the vast building for possible conversion or improvement in order to provide more student bedrooms and staff offices. In 1966 the Lime Walk annexe was stripped out and modernised bedrooms replaced the cabins of the wartime nurses' home. Two further bedroom annexes of temporary construction were added in 1967 and 1968, adjacent to Lime Walk, and with these and with other internal conversions the capacity was lifted to about a hundred and twenty-five students, almost double what it had been five years earlier.

This much increased capacity served to relieve the pressure on the college finances, but more income was needed if permanent buildings were to replace the temporary ones, and if planned expansion was to be continued. Moreover, there was a continuing need to set aside money for the repair of roofs and the stonework of the fabric, and for the replacement and improvement of equipment. So far as the main building was concerned the Historic Buildings Council for England generously agreed to share the cost of repairs to the original Wyatt building on a planned schedule of work, and this has continued. Discussions also started with the Foundation for Management Education, which was established to bring into being the London and Manchester Business Schools, with a view to receiving some support for Ashridge out of the balance of funds remaining. It was perhaps fortunate that Sir John Partridge, the Chairman of the Foundation, was also a college Governor, and understood the requirement from first-hand knowledge. The outcome was agreement to a grant of £7,500 annually for an initial period of seven years, for the development of long-term research projects, and this was renewed for the period 1973–9 with a further generous grant of £175,000.

In November 1968 ill health caused the resignation of Dr. Macrae, and at the end of the year Stephen Manstead resigned in order to resume his business interests. The Governors appointed Philip Sadler, the Director of Research, as the Principal. Reorganisation of the management structure ensued, with the following being appointed Directors: W. A. G. Braddick (General Management Studies), Alan Robson (Financial Studies), Mark Vardy (Executive), Colin Golby (Marketing), and Ross Calvert joined from the Civil Service as Director of Administration. Bernard Barry became Director of Research in 1970.

Any objective appraisal of the work and success of Ashridge is a task for another hand, and since after this relatively short time it could at most be an interim judgement, this is neither the place nor time for such an evaluation. It is sufficient to record that the 10 years since the appointment of Philip Sadler have seen a continuation of growth and improvement, though at a faster pace than before. The number and quality of the academic staff has risen and the administrative support has been similarly increased to cope with the pressures brought about by a rise in the utilisation of residential space from about 84 per cent. in 1968 to 93 per cent. of a much larger capacity in 1979. The financial success of the organisation has proved that Ashridge is able to practise what it preaches and can stand on its own feet. In real terms it has been possible for a non-profit-making organisation to apply earned surpluses to the provision of purpose-built accommodation and to the successful adaptation of older buildings, as well as to the improvement of all the facilities. Thus a total conversion of the old Monks' Barn enabled 32 attractive bedrooms to be added. In 1971 a major new building programme was started, and the following year the Lazell Building was opened, comprising two modern fully equipped lecture rooms, with eight discussion rooms, and a suite of offices which enabled the Research Department to be brought in from the cold. The building was named in tribute to Mr. H. G. Lazell, Chairman of the Governors from 1963 to 1970. A new block of 32 bedrooms facing on to Coronation Walk was opened in 1977, and in 1979 a larger complex of 64 rooms was erected on the site of the old orchard.

A pleasing feature of the second decade of the college has been the development of closer relationships between senior staff and the Governing Body, which has been helpful on both sides. The Governors themselves also introduced a gratifying way of recognising the distinguished services of members of the Trust by instituting the appointment of President of the

Governing Body, with Vice-Presidents. The first President was Sir Hugh Beaver (1965–8), followed by Sir Paul Chambers (1968–74), and by Viscount Watkinson since 1974. The appointment of the late Derek Whitcroft as Executive Vice-President not only recognised his long and helpful connection with Ashridge, but greatly facilitated liaison between the Governors and the college. Other Vice-Presidents have been or are: Mr. H. G. Lazell, Sir Ralph Bateman, Sir Alexander Durie, Mr. D. J. Mann, and Dr. C. Macrae.

Ashridge now provides courses for about three thousand five hundred representatives of industry, commerce and public bodies every year, many of them coming from overseas. Compared with the three hundred or so who attended in the first year this is remarkable growth. It invites the question 'what of the future?' without the prospect of receiving any credible answer at this stage. The limit of physical capacity for enlargement has probably been reached, and this will impose its own constrictions. The extension of certain facilities and amenities is already being planned. Whether there will be a further need for the college to expand will depend on many factors, not least on whether an expansion of the national economy can be achieved and sustained. What form it might take is a matter for conjecture, from which consideration the possibility of a sister or satellite foundation cannot be entirely excluded. In the olden days, if a monastic order wished to expand, it selected its representative brethren and sent them off to colonise a new community in a fresh location. The precedent is there, but whatever the future may hold for Ashridge, it is to the past that we must now turn, and look first and particularly at Ashridge's own monastic origins.

Chapter Two

THE COLLEGE OF BONHOMMES–A NEW ORDER IS FOUNDED

THE END OF THE 13th century was fairly late in time for a new religious order to be brought into being. The peak had probably been passed by the year 1200, though there were notable exceptions in three royal foundations. Henry III had established Netley, in Hampshire, in 1239, and his brother, Richard, Earl of Cornwall, founded Hailes Abbey, in Gloucestershire, in 1246. Edmund, son of Richard, founded Ashridge in 1283.

At the turn of the century, when King John, father of Henry III and Richard, founded the great Abbey of Beaulieu, he brought in French monks from Cîteaux for the purpose, and it was from this prosperous establishment that monks were sent to colonise the new Abbey of Hailes. It has been said that Edmund in his turn brought French monks to Ashridge, though the unlikelihood of this is discussed in later pages. Richard lavished money on his new abbey, and at the time of its consecration in 1251 he had already spent 10,000 marks on it.[1] The occasion was celebrated with enormous pageantry, and was attended by King Henry and his queen and a great gathering of the nobility and churchmen. The great Bishop Grosseteste of Lincoln celebrated the High Mass. Walter de Cantilupe of Worcester was the consecrating bishop. About thirty years later his nephew, Thomas de Cantilupe, Bishop of Hereford, was to become the first bishop of the order of Bonhommes at Ashridge. Afterwards the proceedings were marked by a huge feast, and Richard gave the abbey a further 1,000 marks for the building and to purchase more land.

On the death of Richard in 1272, Edmund, his surviving son, succeeded to the Earldom of Cornwall. Almost his first act was to commemorate his father by giving Hailes Abbey a precious gift, a portion of a relic of the Sacred Blood of Jesus Christ, a treasure which was soon to draw pilgrims in thousands to the abbey. A few years later he bestowed a similar gift on Ashridge, a monastery of his own foundation.

It is with the story of this relic that the history of Ashridge really begins. The circumstances surrounding its acquisition, as recounted by the 16th-century chronicler, Ralph Holinshed, were as follows: 'Edmund, the son and heir of Richard of Cornwall, who was second son to King John, being with his father in Germany, and there beholding the reliques and other precious monuments of the ancient emperours, he espied a box of gold by the inscription whereof he perceived (as the opinion of men then gave) that therein was contained a portion of the blood of our blessed Saviour. He therefore, being desirous to have some part thereof, by fair entreaty and money obtained his desire: and brought the box over with him into England; bestowing a third part thereof, after his father's decease, into the Abbey of Hailes, which his father had founded, and wherein his father and mother were both buried; whereby to enrich the said monastery; reserving the other two parts in his own custody; till at length, moved upon such devotion as was then used, he founded the abbey at Asserugge in Hertfordshire, a little from the manor of Bercamsted, in which he placed the monks of the order of Bonhommes (Good Men), being the first that had ever been of that order in England; and assigned to them and their abbey the other two parts of the sacred blood'.[2]

An interesting variation of how Edmund came to obtain the relic comes from Mantua in northern Italy. It is said that while travelling in Italy Edmund performed some service in the city of Mantua and the citizens rewarded him by giving him a portion of the precious blood of the Saviour that was in their possession. This had been brought to Mantua by a Roman soldier, Longinus, who, it was said, had pierced the side of Our Lord at the Crucifixion. Longinus was a Mantuan and his spear was preserved as a sacred relic in St. Peter's, Rome. Legend has it that some of the sacred blood fell on his hand, and, in touching his eyes, he received Divine Revelation and brought the holy relic to his native town, where it was preserved and worshipped in the church of St. Andrea.[3]

It should not be assumed that this was the first appearance of the Holy Relic. Joseph of Arimathea (1st century A.D.) who settled in Glastonbury, is said in legend to have brought to Britain two silver vessels filled with the blood of Christ;[4] and the legend of the Holy Grail takes various forms. In 1249, according to Matthew Paris, King Henry III celebrated the Feast of St. Edward in St. Peter's church, Westminster, 'in veneration of the holy Blood of Christ lately obtained', obtaining from the bishops present the indulgence of six years and 116 days to all who should come and visit and venerate the sacred relic.[5]

Whatever the merits of the two accounts of how Edmund came to acquire it, the treasured possession of such so-called relics continued to play an important part in the lives of both religious and lay people generally right up to the Reformation. The blood of Hailes even came to be used as an oath:

> Vengeance shal not parten from his house,
> That of his othës is outrageous.
> By Goddës precious herte, and by his nails,
> And by the blood of Christ that is of Hailes.[6]

If eventually at the Reformation most of the relics were broken up and scattered and those of the Blood were denounced as a cheat, who is to say that they had not, for the times, served their purpose? The blood of Hailes was alleged to have been that of a duck, renewed weekly. That of Ashridge, as related by Speed (1611), was exposed thus: 'It was perceived apparently to be only honey clarified and coloured with saffron, as was openly shewn at Paul's Cross, by the Bishop of Rochester, 24 February 1538'.[7] In an age in which scientific analysis had not yet reached the base-line, it was sufficient, in the progaganda war waged by the Reformers, to declare a conviction loudly and frequently for it to become accepted as fact.

Sir Arthur Bryant has observed that at the time of the Norman Conquest the monks in their ordered communities represented a frail link with civilisation, which had withstood the devastating Viking invasions, and they had deeply influenced the people because they were dedicated, disciplined and educated. 'It would be hard to exaggerate the part played by the monastic houses in forming English institutions . . . [they were] teachers and exemplars, not only of learning and of piety, but of the arts of life'.[8] They attracted gifts and concessions. Their wealth and prestige grew, and at their shrines were held great festivals and services which profoundly impressed those who shared in them. At a time when the greater part of the population was ignorant and illiterate, and long before the introduction of printing, communication between ordinary people was by word of mouth and by what they observed. The churches and monasteries offered a range of example and experiences varying from simple devotions and pious living to great religious spectacles and pageants, which moved people deeply. The possession of holy relics acted as a lodestone. These were signs and symbols, visible and tangible, and thus often easier to comprehend than the formal Latin of the Mass. The pilgrims found their way through the muddied lanes to one such relic at Ashridge, staying perhaps en route at the little hospice of Piccotts End,[9] and they received from the Bonhommes both bodily refreshment and spiritual renewal, before the next stage of their self-imposed journey.

There was no dearth of religious vocation at this time and many small religious houses came into being. By the 13th century the sheer number of such houses led to some need for the church to look to its own internal administration. England was a Catholic country owing allegiance to Rome. The monasteries had been developed by those followers of the teachings of such great leaders as St. Augustine of Hippo in the early 5th century, and St. Benedict about a hundred years later. It was as if a great fan hinged upon Rome slowly opened up and extended over France, Spain, Germany and the Low Countries to Ireland, and across the English Channel. Colonies of monks professing the various orders of religion settled in the British Isles, mostly south of the border, and these in their turn threw off more colonies and smaller cells of their brethren to extend their work. For the most part, these were self-perpetuating organisations, observing strict rules, with powers to elect their own abbots or heads, and admitting to membership only those who met certain conditions and were approved by the whole community in chapter. According to the munificence of the endowment or the subsequent gifts of land or money they attracted, so the heads of these societies became the lords of great or small properties, who were required to have (but did not always possess) qualities of good management and sound husbandry, and an ability to direct the devotional duties and to care for the spiritual and physical well-being of their communities. The quality and standing of such communities, as so often happens in institutions of whatever kind, depended much on the ability, integrity and leadership of the man who was for the time at its head.

Ashridge was in many ways a typical example, enjoying generally a very high reputation, but not without passing through phases of deep and worrying depression in the course of its 250 years of existence. If the earlier beneficial influences of the monasteries on all institutions of the country could have been maintained, what might not have been the course of English history in the later Middle Ages? Yet even before Ashridge was established, there were signs that 'in more important matters the King, bishops, the great nobles, the royal administration, and the monastic orders were rapidly drawing apart. The solidarity of the educated ruling class was gone, and relations between monarch and religious were now a personal matter. Less than thirty years after the foundation of Hailes came the statute *De Religiosis* . . ., not a rigid piece of anti-monastic legislation, but a symptom of a new phase of social opinion in which the monks were no longer the animating or invigorating principle of the nation's life, but only one of many bodies of importance, whose private interests must be subordinated to the interests, as conceived by Government, of the King and country as a whole.'[10]

At the same time, and largely on account of this diminishing influence of the monasteries, there came about a gradual unification of policy and a recognition among bishops and scholars of the need to improve the general administration of their dioceses. Episcopal visitations of churches and monasteries became a regular feature by the 13th century, with the purpose of maintaining standards of good conduct and adherence to doctrine.

So many new monastic houses had been established, or older orders invigorated, that new and often quite elaborate constitutions had been adopted. To make for greater unity the Lateran Council decreed that any new religious societie founded must adopt the Rule of St. Benedict (for monks) or of St. Augustine (for canons). Thus Ashridge, when it was founded, followed the Rule of St. Augustine. Quite a strong similarity existed between the orders in their monastic and liturgical observances, in which stability and the permanence of a family unit was taken for granted. Then came the new teachings of St. Francis of Assisi, challenging all the traditions of stability and replacing them with a call to the friars to go out into the world, to make contact with and preach to the people, and this offered a new and stimulating form of religious life for which the country appeared to be ready. Some earlier authorities attempted to classify the Bonhommes of Ashridge as friars, but there is no justification for this. They were Augustinian canons,[11] established in a stable community and bound by rigid, though not harsh statutes, where absence from the college was not encouraged, and was only allowed with the special permission of the rector.

* * * * * *

The early life of Edmund, founder of Ashridge, cannot be totally separated from the events of his father's career, although the course it followed subsequently bore few marks of similarity. When Richard, Earl of Cornwall, was only 16, his brother Henry III sent him, accompanied by his uncle, the old Earl of Salisbury, on a mission to Gascony, then an English-ruled province in France. He performed his task with distinction, and when he returned two years later in 1227 he was granted the manor and castle of Berkhamsted, and began to build up big estates and great wealth. He married Isabella, the widowed Countess of Gloucester, in 1231, and their first son, Henry, was born in 1235. Isabella died in childbirth at Berkhamsted five years later and Richard went on a crusade to Jerusalem in 1240-1, where he distinguished himself nobly. After his return to England he married the beautiful Sanchia, daughter of the Count of Provence, and sister to the queens of both England and France. Of this union Edmund was born at Berkhamsted on 26 December 1249. Richard's first marriage had brought him closer to the barons of England, and in their struggle for power with Henry III they urged Richard to lead their opposition, but as the King's brother he was unwilling to join them and preferred to attempt to mediate in their disputes. His reputation as a mediator and skilled diplomat grew and became widely respected, so much so that when, following the death of Conrad IV in 1254, the Electors of the Holy Roman Empire were seeking a successor as emperor, Richard was invited to accept the honour. 'The Archbishop of Cologne advised his brethren the Electors (seven magnates of the realm) to choose someone rich enough to support the dignity but not strong enough to be feared by the electors.'[12] Richard, apparently meeting both requirements, was elected King of the Romans, the only Englishman ever to hold that office. This was the title given to aspirants to the dignity of Holy Roman Emperor, which only the Pope could confer, after gaining the approval of all the interested parties.

With the support of his brother Richard went to Germany in 1257 where he was well received. He was seen as one who could counter hostile Italian and Spanish influences. Richard himself hoped for the greater stimulation of trade within his kingdom, while Henry hoped that stronger and more unified German states might be a means of exercising a restraint upon France so that he could regain the lost province of Normandy. Richard failed to achieve the highest title, because pressure by the barons (under the leadership of Simon de Montfort) on his erratic brother the king caused him to spend longer in England than in his new kingdom, bolstering up the monarchy and draining his personal finances in the process. The involved story is well told by the late T. W. E. Roche in *The King of Almayne.*[13] When war with the barons in the south of England appeared to be going in favour of the royalists, de Montfort's troops won the battle of Lewes in 1264. Henry and Richard were both taken and imprisoned, not to be released until the following year after the royalist victory at Evesham. Richard's wife, his beloved Sanchia, had earlier died at Berkhamsted in 1261. England's uneasy peace saw Richard having to wrestle mainly with constitutional problems, but he could now begin to think of returning to Germany after a very long absence. The Pope was delaying a decision on the appointment of a Holy Roman Emperor, and the Spanish contender for the title, Alfonso of Castile, appeared to be gaining ground. Richard sent his son, Henry of Almayne, to plead his cause in Rome, while he returned to Germany in August 1268, taking with him his second son, Edmund, now 18 years old. The following year in Germany Richard married for the third time, his bride being the 16-year-old Beatrix, daughter of one of his staunchest supporters. They returned to England to be present at the consecration of Westminster Abbey in October 1269, and in the following New Year King Henry was taken ill, and Richard was made Regent. His son Henry was sent to be the English Ambassador to the College of Cardinals at Viterbo, Italy, and here he was murdered in a revenge killing by the two sons of the defeated Simon de Montfort. This was a grievous shock for his father, and Edmund was ordered back from Germany for fear of a similar attack on his life. This is presumed to be the occasion when he brought back with him his precious relic, which he is said to have purchased from the Count of Flanders. The King remained ill through 1271, with Richard presiding at the June parliament. Then Richard himself fell ill in the autumn and suffered a stroke at Berkhamsted Castle, from which he eventually died on 2 April 1272, at the age of sixty-three. He was an able and likeable man, of refined tastes, which had secured for him three very beautiful wives, and he was rare for his time in preferring mediation and diplomacy in the settlement of differences to resorting to war. His brother, Henry III, outlived him by only a few months.

Edmund, the only surviving son, inherited the earldom and the estates of Cornwall and Rutland. Within a few months of his father's death he married Margaret, a sister of Gilbert de Clare, Earl of Gloucester and Hertford, but, although the marriage lasted for 22 years, it ended in separation and without children. England, under the more statesmanlike rule of his cousin, Edward I, began to achieve a calmer mood. Edmund played very little part in public affairs, except that in later years he acted for the King during his absences in Europe. Like most men of his rank, he bore arms and led a body of knights in 1284 when Edward was campaigning in Wales, but he declined to join the King in Scotland and paid the customary fine for his knights in lieu. Without the ambition of his father, and free from the need to dig deep into his finances to support a kingship in Germany, Edmund was in a position to apply his wealth for other purposes, even if this sometimes involved him in having to act as banker for the King, helping him out with large loans. The most creative part of his life was given to the founding and endowment of religious houses. Although he is best remembered for his foundation of Ashridge, he was concerned with aiding and developing four other similar institutions before starting on his principal work. At Hailes, founded by his father, in whose memory he gave the abbey part of the relic of the Holy Blood, there was a disastrous fire in 1271 and Edmund bore the cost of rebuilding, which took six years. At Wallingford, his father's castle, he endowed the collegiate chapel of St. Peter's so generously that he was often regarded as its founder. There is a comparison to be drawn here with the action of the Black Prince at Ashridge in the following century. Edmund endowed the Trinitarian Brethren at Knaresborough, and in 1280 founded and endowed the Cistercian abbey of Rewley, Oxon, where his father had intended to found only a small chantry. His last large bequest was for the building of a small chantry and house for the Trinitarians at Oxford in 1291.

His greatest work, however, was Ashridge. He gave his whole energy to it, even preferring residence there to living in Berkhamsted Castle, which he neglected. It became the adminstrative centre for all of his estates and extracts from the accounts support this, with reference to special quarters for the Earl, such as the Great Chamber, and to the purchase of wood for benches. Money collected from his other estates, as far apart as Knaresborough, Yorkshire, and Lydford, Devon, was brought to Ashridge. The sum of 24 shillings was paid for new wine brought from Cornwall for the festival of St. Martin (15 Anno Edw. I). Richard Spronk was paid £83 for one year's work on the 'castles' of Ashridge and Hudnall. The Earl's steward received three shillings a day for expenses of travel as a messenger from Ashridge to Henley and back, and then to Oakham in Rutland—in all nine days.[14]

It was at Ashridge that Edmund died on 25 September 1300.[15] In the manner of the times for great noblemen, his burial was, at the least, somewhat piecemeal. His bowels were immediately removed and placed in the sepulchre of the Chapel. His heart and flesh were solemnly buried there on 12 January 1301 in the presence of Edward, the King's son, and an array of worthies of the realm. The significance of giving the heart was a special one. It symbolised the absolute and eternal association of the patron with the foundation and its community, and Edmund's heart was to rest alongside that of Thomas de Cantilupe, the first bishop of the order. His bones reached their final resting place in Hailes Abbey some six months after his death, when they were interred with great ceremony in the presence of the King himself on 23 March 1301. Since there was no heir to succeed him, his titles and estates in Cornwall and Rutland automatically reverted to the Crown.

* * * * *

The site chosen at Ashridge may have been that of an earlier royal house, though the evidence is rather circumstantial. John Leland, library-keeper to Henry VIII, visiting Berkhamsted about 1535, before the final dissolution, related that 'the house of Bonhommes, caullid Asscherugge, of the foundation of Edmunde, Earl of Cornewale, and owner of Berckhamsted Castel, is about a mile of, and there the King lodgid'.[16] Newcome, the historian of St. Albans, was more specific, stating that Richard of Cornwall, while at Berkhamsted 'had chosen the spot at Ashridge, in the midst of woods, for a house of pleasure; and perhaps as commodious for the sports of the field: and it thus became an occasional residence'.[17] This seems a very possible explanation.

The endowment was completed by 1283, which is accepted by all later authorities as the date of foundation.[18] The building was completed by 1285, and the conventual church of St. Mary was dedicated by Oliver Sutton, Bishop of Lincoln, in whose diocese Ashridge was, in 1286.[19] On 17 April 1286 Edmund obtained at Kings Langley from Edward I confirmation of his charter to establish a college for 20 brethren, of whom 13 at least were to be priests, endowing them with the land and rents, including the manors of Ashridge, Pitstone, Little Gaddesden, and Hemel Hempstead, but excepting the rent of the church from the last. An earlier charter of 5 November 1285 (13 Edw. I) which provided for the support of 13 brethren, of whom at least seven were to be priests, is marked as having been vacated and superseded by the 1286 charter.[20] The reasons are far from clear, as records found at Lincoln and noted by Todd[21] show that the number of priests at the foundation was in fact only seven. The final establishment of 20 brethren was not filled until the Black Prince's bounty made this possible some eighty years later. The priests were to receive their habits and six marks each yearly for their support. The project seems to have had a rather shaky start. The chronicler of Dunstable recorded that there was at the time 'little hope that the house would continue as the foundation was so insufficient; and some of the brethren had not at first a very good character in spite of their name'.[22] Even in 1297 Bishop Sutton allowed the Archdeacon of Huntingdon to examine an election of rector because the house was so poor that he thought the canons should be spared the expense of so long a journey to Lincoln.[23]

Their name, the Bonhommes, a corruption of the Latin *Boni Homines,* has given rise to varying theories about the origins of the order, not all being free from bias. There is not space to elaborate them, but only to indicate the conflicting lines of evidence. Thus when Todd asserts that the monks 'were brought out of the south of France, at a time when there prevailed a sect who called themselves *Boni Homines,* and were termed in the Gascon dialect of the vulgar, Los Bos Homes', he appears to rely only on an unsupported statement in Newcome's history of St. Albans.[24] It has also been claimed that because the founder's mother, Sanchia (Cynthia), was the daughter of Raymond Berengar IV, Count of Provence, one of whose descendants was Raymond VI of Toulouse, a notorious protector of the Albigenses, who were locally called Boni Homines, therefore Edmund must have recruited monks having the same sympathies as the heretic Albigensians. Another theory was that they were Friars of the Penance of Jesus Christ, or Friars of the Sack. This order originated in 1245 but was condemned in 1274, some years before Ashridge was founded, by the Council of Lyons and was forbidden to receive novices, and it accordingly died out. The Ashridge Bonhommes were not friars and their way of life bore no resemblance to that of the Friars of the Sack.[25]

Newcome, without evidence, took the view that they were closely allied to the Albigensians, and sought to deduce that the wall paintings which decorated the old cloisters at Ashridge,[26] which he was able to see on a visit in 1794 or

1795, were of subjects chosen to deride the Preaching Friars and Minorites. These two orders, introduced in 1272, affected a superior holiness and purity, pretended to absolute poverty and self-denial, and thus called down on themselves the ridicule and odium of the older orders, especially of the Albigenses because, as Newcome tells us, these orders of Friars had been instituted and encouraged to preach down 'their antipapistick doctrines'.

The Albigenses comprised a variety of sects living in the South of France in the early 13th century, deriving their name from the city and cathedral fortress of Albi, near Toulouse. This part of France had long had commerce and trade with Spain, a Moslem country, and with the countries of the Balkans and the Eastern Mediterranean. The religion of the people of southern France was much affected by these contacts and sharply differed from that of northern France. It was influenced by the doctrines of Manichaeism, spread from the eastern Mediterranean, whose Persian founder Mani sought to establish a universal religion based on a synthesis of the teachings of Buddha, Zoroaster and Jesus Christ. Its objects could only be achieved by complete asceticism, by abstaining from sexual intercourse, meat, wine, and the ownership of property, because these bound the soul to matter, and it required its followers to lead the life of wandering preachers, sustained by their disciples, who were permitted to marry and remain in the world. The Albigenses divided their followers into the *Credentes,* the believers or disciples whose obligations were very light, and the *Perfecti* (also known as Boni Homines) who were expected to lead a life of extreme asceticism. St. Augustine himself, in his younger days before his consecration as Bishop of Hippo, had been attracted to Manichaeism for a few years, but had wrestled with the problem and came down on the side of Christian orthodoxy, founding a monastery and living quietly there until he was ordained priest at Hippo at the age of thirty-seven.

The Albigensians were complete heretics in the eyes of the Holy See. When a papal legate of Innocent the Third, sent to extirpate the heresy in the lands of Count Raymond the Sixth of Toulouse, was murdered, a Crusade was mounted against them in 1209 led by Simon de Montfort, whose son was to unify the barons against Henry III, and they were severely persecuted and harassed for years until they were defeated in 1229. The *Perfecti* were pastors or teachers of the Cathars or Albigenses, and were supposed to have attained spiritual perfection by their approved practice of the ascetic doctrine of the sect. 'They were generally distinguished by their superior learning and intimate knowledge of the scriptures . . . The *Perfecti,* generally speaking, abstained from intercourse with mixed society and often passed several days together in complete isolation from the world'.[27]

From 1229 the history of the Albigenses became mainly associated with the proceedings of the Inquisition, and with the advance of the 14th century the Cathars almost disappeared in Western Europe. There were other French orders known as Bonshommes, notably the Abbey of Prémontre, near St. Gobain, which followed the rule of St. Augustine, more severe than that of the Benedictines of Cluny, and the order of Grammont (or Grandmont) in the south. Both were successively reformed by stricter observances and the Grandmontese were said to practice 'an almost inhuman austerity'.[28]

It is difficult to see how the Bonhommes of Ashridge could be fitted to any of these moulds. There is one more curious clue, however, of a later date. John Leland, writing about the other foundation of Bonhommes at Edington, Wiltshire, related that the Black Prince 'Had a great favour to the Bones-Homes beyond the se[a]. Whereupon cumming home he hartely besought Bishop Hedington to change the ministers of his College into Bones-Homes'.[29] We do not know the nature of that favour, but must assume that an account, handed down through more than two centuries, had been retailed to Leland, suggesting a foreign connection. The most that can be said is that it is not impossible for Edmund of Cornwall, through his French connections on his mother's side, to have been tolerant towards the Albigenses and their teachings; and although the Cathars had been defeated and dispersed by the middle of the 13th century, it is probable that small cells survived in many parts of Europe. There was at this time a considerable movement of clerics, monks and scholars between Europe and England. If Edmund really did bring his founding monks from the South of France, these might have included men of heretical beliefs, refugees from persecution, but there is no evidence to support this theory. Moreover, the Original Statutes of the College, whose ordinances were fairly strict, certainly do not suggest an ascetic regime.

The names of the seven foundationers have not been preserved, other than that of the first rector, Richard of Watford, which is English enough. David Knowles, the leading modern historian of the monastic orders in this country, asserted 'that the religious of Ashridge were unconnected with any other body, and seemingly, pure English'.[30] Certainly the names of later rectors and monks, such as Richard of Sarratt, Ralph of Aston, John of Tring, right up to John Malden and Thomas Waterhouse in the 16th century, could not have been anything else. There is therefore so much doubt about the French origin that the theory can be discounted, and it seems more likely that what Edmund, Earl of Cornwall, established was simply a new order, a *novus ordo,* as it is described in his epitaph.[31]

Chapter Three

THE FOUNDATION OF A COLLEGE

THE TERMS OF THE CHARTER of Edmund, Earl of Cornwall, confirmed in 1286, declared his intention to found a church in honour of God and the Blessed Virgin Mary and of the Precious Blood of Jesus Christ, for which he gave the rector and brethren in perpetuity 'our manor of Ashridge with Pitstone, with all their possessions which we formerly had by gift and concession from Julian Chayndut, with the enclosed park of the same manor of Ashridge lying in the parish of St. Peter Berkhamsted and in the parish of the church of Pitstone'; also the manor of Little Gaddesden, and the manor of Hemel Hemstead, except for the rent of the church. Together with these were given a number of rights which illustrate the very tight control under which our medieval forefathers lived; such as the fees and payments of penalties, the 'return of writs to our Lord the King', with plea of distraint, with criminal or civil pleas in the King's Court, the chattels of felons or fugitives, with inspection of frankpledge (surety for the behaviour of freemen), regulation of the quality of bread and ale and broken casks, and fees for calling hue and cry, and bloodshed.

The Latin deed recites in great detail the rights to which the monastery was entitled in all these manors, as to dwellings, buildings, homages, trusts, custody of impounded animals, feudal reliefs, death duties *herietis* (i.e., the right of the best chattel), scutage, and all other foreign service, (i.e., payment in lieu for military or foreign service), escheat, rents and services, not only in respect of freemen, but also of the villeins (customary tenants) and their chattels and households. The extent as to land is listed very precisely as parts of courts, cottages, yards, gardens, woodlands, open lands, meadowlands, pastures and rights of pasturage, roads, footpaths, ditches and hedges, streams, fishponds, rights of fishing, dams, mills, naming especially Piccotts Mill, Bury Mill, Two Waters Mill, Felling Mill, and Welpesburn Mill, with the lands adjoining them.

Bury Mill and Piccotts Mill were located on the upper River Gade, the former not far from Bury House, Hemel Hemstead. There is still a mill building at Piccotts End, though no longer in use for that purpose. The original was the principal mill for corn grinding in the area.

Welpesburn Mill was on the River Bulbourne, near Bourne End. Two Waters Mill and Felling Mill (sometimes Fulling) were near to where the two rivers merge. The latter was a fulling mill which processed cloth for the local clothmakers.[1]

The founder reserved to himself the rent of the church at Hemel Hempstead, and the rights of warrenage in that manor, though there was provision that 'the brethren shall not be troubled for taking hares and rabbits in the warren', but if their servants or tenants did so the brethren should receive any amends or fines. The brethren were to enjoy the rights of pasturage in 'our woods of Berkhamsted, called the Frith', and of putting their pigs into the same wood in due season, as well as taking hay. The rector and brethren and their tenants and servants were to be quit 'of all suits of court, of hundreds, views of frankpledge, and other exactions and demands' so that in future all men should 'do their suits' to the rector and brethren for the appropriate fees. Likewise the brethren were given the right of buying and selling without payment of toll in the honours of Berkhamsted and Wallingford and 'shall everywhere be free from toll, whether from pontage (upkeep of bridges), stallage (market stall rents), passage, lastage [*leistagii*-payment for incontinence!] and from all fines and duties as are the men of Berkhamsted and Wallingford'.

The earl contracted for himself and his successors that on the death of the rector they would have no rights of entry nor would they interfere in any other matters affecting the brethren at a time when a vacancy should arise. 'And when the brethren elect a new rector by canon rule the bishop of that place may confirm him even if he should not have been first presented to the patron'.[2] The principal witnesses to this deed were the lords Bishops Oliver of Lincoln and Peter of Exeter. Among other witnesses[3] were Randolph Pippard, John

Neirnuyt, whose family owned all the lands around Pitstone, and John of Gaddesden (the elder). The editors of the 1830 edition of Dugdale give the full list of witnesses printed in the first edition, which curiously included 'Richard of Cornwall, our father', who had died in 1272. Todd (page 7) gives him as 'Ricardo de Cornubia, fratre nostro', which is equally strange if read literally, as Edmund had only one brother, Henry, who had been killed at Viterbo several years earlier. John of Gaddesden was probably the father of the more famous physician of the same name. The younger John was born in 1280. He studied 'physic' at Merton College, Oxford, and achieved great esteem and recognition abroad, especially in Italy, where his books were first published. He practised in London and treated a son of Edward I for smallpox. He is the 'Gatesden' referred to in the *Prologue* of *The Canterbury Tales*. Thomas Fuller (1608-61) paid graceful tribute to one of his books:

> the first treatise . . . is termed *Rosa Anglica* (the English Rose) and I doubt not but, as it is sweet in the title, so it is sovereign in the matter there contained.[4]

On 5 November 1285, Edward I confirmed the first Charter[5] at Swanston; an additional grant was included that the brethren should enjoy all the liberties in respect of chattels of fugitives and felons, and amends of the assize of bread and ale, pleas of hue and cry and bloodshed, and other rights in the manor of Hemel Hempstead, because an inquisition had found that Isabel, former Queen of England (mother of Henry III) and Richard, King of Almayne, and the Earl Edmund in his turn, had all enjoyed these liberties. Lands in the parish of Pitstone, owned by John Neirnuyt, who had witnessed the Charter, were released to the monastery in a deed dated 25 January 1285:

> Fulk Neyrunt, Rector of Pichelesthorn, with the consent of Lord John Neyrunt, my brother and patron of my church, as rector of the church, to Ralph, Rector of Essherugge, founded in honour of the precious blood of Jesus Christ and the good men brothers of that place:
>
> Of right to common pasture housebot in the park and new close of Ashridge and its old and new hedges, but reserving tithes, and they may fence twelve feet round the park. 6 marks paid.
>
> Witness: Lord John de Gatesden, Will de Enneyse, Stephen Cheyndut, Knights (and eight others).[6]

On 20 June 1287 the king inspected and confirmed a further charter allowing the rector and brethren to have without impediment the amercements and fines of the men and tenants in all their manors 'for the increase of the worship of God, and the happier fulfilment of the vow of the said earl'.[7]

The following year the brethren received a grant of the manors and churches of Ambrosden and Chesterton in Oxfordshire, and on 27 July 1290 (18 Edw. I) at Kings Langley, the Earl of Cornwall endowed them with further grants of lands and the rent of the Church of Hemel Hempstead. In 1291 the monastery benefited from additional rights in Edlesborough and Pitstone, and certain hamlets, including Cheddington, which lay within the honour of Wallingford, and further lands in Berkhamsted and Aldbury, in charters confirmed by the king at a parliament held at Ashridge in January of that year.[8] Further grants were made by a charter, confirmed at Westminster on 28 October 1293[9] of liberties respecting justice and order within the honour of Berkhamsted. This laid certain judicial obligations on the rector and brethren. They were given power to plead in their courts of Hemel Hempstead, Ashridge, Berkhamsted, and Pitstone, all pleas which the sheriff of the county could plead, except appeals and outlawries. Through their bailiff they were given power to seize for the preservation of the peace all attachable persons, and to arrest all who ought to be arrested, and take them to their prison in Berkhamsted. They were to have the powers and duties of coroners. If the king's justices either assigned or itinerant, should come into Hertfordshire to hold pleas, they were to come to Berkhamsted, and when they came to the county of Buckingham they were to come to Pitstone, 'and on the soil of the said rector shall hold all pleas belonging to their office which touch the rector and brethren and their tenants'. The brethren were to have the chattels of all persons condemned and fugutive, and the justices were to deliver to them such fines as were imposed: 'and the said rector and brethren and their tenants shall be quit of paying money for murder or contributing to the common fines or amercements of the county'.

It may be seen from all these grants that within a short time from the foundation the Bonhommes, though by no means finally secure, had become large landowners, and they were expected to play a significant part in the administration of justice within the boundaries of their lands. The judicial and custodial responsibilities were not a mere formality, for it was recorded at Westminster: '9 July 1290. William Rose, imprisoned at Assherugg for the death of John Everard whom he slew in self-defence, has letters to the sherriff of Hereford to bail him'.[10] In the same year on 30 July, while en route from King's Langley to Northampton, the king stopped 'and granted pardon to John de Asserugge for his outlawry for the death of Robert Spileman'.[11] There was no suggestion that either of these men was a Bonhomme.

The Earl of Cornwall's successive gifts and grants to the new foundation were designed to reinforce the insufficient initial income of the house and must have helped it greatly to recover from its hesitant start. Edmund also improved the roads in the park, enclosing the king's highway and cutting a new one, though apparently not without having to obtain the necessary authority.

> 13 February 14 Edw. I (1286)
>
> To the sherriff of Buckingham, Friday after St. Mathias.
>
> The road, which is to the hay of the park of Esserugge which Edmund Earl of Cornwall caused to be made through his wood, is safer, smoother and lighter, and of greater width than another which he has caused to be enclosed in the said park.[12]

This report was evidently sufficient to secure *post facto* approval:

> 1286. Langley, 18 April. License to Edmund Earl of Cornwall to enclose the King's highway through the park at Ashridge and make a new one.[13]

The Rev. F. H. Cobb summed it all up in the words, 'he neglected the Castle and spent all his energy on Ashridge, his new foundation'.[14] King Edward I, cousin of Edmund, was also deeply interested in the new monastery, and found solace there after the death of his wife, Queen Eleanor, in 1290. The queen was taken ill at Harbey, Notts., while they were travelling, and on 28 November she died. The king ordered a solemn procession back to Westminster and at each village where the bier rested Edward vowed to raise a cross to her memory.

As Sir Arthur Bryant has recorded:

> A week before Christmas her body was laid in the Abbey, then having bidden farewell to all that was happiest in his past, the King rode to the Monastery of the Bonhommes at Ashridge which his cousin Edmund of Cornwall had founded. There in the cold solitude of the Chiltern beechwoods he spent his Christmas.[15]

The king's business had to go on, however, despite the mourning, and immediately after Christmas parliament met at Ashridge, the first session being on 27 December and the last entry recorded being for 26 January 1291.[16] No business of any great moment was transacted, and apart from *inspeximus* and confirmation of the Charters affecting Ashridge, already noted, the principal matters were concerned with letters patent, with licences, with appointments and the like, and a long debate on the origin and use of fines and their necessity.[17] Lipscomb noted that the king 'remained here five weeks: and the chronicle of Dunstable Priory records the grievances endured by the inhabitants of that town, by being compelled to supply provisions for the Monarch and his Court'.[18] Edward returned to Ashridge for a short while on 5 February 1291. The custom of royal progress through the towns, staying here and there at the houses of the great or in traditionally hospitable monasteries was much more than a matter of conferring an honour on the hosts. It was essential if the costs of keeping the Court were to be met, for the burden to be reallocated, as it were, and this was a calculated and long-practised method of doing so. Similarly, the receipt from the king of special benefits or protection would imply that the recipient would at the appropriate time make a suitable contribution to the king's purse, and although these contributions were termed voluntary, they were, in fact, compulsory. In such a way were the costs of new wars or expeditions financed. Anyone who failed to acquiesce in these arrangements was liable to be dealt with as an enemy of the king and nation. If a benefice was granted to a monastery, up to one half of the yearly profits from it would be expected to be given to the king.

Bishop White Kennet, whose *Parochial Antiquities* records many such instances, was formerly vicar of Ambrosden, one of four churches granted to the Bonhommes soon after their foundation. He remarked that the revenues from the churches bestowed on religious houses were not originally designed to be converted for the use of these particular houses, 'but to be entrusted to religious men that they might better execute the office of patron, and more incorruptly provide an able Incumbent. Yet without regard to the real intention of the Donors, the convents soon resolved that the inheritance should be their own: and so purchasing a deed of gift from the Pope, they quickly made themselves Perpetual Rectors!'[19]

Lay patrons would devoutly resign their right of presentation to religious houses. The latter would procure by purchase from the Holy See the annexation to themselves of the tithes, with an arbitrary small reserve for presenting a nominee of their own, called a vicar.

Three records in the Papal registers are relevant:

> *1300. 7 Kal. Oct.*
>
> Grant to the rector and brethren of the Augustinian house of the Blood of Christ at Asserugge, commonly called *Boni Homines,* in the diocese of Lincoln, of certain lands and possessions with the patronage and advowsons of the church of Hemel Hempstede . . .[20]
>
> *1308. 4 Non. Aug.*
>
> To the rector and brethren of the house of Hassherugge, in the diocese of Lincoln, commonly called *Boni Homines,* confirmation of the gift by Edmund, Earl of Cornwall, founder and patron thereof, to them of his manor of Ambresdon, and advowson of the church of that place, value 40 marks, sufficient stipend being reserved for a chaplain'.[21]

A similar appropriation for the Bonhommes of the parish church of Chesterton, made originally in 1288, was reconfirmed at St. Peter's Rome, in 1401, 'the value not exceeding 40 marks'.[22]

The relationship of the Holy See to the monastery of Ashridge appears to have been restricted for the most part to occasions such as these, or to the granting of special licences and indulgences, after payment of an appropriate fee, and to disciplinary matters. There is nothing to suggest that the Constitutions of the Bonhommes were ever submitted to Rome for approval. This aspect of the administration was left in the hands of the bishop of the diocese. What these Constitutions embraced and how the system of episcopal oversight worked are examined in the following chapter.

Chapter Four

THE CLOISTERED LIFE

THE ORIGINAL STATUTES of the college were reproduced in their medieval Latin by Todd from the Martyrology of the college, which cannot now be identified as having been preserved. The brethren were required to acknowledge and observe the Rule of St. Augustine. In contrast with the Rule of St. Benedict, the other principal Rule by which monastic houses were guided, and which is clearly set forth, St. Augustine did not actually write down his Rule in precise terms. The Rule owed its origins principally to two sermons in which he taught that the guiding precepts to be observed were a love of God and one's neighbours, a common life, and the virtues necessary for such, abstinence, care of the sick, respect for authority and weekly readings for followers of divine grace. These principles were adopted extensively by canons regular from the 11th century onwards.[1]

The form of the monastic services and ceremonies was to be according to 'the use of Sarum', a pattern of worship and singing that had been initiated earlier at Salisbury, which had become so renowned as to provide a model for many churches throughout the land. The normal hours of service were: Mattins at midnight, but often combined with Lauds at 2 a.m.; Prime (6 a.m.); Terce (9 a.m.); Sext (noon); Nones (3 p.m.); Vespers (6 p.m.); and Compline at 9 p.m. After sung Mattins the brethren were allowed to study or pray, or rest quietly if they were fasting until Prime. Before Terce they went to Chapter, where any brother might confess his manifest faults and be liable to a fine or penalty at the discretion of the rector. If any did not confess the rector might still punish transgressors appropriately. Strife and contention were always to be avoided in Chapter. After Correction prayers were to be said for the founder and for all benefactors living or dead, and psalms and prayers were prescribed.

After Chapter, those who had no outside duties might study, pray or sing and say their private masses until the bell was rung for Terce. This, in fact, was the purpose of the Order and, as the name 'College' implies, study was one of its chief ends. Normally dinner was taken between Sext and Nones. There followed in the statutes a number of variations for times of fasting, for Lent, and for the principal feasts and vigils. After Vespers the brethren might take supper, and then, after a reasonable interval, the bell was to be rung for Compline, which was said by all.

Directions were given as to when to incline the head, when to face the altar, or when to prostrate themselves. The festivals, particularly those of the Blood of Jesus Christ and Edward the Confessor, are specified. The brothers were to fast during Lent, on every Friday throughout the year, on every Thursday and Sunday during Advent. Except for fast days meat might be eaten on four days a week, and on the other three fish or milk foods.

Silence was to be observed in the refectory during meals, in church during the singing, and also in the dormitory during the hours of sleeping.

When a vacancy occurred in their numbers it was to be filled as soon as possible, but certainly within six months, from men of honest character, sufficiently literate, of good reputation, free men (i.e., not villeins), not married, not in debt to anyone, and not professed in any other Order. A probationary period of one year was ordered, after which, if the brothers agreed to the election, the novices were to take the vows, receive their habit, and their first tonsure.

The uniform habit consisted of a tunic of ash-grey colour[2] with scapular of the same colour but shorter than the tunic, and a cowl of suitable size. They were to have cloaks of the same colour, reaching to the feet, and a round cape for journeys away from the House. Linen was not to be worn next to the skin, except around the thighs, but a linen or woven shift might be worn for sleeping.

Absence from the House was allowed only by permission of the rector and then within fairly strict limits.

Women were not allowed within the gates, except for the queen, the wife of the founder, or mothers or sisters of the brethren. Sometimes, however, women might come in festal processions and, subject to the absolute dispensation of the rector, they might be permitted to enter. If the brothers wished to speak to them they might do so briefly, but always accompanied.

On the death of the rector, the constitutions provided that the brethren should proceed to elect a successor within 15 days, and should humbly ask the bishop to confirm the election. The details of one such election have been preserved and are shown in Appendix I.

When a brother lay dying, the chapter bell was to be rung and all the brethren gathered in the infirmary for the administration of the sacrament. After which, attired in his habit, the deceased was to be carried reverently into the church, and on the morrow, after a Mass for the dead, his body was to be laid to rest in the sepulchre.[3]

Special anniversaries were set down to be solemnly celebrated, especially those of Edmund, the founder, and his father and mother. Finally, once a week either in Chapter or at table, whichever was better, the brethren were to be reminded of the Rule of the blessed Augustine and the Statutes were to be read out to the assembled community. With the passage of time it was natural that minor changes should be made in the Statutes, but these served to guide the College of Bonhommes through the 250 years of its existence. The principal variation occurred at the time of Edward the Black Prince, and followed his review of the College's general organisation. The revised Constitution, dated 20 April 1376, preserved at Lincoln, showed that Bishop John Bokyngham had expunged the provisions relating to confession and correction and praying for the founder, and in a new clause acknowledgement was made that the Prince of Wales, Edward, 'is now their patron'. The prince died only a few weeks after this, and in his will made substantial bequests to the college:

> We give and devise our great table of gold and silver furnished full of precious relics, and in the middle of it a holy cross of the wood of the True Cross; and the said table is garnished with stones and pearls, that is to say 25 rubies, 34 sapphires, 15 great pearls and several

> other sapphires, emeralds and small pearls, to the High Altar of our House of Ashridge, which is our Foundation: for the perpetual service as the said altar and for no other purpose. And we lay it on the soul of the Rector and the brotherhood to answer for this before God.

The interest of the Black Prince in Ashridge must have dated from his early years. Under his father, Edward III, Berkhamsted Castle had become a regular place of royal residence, and had been put into a good state of repair. He spent much of his youth there, and the king gave him the castle on creating him the first Duke of Cornwall in 1337. It became his normal residence as often as his military exploits allowed. Edward was created Prince of Wales in 1343 and over the next 15 years he took part in major military campaigns with distinction. He was regarded as the model of the conventional chivalry of his day. Crécy was followed by Poitiers, where the prince captured King John of France, and brought him to England where he remained imprisoned in the Tower of London for 25 years until the huge ransom for his freedom could be paid.

The prince began to involve himself in the affairs of Ashridge in the years during and following the Black Death, as he wished to see the community strengthened.

> 2 Nov 1353. Notification to all that, at the instance of William, rector of the church of the house of Ashridge, of which the prince is patron, and of his brethren the other chaplains there, the prince has caused . . . examination of the divers previous charters of Edmund . . . has caused an abstract of the liberties to be compiled, and grants:
>
> (a) On the death of a rector, power to elect a successor within 15 days, [with] confirmation by the bishop
>
> (b) freedom from interference into the manors of the brethren.[4]

Patronage, however, was not to be enjoyed without the brethren having to undertake reciprocal obligations. Most monasteries suffered to a greater or lesser degree from corrodies, that is, the requirement by a patron to provide meat, drink, clothing and often accommodation or money for the sustenance of such of his servants as he chose to nominate. Thus later in the same year 1353 we find the Black Prince terminating an earlier corrody: 'When the rector and his brethren have at the Prince's request freely and unanimously given to Master

Richard Raven, his cook, for life a certain sum of money yearly and a robe of the suit of the rector's esquires, or a mark of silver in lieu thereof [the Prince grants] freedom from any future payments of such kind'.[5] Four years later the same Richard is to be found as the Yeoman and Keeper of the game at Berkhamsted.[6]

The prince maintained a watch on other affairs also, for in May 1359 the rector and brethren were summoned to appear before his court 'at the quinzaine of Easter next' to show why they had seized goods in Hemel Hempstead of William de Garton.[7] It is not recorded how they acquitted themselves of this charge.

During the same period the Black Prince interested himself in the secular college of Edington in Wiltshire. The college had been founded in 1351 for a dean and 12 ministers, but this was changed in the next year, at the desire of the prince, to a house of Bonhommes. A small cell was sent from Ashridge to direct it under a rector, John of Aylesbury.[8] John Leland relates that Bishop Edington of Winchester 'builded a fair new church' here (Edington was his birthplace) 'and there made a College with a deane and twelve men'. Edington had long been a prebendary belonging to the Abbey of Romsey, and the bishop had appropriated the title to his new college. Leland's account continues:[9]

> Prince Edward caullid the Black Prince had a great favour to the Bonhommes beyond the se[a]. Whereapon cumming home he hartely besought Bishop Hedington to chaunge his ministers of his college into Bones-Homes. Hedington at his desier entreated his collegians to take that ordre. And so they did all saving the deane.
>
> Hedington sent for two of the Bones Homes of Asscherugge to rule the other 12 of his college. The elder of the two that came from Asscherugge was caullid John Ailesbyri [Aylesbury] and he was the first rector of Hedington.

The new monastery was founded in 1352 and the brothers received their first tonsure on 16 October 1358.[10] The connection with Ashridge was established and there is evidence of later interchange between the two houses.

A few years earlier another house of Bonhommes had also been established at Ruthin, in Denbighshire. Not a great deal is known about this house, and no direct evidence of a cell having been sent from Ashridge can be found. According to Leland, 'A priest of Saresbyri [Salisbury] told me there was a celle of Bonhommes at Ruthin by Denbigh land, and that sins it was translated into a paroche church'.[11] Knowles and Hadcock made the point that the Salisbury priest probably knew about the Bonhommes of Edington. Dugdale says Ruthin received a charter in 1310 for an establishment of seven priests (this was the same as at Ashridge).[12] It was founded by John de Grey, whose father, Reginald, had been created Lord Ruthin by Edward I in 1282, and whose family estate was at Bletchley, not many miles away from Ashridge. The connection is the more interesting since John William Egerton, 7th Earl of Bridgewater, was the son of John Egerton, Bishop of Durham, and Anne Sophia de Grey, a daughter of the Duke of Kent. The de Grey armorial bearings are represented on the south frieze in the Great Hall at Ashridge. Ruthin was dissolved along with the smaller monasteries in 1535. Edington, whose annual value (£442) was slightly more than Ashridge (£416) at the time of suppression, was dissolved in 1539.

In 1367 Prince Edward married the beautiful widow Joan, 'the fair maid of Kent', a match which did not please his father, who decided that they should go abroad, and sent his son to rule over Gascony as Prince of Aquitaine. It seems to have been an amicable displeasure since the couple entertained their royal parents at Berkhamsted Castle for Christmas that year, and it was not until the following year that the prince and his wife left for France. Here he proved to be less successful as a ruler than he had been as a soldier. He spent money lavishly, and his imposition of heavy and unpopular taxes to meet his expenses caused the French lords to appeal to their king. War broke out again and gradually the French provinces slipped from his grasp. He returned to Berkhamsted in 1371, cripped in health and almost ruined in fortune. Five years later, at the early age of 46, he died at Westminster.

The bequest in his will, already mentioned, showed the strength of his feelings for Ashridge. Although he had claimed the house to be 'de notre fondation' there is no doubt that his patronage and support revived Ashridge at a time when it badly needed help, and though the intended full establishment of 20 brothers may not have been consistently maintained, it did not fall below 17 during the remaining 160 years of its existence.

Chapter Five

CHANGE AND ACHIEVEMENT

THE PHYSICAL EFFECTS on Ashridge of the Black Death or the Great Pestilence in 1348-9 and the later recurrences of 1361 and 1369 are not known in any detail. Yet it is difficult to imagine that with the comings and goings of pilgrims and visitors, and of the lay servants and workers on the estates, Ashridge and the surrounding areas escaped totally unharmed, although the incidence of the plague was very uneven. St. Albans lost its abbot, its prior and 46 monks within a few days in 1349. In Abbots Langley 71 inhabitants perished. In Little Gaddesden tradition has it that disease-stricken parishioners fled from their cottages around the church, and there is circumstantial evidence that there was a change of priest here in 1361. At Ashridge, however, Gilbert Bowles was elected rector in 1346 and remained in office for the next 27 years. If the plague did not actually reach the gates of the monastery, its economic effects were widespread and were to be felt for many years, and it brought great social changes in its wake.

In England as a whole, one fifth of the population perished. The church lost half its clergy. There were many fewer men available for work, and labour costs rose steeply. There were other changes, too. Most of the estates held by the monks were demesne lands (held with unrestricted right of use). The more ambitious villeins working the Ashridge lands to produce food and stock for the Bonhommes to sell in the markets of Berkhamsted, Wallingford and St. Albans, or for use in the monastic kitchens, were beginning to question why they should not be receiving direct payment for their products, or at least be allowed to rent the lands for cash and then market their own products. During the Peasants' Revolt of 1381, considerable losses were caused to the Bonhommes in their manors of Berkhamsted and Hemel Hempstead from the violence of the peasantry, who marched on Ashridge to demand a new charter. The rector, as happened with the heads of so many other religious houses, was obliged to grant new liberties, and eventually he had to petition the king to allow demesne lands to be leased for lack of adequate labour to work the land properly.

The new endowment of the college by the Black Prince in the mid 14th century no doubt had seemed both generous and timely, but in the light of events of the following few years all the indications are that it was far from sufficient. With fallen rents and rising war taxes, by 1413 the monks found themselves 'overwhelmed with great necessity'. Benefactors there had been in plenty during the preceding 100 years and were yet to come, mostly, it must be said, with the object of securing their own spiritual comfort by arranging for the celebration of masses for their souls.

Todd reproduces a long list of these, culled from the Ordinances and the Martyrology.[1] We know from published wills that the practice continued into the early 16th century. White Kennet tells us that the veneration accorded to the Holy Relic 'inclined many to appoint their burial in the Church of Ashridge, to the great advantage of the Brethren there'.[2] He named Sir Thomas Bryan, Chief Justice (1500), Sir Thomas Denham (1519) and his son, Sir John Denham (1535). Several of the well-known Verney family of Claydon, Bucks, were also buried there. Sir John Verney was buried in 1505 at 'the beautiful convent at Ashridge with his wife's relations and in 1509 his wife was laid to rest beside him'. Later Sir Ralph Verney (1525) and his son, also Sir Ralph, a supporter of King Edward IV and a former Lord Mayor of London, were to be buried there, followed by Sir Ralph Verney (the third). He was a soldier of some note, who died at the early age of 37 years, and directed in his will: 'I will that oon honeste prieste shall synge for the sowlles of me, my father and mother, of Rauff Verney, etc., and of all cristens'. This was to go on 'for oon holl yeare'. The priest was to have a stipend of six pounds sterling and 'is to find himself wine and ways to say every Wednesday and Friday Diriches [dirges] and commendaciouns for the sowles aforesaid'.[3] The Verney memorials were removed in 1575 to the church at Aldbury by Sir Edmund Verney, and set up in the Pendley chapel, which he had there created, paved with tiles and enclosed by a 15th-century screen of carved stone brought from the chapel at Ashridge. A benefactor of importance who appeared on the scene at the turn of the 15th century was Richard Peteworthe, clerk, one of the staff of the Bishop of Winchester, who gave the brethren £100 for the rebuilding of the choir, at a time when not only the choir, but the cloisters and dormitory also stood in great need of repair. This generosity was followed by a grant in 1413 by the bishop himself, Henry of Winchester, uncle of the newly-crowned King Henry V. He granted the Bonhommes the rectory of the church of Ivinghoe in Buckinghamshire. The bishop's support did not end here, for he also gave £500 for the repair of the cloisters, the dormitory, the infirmary and the sacristy.[4] The bishop had an affection for Ashridge, and John Amundesham noted that he visited it in 1429 on his way to St. Albans 'directing his steps to that place of Ashridge so dear to him'.[5] This interest of Winchester in the welfare of the Bonhommes may well have derived from the fact that the Edington monastery, within the diocese, had been established about sixty years earlier under the leadership of two of the canons from Ashridge. With such aid the college was beginning to recover its position and its poise, and the building of the big tithe barn towards the end of the century was sure evidence of a revived prosperity.

Other changes were also evolving. With possibly as many as half of every land-owning religious community engaged in the administration of the estates, all over the country there was beginning to be seen a move away from the fully monastic life. Exemptions were given for regular attendance at every daily service and the prescribed readings. There were relaxations of the rules of common life. The more senior monks had their own offices and servants. Some enjoyed private rooms, and it was possible to retire from the silence of the refectory to the infirmary with the advantage of conversation and a more varied diet.[6] The rules for drinking were being relaxed too. At times when only one daily meal was prescribed, an evening drink of beer or wine was permitted from quite early days, and in summer months an afternoon drink was allowed also. As Knowles remarked, 'there was a tendency, as in all large establishments of every age, for one refreshing drink to follow another'.[7]

The gradual relaxation of the rules of silence took the form of providing more time for social and recreational conversation in the daily timetable. This probably recognised the stimulus of mental activity and the value of an exchange of ideas, because, in the outside world, change had begun to accelerate. By the middle of the 14th century French and Latin had virtually disappeared except for formal documents. The English vernacular became the normal language of conversation, and English was being taught in the grammar schools in place of French. In literature the poems of William Langland and Geoffrey Chaucer were commenting caustically on the social problems of the day. Both they and John Wycliff condemned corruption and greed in the church, but, while Langland and Chaucer relied on satire and ridicule, Wycliff, a theologian and scholar of Oxford, aimed at a greater reformation to reduce the power of the Pope and the clergy. In translating the complete Bible into English for the first time, he asserted the right of every man to examine the Bible's teachings for himself. This deeply offended the church leaders, who saw in such a move nothing but a calculated assault on their entrenched influence.

Half a century or more was to elapse before the printing of books from movable type began in Europe, to be followed in 1476 by Caxton's first press at Westminster for printing books in the English language (and in 1480 at St. Albans), but everything was moving forward to a much easier and wider dissemination of ideas. More grammar schools were being founded, more colleges being established at the universities; more students had opportunities for travelling both in England and in Europe, and few monasteries could so shut themselves off from outside contacts as to be unaware of what was taking place.

Within the cloisters it eventually came to be recognised that the brethren needed occasional rest periods away from their surroundings. St. Albans Abbey had maintained a rest hotel for their monks at Redbourn from quite early days. The smaller monasteries like Ashridge were not able to match this, but the number of lay brethren brought in to help as teachers, stewards, clerks, waiters, painters and building craftsmen increased and this lightened the load.

The long-standing custom that the monks did not own personal property began to change. They had always been allowed to receive gifts to distribute to the poor and needy, and later small sums would be contributed to be divided between the monks to provide for alms, medicines, or even holidays. Normally clothing was issued as required by the cellarer or chamberer, but a custom grew up, and became fairly general, of giving a small allowance of money in lieu of clothes. This might average about a pound a year (at St. Albans *c.* 1475 the sum was £1 7s. 8d.). Gradually the idea of a small fixed wage became the accepted form, and though this greatly displeased the Pope, it was clear that he could do little that was effective about it. In fact, Knowles stated that shortly before the dissolution the tariff of each monastery was known sufficiently well to attract or repel recruits. At the dissolution it was common practice for the Commissioners to award a year's wages as part of the compensation for the displaced, in addition to a pension. The settlement made at the closure of the College of Bonhommes followed this pattern.

* * * * *

In preceding chapters, as in this one, mention has been made, usually by way of comparison, of the Abbey of St. Albans, sufficient to make it interesting to speculate on the influence which its proximity to Ashridge might have had on its smaller neighbour. There are a few pointers. Certainly their lands shared a common boundary, and when a dispute arose in 1380 about the pasture rights under the hedges along Redbourn Road, Abbot Thomas and the rector, Ralph of Aston, settled this in truly British fashion by drawing the boundary down the middle of the road, though it later transpired that the Ashridge rights in the matter were at least questionable. When Abbot Thomas died in 1396, Ralph of Aston was among those who greeted his successor, the Prior, John de la Moote, at St. Albans after returning from his installation at Boreham. Ralph himself died later the same year having been rector for 23 years.[8]

Offa had generously endowed the Abbey of St. Albans to become a Benedictine house for 100 monks in 793, and by the mid 13th century it had reached a leading position in the leadership of literary, cultural and intellectual thought. While it was not the largest, nor the wealthiest, of the monasteries, it had established a premier position by the distinction of its succeeding abbots, and it attracted many scholars from abroad. 'Abbot Thomas de la Mare of St. Albans, whom the Black Prince loved as a brother, was a power in the land.'[9] St. Albans enjoyed a great reputation not only for having set a tradition of historical writing, by keeping extensive domestic records, but for its encouragement of artists and craftsmen. Roger of Wendover, and later Matthew Paris (d. 1259) were its most distinguished historians. It was natural that the influence of French architecture, sculpture and painting was strong and the men employed were usually professional craftsmen, such as masons; but a few, some of whom were the most accomplished, were monks or became monks.

A small group of artists from Colchester settled outside St. Albans Abbey. They included painters and craftsmen in wood and metal. Matthew Paris himself, though he became famous as an historian, was an artist of great talent, and expert in the art of book illumination. These attracted many pupils and small teams of such craftsmen began to go out into the surroundings to enrich and decorate churches and religious houses. At Ashridge, the cloisters of the old monastic buildings were decorated with a series of paintings[10] that might have been the work of artists inspired by the St. Albans school, though there is no proof of this. The tradition of fine calligraphy and book illumination found a response at Ashridge in the beautiful work of Brother Simon de Wederore of Tring, whose copy of a book by Martinus Polonus was made in 1368. It is written on vellum with the index 'curiously and beautifully decorated in red and violet' with other graceful illumination. Though it is not clear when the book came to leave Ashridge, it is now in the ownership of the Huntington Library, San Marino, California. An interesting feature was a personal note inserted by the scribe, which included a dire warning to anyone who should remove the book from his possession. Translated,[11] it reads:

> To the glory of God, and the glorious Virgin Mary and blessed Peter chief of the apostles and of all the saints, Simon de Wederore of Tring, brother in the house of Assheruge, of the order of St. Augustine, in the diocese of Lincoln, wrote this book, and he presented it to God, and to the church of the aforesaid house, . . .

> for the benefit and use of the brethren, and not to be removed from that place, in memory of Philip de Wederore his father and of Petronella his mother and of his brothers John and Thomas and of Katherine the wife of the aforesaid Thomas and in memory of brother Simon himself and of all and singular whom they are in duty bound to serve, on 29th June in the year of our Lord 1368. The use of this book, however, is reserved for the aforesaid brother Simon, as long as he shall live, by permission of his Superior. And if anyone shall remove this book, or destroy the titlepage, let him be accursed, and may he be separated from the most holy Body and Blood of God and the Lord and Saviour Jesus Christ (in whose honour the aforesaid house was founded) and in the last Judgement may he receive the most extreme penalties. So be it. So be it. AMEN.

Other fine illuminated books from Ashridge are preserved in the British Library. The *Historia Scholastica*[12] of Petrus Comestor of the late 13th century (1285-1300), was a book almost certainly executed for Edmund, Earl of Cornwall, and presented by him to the college. The chapter headings, initials and page headings are delicately flourished in red and blue with beautiful representations of birds and beasts. An illuminated border on fol. 234 depicts four shields of arms—those of Edward I, Edward, his son, Richard, King of the Romans, and Edmund, his son, Earl of Cornwall. It is inscribed on fol. 1 'Liber domus de Assherugge'. The 15th-century *Florarium Bartholomei,*[13] a compilation on vellum by John de Mirfield, Augustinian canon of St. Bartholomew's, Smithfield, London, was a collection of excerpts from theological and canon law writers. It bears a note on fol. 259 of the names of Thomas Baxter, vicar of Stickford, Lincolnshire and of Richard Hutton, a Bonhomme of Ashridge, *qui Ricardus, contulit istum Librium domui religiosi de Assherugg . . . ibidem in biblioteca permansurum, A.D. 1518.* A third was *Ovid Moralised,*[14] a collection of historical romances, in Latin, including Richard de Bury's *Philobiblion,* a 15th-century book written on vellum with initials in blue and red. This belonged originally to the Hospice of St. Thomas of Acon, London, and was for a long time loaned to the library at Ashridge by John Nele, the rector of the hospital in 1463. It was this hospital, as related in the next chapter, which, 150 years earlier, Ashridge had attempted to annex to itself.

¶ Here begynneth a lytell treatyse in Englysshe / called the Extripacion of ignorancy: and
it treateth and speketh of the ignorance of people /
shewyng them howe they are bounde to feare god /
to loue god / and to honour their prince. Which trea
tise is lately compyled by sir Paule Busshe preest /
and Bonhome of Edyndon: and dedicate vnto the
yong and most hye renomed lady Mary / princes &
doughter vnto the noble progenytour / our worthy
soueraygne kyng Henry the eight / kyng of Englāde
and of Fraūce / & hye defēder of ỹ christenfaithe. &c.

Fig. 1. From Paul Bush's *Extirpacion of Ignorancy*

Another Bonhomme, Paul Bush, of Edington, spent part of his time at Ashridge in about 1530. Todd attributes to him the role of visitor to the college,[15] that is, one through whom disputes between the brethren might be settled, but this is speculative and there is no known evidence for this appointment. It would, however, seem likely that Bush, described as 'a wise and grave man and well versed in divinity and physic' lent strength to the community at a time when there were signs of tension between some of the brethren, as the reports of successive bishops' visitations testify. Paul Bush was the author of a number of short devotional treatises and poems. He is remembered chiefly for two works, *A lyttel treatyse in Englysshe, called the Extirpacion of Ignorancy* and *Certayne Gostly Medycynes*. The former was in verse and was dedicated to the Princess Mary. It is undated and consists of a small quarto of 18 leaves, printed by Pynson, and is now in the possession of the Cambridge University Library. *Certayne Gostly Medycynes*[16] consists of only 12 leaves, bound together with four other short devotional tracts by other authors under the title of *Devoute Prayers in Englysshe for th'acts of our redemption*. The Bush treatise bears the same imprint as the others, namely, of Robert Redman at the sign of the *George* in Fleet Street, London; but while these are dated 1531, his is undated and probably belongs to 1532. The author explains: 'This lyttel book contayneth certain gostly [i.e., spiritual] medycynes necessary to be used among weldisposed people to eschew and to avoyde the comen plage of pestilence/thus collects and sette forth in ordre by the diligent labours of the religious Syr Paule Bushe in the good house of Edyndon'.

There follow the various prayers and injunctions, and he ends with this bidding:

> Syr Paule Bushe to every well dysposed pacyent/willing to recover gostly helthe:
>
> When this is done/and brought to passe the next day enthewynge/ with good devotion use these medecynes agayne/herrynge [hearing] a masse in the temple of Christe/clene of all corupcyon and thus vertuously continue/all thy lyf season for whan all medecynes/shall faynte and fayle these evermore/shall do good and prevayle.
>
> Thus fayre thou well.

Paul Bush later became Corrector and, finally, head of the Order of Bonhommes at Edington. After the Dissolution he was made Chaplain to King Henry VIII, who later appointed him to be the first Bishop of Bristol. Somewhat surprisingly for a Catholic bishop he married, and when Queen Mary came to the throne, he was much in disfavour for having broken his vows of celibacy. He resigned his see in 1553, and ended his days as rector of Winterborne, near Bristol, where he died in 1558, and was buried in his cathedral.[17]

Chapter Six

DECLINE AND FALL

REMOTE THOUGH IT WAS, the Holy See in Rome exercised its authority in many matters affecting discipline, often without reference to the bishop of the diocese. It caused to be heard cases of dispute between religious houses, and it granted dispensations and indulgences in return for an appropriate fee.

Not long after their foundation the Bonhommes were in trouble with the Pope for attempting to appropriate to themselves the Chapel of St. Thomas the Martyr in the City of London. There existed in Berkhamsted two hospitals, both founded at the beginning of the 13th century: that of St. John the Evangelist cared for the sick and the poor; and the hospital of St. John the Baptist cared for lepers. Both were dependent on the rule of the Order of St. Thomas the Martyr, Acon, in London.[1] Ashridge had somehow acquired the custody of the chapel and hospital of St. Thomas, but in 1307 it was alleged that the brethren had done so by falsehood during the absence of the master, and the matter was referred to Rome. In 1310 the Bishop of London received from the Pope a mandate 'to cite the rector and convent of the Augustinian house of Asserugge in the diocese of Lincoln, to appear before the Pope in person, or by proctor, within four months, with all papers touching the cause between them and the preceptor and brethren of the chapel of St. Thomas the Martyr in Acon, commonly called the Hospital, in the city of London, who have complained that the said chapel, situated in the place called "Alto Vico" [Old Street] and the church of Calcherche, near the said chapel have been taken from them by the said rector and convent. The Pope has appointed William, Cardinal of St. Nicholas in Carcere, to hear the cause'.[2]

The college lost this case and the chapel and hospital reverted to their rightful owners. Little else about Ashridge appears to have disturbed the Holy See for some years. The confirmation of the transfer to the brethren of the churches of Ambrosden (1308) and Chesterton (1408) has already been mentioned. Three interesting indulgences or dispensations are noted:

Indults to the following to have a portable altar . . .

1423. 18 Sept. John Northampton, brother of the house of Asserugge . . . [the fee was 10 grossi for one person, 12 for two].[3]

1442 July

To John Planysted, a brother of the house of Asserych in the diocese of Lincoln, living under the rule of St. Augustine.

Dispensation to him who is a priest and has made an open profession by the order of canons regular of St. Augustine to receive and hold any benefice with cure (only), wont to be held by secular clerks.[4]

1462–63. 7 Id. Oct.

To Thomas Cowper, a bro. of the confraternity of the Augustinian house of the Bonshommes of Asscherugge in the diocese of Lincoln. Dispensation to him, who suffers so much from a grave and incurable bodily disease, that he cannot fulfil the austerity and regular observances of the same order, to receive and retain (for life) a benefice with cure or a service, resign it, simply or for exchange, as often as he pleases, and retain for life a like benefice or service.[5]

If there had been a popular press in Berkhamsted in those days probably the most sensational case would have been that of Philip Harewell, following the slaying of brother Nicholas in about 1475. The circumstances and dispensation merit reproduction:

1476–7. 5 Jan. St. Peter's, Rome . . .

To William Johannis, a canon of Llandaff. Mandate, as below. The recent petition of Philip Harewell, professed [brother] of the house of Asserugge called the house of Bonshommes living under the rule of St. Augustine, in the diocese of Lincoln, contained that lately, after he and the late Nicholas, a brother professed of the same house and in priest's orders, had long hated one another by reason of the blows and wounds which Nicholas had at divers times inflicted on two brothers of the same house and of the threats and assault which he had made against Philip, even drawing his knife, both in choir and elsewhere, and after Philip, perceiving Nicholas's fury and malignity, had made up his mind as far as he could to

> avoid quarrelling with him, and, if that happened, to slay Nicholas rather than let himself be slain, it happened that Nicholas, after being charitably monished and corrected by the rector of the said house about certain excesses, uttered insulting and improper words against the said rector, whereof Philip and Nicholas fell to quarrelling so that, as Philip was trying to go through a certain door of the said house, Nicholas aimed a blow at him with a staff and Philip, fearing violence and remembering Nicholas's fury and malignity, drew his knife and wounded him, which done, after receiving the sacraments and pardoning Philip, Nicholas straightway departed this life. The said petition adding that the said house has few priests who have professed the said order, and that Philip fears that, even after absolution granted to him, he will be unacceptable to the other brothers in the said house, and that if he were not accepted therein he would be obliged to wander about and beg, to the shame of the priestly dignity, and he intends to offer prayers to God in the orders which he has received, the Pope hereby orders the above canon to absolve him from the crime of priest-slaying, enjoining a salutary penance, etc., rehabilitate him and dispense him on account of irregularity incurred, if any, dispense him to minister in the orders which he has received, except in the ministry of the altar, and, in the event of so doing, cause him to be received or to remain in the said house, and to be treated therein with sincere charity, and to have his commons like another brother thereof. *Sedis apostilice graciosa benignitas.*[6]

William John of Llandaff was presumably acting in the capacity of 'prisoner's friend' and intermediary, since the rector and canons of Ashridge could scarcely have interceded in an independent manner.

The historian of today is fortunate that many episcopal records have not only been preserved but, as at Lincoln, they have also been printed and are thus more readily available for study. These help to give a living and, at times, a lively picture of monastic life as revealed in the accounts of bishop's visitations, ordinations and court rulings.

Ordination lists show the progression through the various stages of the priesthood, and illustrate that it was possible to rise within the same community to become *magister* or rector.

27 May 1290.

Subdeacon William, from Ashridge Priory. At Hertford All Saints.

23 Dec. 1290.

Subdeacon William of Wheathampstead, from Ashridge Priory. At Wycombe.

12 March 1291.

Priest — William of Wheathampstead. At Northampton.

22 Dec. 1291.

Subdeacons — Wm. of Broughton, Richard Tenerey, John de Russe, Ralph of Aston, Walter of Dunstable, from Ashridge Priory. At Wycombe.

20 Dec. 1292.

Deacon — Ralph of Aston. At Dorchester-on-Thames.

19 Dec. 1293.

Priest — Ranulf [Ralph] of Aston. At Wycombe.[7]

Four years later Ralph of Aston was elected Rector of Ashridge and remained its head until his death in 1336.[8]

* * * * *

The form of a bishop's visitation was fairly consistent from the 13th century. In a diocese as large as Lincoln, stretching from the Humber in the north to the Thames in the south, it was not to be expected that visitations would be frequent, and this placed a particular responsibility on the rector or head of the house for keeping up standards. The general pattern of a visitation was:

Reception of the bishop.
Examination of the evidence of foundation, presented by the rector.
The current state of the finances of the House.
A sermon by the bishop.
Interview with every member of the community at which complaints and requests were heard. Each member was asked if the Rule and customs were being obeyed,

and this provided evidence of the state of religious discipline and the standard of management of the order.[9]

Two Archbishops of Canterbury are known to have visited the Bonhommes. William Courtenay, in the course of a lengthy tour starting on 17 September 1389 at Baldock, and proceeding through Huntingdon, Ramsey, Peterborough, Spalding, Boston, Leicester, Bicester, and Oxford, reached Ashridge on 25 November, almost at the end of his journey.[10] Archbishop Henry Chichele visited the college on 7 July 1424. The more interesting records, however, come from the early 16th century, partly because they are more complete, but also because they begin to show how the progressive relaxation of the earlier strict observances was leading towards a breakdown of standards of discipline and administration.

Bishop William Smith of Lincoln, visited Ashridge on Tuesday, 8 October 1505, and made various injunctions which, except by implication in reports following in 1515 and 1518, have not been preserved.[11] A certificate acknowledging the bishop's citation for the visitation was given by the rector, John of Berkhamsted, and to this he added a list of the 18 members of the college.[12]

Bishop William Attwater visited the Chapter on the 12–13 June 1518, and in his report noted:

> It was asked that no women be allowed to make stay inside the College.
>
> The Lord Rector in Chapter has been wont to grumble at the brethren as a body, instead of naming both the delinquents and those who were innocent, and because of this there was murmuring among the innocent brothers.
>
> Let bellringers be provided other than the brothers of the House, for the brethren find the bellringing too much in addition to their other duties; or else let a small bell be provided so that one brother be able to ring it by himself.
>
> It is laid down that the ancient injunctions of the time of our Lord (Bishop) William Smith (of blessed memory) be carried out in every particular, and that an Instructor in grammar be provided.
>
> *xiiii day* of the aforesaid month, before the Lord Bishop sitting in the church of the monastery in his judicial capacity. William Clark and Robert Wilson of Bekonsfield were summoned to appear and were sworn on the Holy Gospel that they would come up when called to appear before the said Lord, and that they would carry out the penance then laid down upon them. And, after that is done, he will loose them from the sentence of suspension which they had incurred through fighting in the cemetery. The xiiii day the said Lord dissolved the visitation.[13]

This instance of the bishop sitting in a judicial capacity is not unusual. The same Bishop Attwater, sitting at Missenden, imposed a penance on Thomas Hardynge and his wife Alice for heresy:

> Either of them shall wear a signe of fagot of diverse colours upon their uttermost garment during their lyffes. [They were later pardoned from this.] Either of them shall fast bred and ale every Corpus Christi even during their lyffes.

On 14 April 1515, he granted them a remission:

> Either of them shall every Corpus Christi day during their lives go in the procession at Asherige barefote and bareleged beryng a taper of wex in their hand bryning in such place as shall be assigned unto them by the prior or sub-rector ther.
>
> Item. They nor neyther of them shall never during their lyves dwell out of the parish of Hamersham.[14]

There was a sequel to this a few years later, for Harding was again apprehended for heresy. He refused to recant and was sentenced to execution in 1532, at a trial in which Thomas Waterhouse, the rector of Ashridge, assisted. He died awaiting execution.[15]

But to return to the visitations, Bishop Attwater went to Ashridge again in 1518, arriving on 21 April and remaining for two nights. He found, among other things, that:

> The brethren do not observe silence after meals nor at other times and in places (adjacent to the refectory).
>
> The brethren are not fully aware of the rules of the house.
>
> The Bishop enjoins the Rector that the injunctions made by Bishop William Smyth (1505) have not been observed and should be displayed in the dormitory so that all the brothers can see them and carry them out.
>
> When the Rector and Co-Rector reprimand the brothers, words are used which are harsh and opprobrious. They are instructed to correct this.[16]

This is, on the whole, fairly mild comment and made in kindly terms.

It was about this time that the court poet, John Skelton, stayed at Ashridge, probably for recuperation, and he appears to have found his stay congenial. He commemorated his visit in *A Garland of Laurel,* published in 1523:

> Of the Bonhoms of Ashridge beside Bercamsted,
> That goodly place to Skelton most kind,
> Where the sang royal is, Christes blood so red,
> Whereupon he metrified his mind,
> A pleasanter place than Ashridge is, hard were to find,
> As Skelton rehearseth, with wordes few and plain,
> In his distichon made on verses twain:

Fraxinus in clivo frondetque viret sine rivo,
Non est sub divo similis sine flumine vivo.[17]

(The Ash tree on the hill comes into leaf without a brook,
There is not one like it under the sky without a living stream.)

However, by 1531, the domestic composure of the Bonhomes seemed again to be in some disarray. John Malden had died in 1529, and had been succeeded as rector by Thomas Waterhouse. A mandate of Bishop Langland to the new rector announced that a visitation would be held on 4 May 1531, in spite of the fact that one had recently been held by his Vicar-General, 'the state of affairs being scandalous'.[18] The rector acknowledged the mandate in a certificate of 2 May 1531, and sent it with a list of the brethren. It is interesting to compare the 1505 and 1531 rolls of brethren and to find that seven names are to be found in both lists. These were Thomas Hill (co-rector), Nicholas Edyngton (presumably from the other house at Edington), Elias Barnard, Michael Draper, Robert Ewar, John Hatfield, and Robert Hitchin.

The bishop found a fairly unhappy state of affairs prevailing, as the following extracts suggest:

> There is very little love [*minime caritas*] between the brethren.
>
> The statutes of the College in regard to eating and drinking are being broken.
>
> The number of the brothers is reduced. [There were only 17.] Brother Robert Ewar practises physic. [It is not clear whether this was a stricture or not]. The same Robert is the cellarer of the college and is troublesome.

The reports of the personal interviews are revealing:

> Draper. Says that all is well.
>
> Ewar. The granator [farm manager] goes out of college without cause on many occasions.
>
> Hatfield. The granator is useless to the College.
>
> Hitchen. The office of granator is burdensome. Hatfield is disobedient.
>
> Downham. The seniors are not held in repute. The juniors do not give the seniors the respect due to them . . .
>
> Knighton. Has an impediment in his voice and cannot sing the masses. He says that the wife of a certain Hugo of St. Albans comes to the college frequently and stays overnight.
>
> Canan. Hatfield was disobedient and argued with the Rector.

Other allegations were:

> Women come to the college and eat in *camera cellarii.*
> Hatfield is often absent from Mattins.
> Hitchen often leaves the choir, even at the time of exsequies, and frequents the ale-houses. He is in debt to divers persons.

There were other observations in the same vein, including a mild one from the bishop himself that the brethren sang too hurriedly at worship.[19]

It was clear that Ashridge was not a happy and composed community, though the complaints seemed to centre on only two or three people. While the standing of the college remained high in the eyes of the outside world, within the brethren were troubled with problems, often petty perhaps, and they were unsettled. The great burdens of looking after the estates and finances, coupled with growing disillusion about the prospects and future of the monastic calling were probably the major causes, and there is no indication that the new rector, Thomas Waterhouse, possessed the stature to be able to arrest the coming decline.

* * * * * *

Compared with the visitations of the bishops, a royal visit must have seemed a very different affair. Thomas Waterhouse seems to have enjoyed the friendship of King Henry VIII, who referred to him as 'our gentleman priest'. He had been elected in 1529, and he was to remain at the head of the college until its final extinction in 1539. The interesting process of his election is preserved in documents at Lincoln, and a transcript of these is given in Appendix I. In 1530, the year following his election, Waterhouse entertained the king at Ashridge, no doubt in royal style. According to the account books[20] the visit lasted over several days, as entries show:

1530.	Aug. 7.	The King's offering at Ashridge to the Holy Blood there.[21]	7s. 6d.
	Aug. 17.	To a servant of Sir Edward Donne's for bringing a bucke to the King at Ashridge.	7s. 6d.
	Aug. 18.	To Edmonde the footman for so moche by him given in rewards at Ashridge to one that made the dogges to draw water.[22]	3s. 8d.

Henry was preoccupied at the time of his visit with trying to divorce Queen Catherine in order to marry Anne Boleyn. He was in something of a quandary, not wanting to offend the all-powerful Emperor Charles V, whose aunt was Catherine, not wanting to break with Rome, and seeking mostly to come to terms with his own conscience. Unaccustomed to being thwarted, he was smouldering under the obduracy of Rome and irritated at the failure of Cardinal Wolsey to advance the progress of his divorce. Wolsey, a committed supporter of the supremacy of the Pope, had little liking for his master's business. When a comparatively unknown Cambridge don and churchman, Thomas Cranmer, suggested that a better approach might be for the king to build up an enlightened opposition to the supremacy of the Pope among thinking men, on the lines of the Reformation spreading in Europe, which could lead to a peaceful transition of the Church of England from the power of Rome, Henry was immediately attracted, and Cranmer was given the task of building up the propaganda machinery. Henry hesitated to move against Wolsey for his failure because he had been his main counsellor, but there were too many other of his advisors who wanted to see a clear break with Rome. Wolsey was dismissed from his state offices and his possessions were confiscated. He had been assisted by one Thomas Cromwell, first as a collector of taxes for the see of York and then as his agent in suppressing some of the smaller monasteries to provide for the endowment of his colleges in Oxford. Cromwell was loyal to his master, but was unwilling to accept that Wolsey's downfall should signify the end of his own career. He had become too fond of power and was determined to fight for his own future. Within a year of Wolsey's death, Cromwell had so successfully managed to win the king's favour that he became Chancellor of the Exchequer, and then the king's Secretary and Master of the Rolls.

The death of the sick and aged Wolsey, on his journey from exile in York to face trial for treason, gave encouragement to the Boleyn faction, but it left a gap in the conduct of national policy which Henry found difficult to fill. He did not really want another strong adviser to curb his intentions. Cromwell, from his vantage point as Secretary, gained the ear of the king, and by supporting Anne Boleyn was able to insinuate himself quietly into the role of policy adviser. Yet the royal divorce was not his main objective. 'He had one scheme in view: to carry out on a grand scale the dispossession of the Church of Rome.'[23] So came to power the man who, more than any other, was to bring about the downfall of the monasteries in England. He saw as one of his aims making the king the richest monarch in Europe. The power of the state would then become unassailable, and by concentrating this power in England, the thorny problem of Scotland, Ireland and Wales could be kept under control. Anne Boleyn could become queen. Cromwell was convinced that things could be so managed that the king could become the head of the church quite legally without provoking more than an emotional unheaval. Henry was less sure. He was wise enough to see the difficulties ahead. He had a deep feeling for the faith in which he had been reared, but the opposition of Pope Clement to the annulment of his marriage to Queen Catherine hurt him deeply. He could not understand how the Pope could so treat the Defender of the Faith. Henry decided on an outright challenge. His first move was against the clergy at the Convocation of 1531, and by threats of confiscation and by exacting large fines he set out to obtain recognition of himself as Supreme Head of the Church. He had many things in his favour because none of the institutions of the realm could mount any effective opposition. The Church certainly could not, because in spite of its great wealth and estates it was only too well aware how much others wanted to lay hands on them. Individual thinkers opposed to the king were easily suppressed: they either fled to Europe or paid the supreme penalty. 'As for the rest, Parliament, the nobility, clerics and monks, court followers and civil servants were concerned less for principles than for their lives and the safety of their families. Most were prepared to settle for what they could get.'[24]

Parliament was encouraged to increase legislation against the clergy. Papal taxes were suspended and the benefit of clergy was restricted. Thomas Cranmer, meanwhile, had returned from Europe and been made Archbishop of Canterbury, and at his consecration he swore that in all his acts he would place the king above everyone as Supreme Head of the Church of England. The way was thus soon opened up for parliament and Convocation to pronounce Henry's divorce legal, and Anne Boleyn became queen. Parliament eventually passed the Act of Supremacy and Thomas Cromwell was made Vicar-General to enforce it. He was given a commission to carry out a general visitation of churches and monasteries. This was the power he had schemed for, and he entered on his plans to abolish papal authority and reform the Church not only with zeal but with utter ruthlessness.

The idea of confiscating the wealth of the monasteries was not by any means a new one. Henry V had suppressed many small orders of foreign origin, such as those of Cluny and others founded by the Norman conquerors and their sons. Switzerland and Sweden had already dispossessed religious houses, though generally without persecution. This was one telling way to strike at the power of Rome. There had long been antagonism in England to the system of Papal taxes, and even in 1464 the Archbishop of Canterbury had advised his clergy to seek the protection of the king against their claims.[25]

County commissioners were instructed by Cromwell to visit all religious houses to investigate the internal conditions. It was essential to know precisely what resources and wealth the Crown could count upon, and this was the first systematic survey to be carried out for nearly two hundred years. Interrogations about finances and administration were searching, and were followed by injunctions as to behaviour, often peremptory and severe, sometimes even crude and cruel. Professed monks under a certain age were interviewed and were given an opportunity, if they wished, to be dispensed from their vows. The way was being cleared for the Acknowledgement of Supremacy. In due course worse terror tactics were to be employed against certain larger monasteries, such as the looting of Canterbury and the murder of the heads of the abbeys of Colchester, Reading and Glastonbury. If the Crown could by such means gain possession of the monasteries, this would enable the king to dispose of their lands cheaply to the laity and so gain support for his policy of religious reform.

Cromwell grew in power and became Lord Great Chamberlain, and was created Earl of Essex. In the process of spoiling the churches and monasteries he had not hesitated to enrich his own wealth and possessions, but the end of his power and influences was signalled when, having negotiated the king's marriage to Anne of Cleves, Henry found her impossible as a wife. Once the divorce was in train he had no further use for his Chamberlain. Cromwell had enemies in plenty who hated him and his policies, and it was not long before a case was built against him and he suffered a rapid change of fortune. Judgement, right or wrong, was seldom dilatory. He was arrested, charged with high treason and heresy, and beheaded on Tower Hill. A comment of Sir Walter Raleigh about Henry VIII seems very apt: 'To how many he gave the abundant flowers from whence to gather honey and in the end of harvest burnt them in the hive'.[26]

Cromwell, the efficient and ruthless administrator, was the mastermind and main agent for destroying the monasteries and the authority of the Pope in England. Apologists have held that he and his commissioners were merely over-zealous tax collectors, concerned mostly with raising money to enable the king to maintain his armies in France. Even if they were partly such, the shameful means he employed to gain his objectives hardly excuse his actions; and since it is not conceivable that a monarch so shrewd as Henry VIII could have remained in ignorance of what was going on, he must be accounted guilty of acquiescence if not of actual complicity.

* * * * *

The final valuation of the Ashridge estates, as returned to the king's commissioners in 1534, five years before the Dissolution, was £415 16s. 4d. per year.[27] This consisted of:

Outgoings	£	s.	d.
To Thomas Waterhouse, rector, per annum	110	6	8
To 17 brethren at £8 per annum each	136	0	0
To the clear outgoings of Temporal and Spiritual possessions of the College	150	9	8
The College paid yearly tenths to the Crown of	41	13	4

The Rental was valued at:

In Temporals	£	s.	d.
In Co. Hertford			
By farms in Hemel Hemstead	137	10	3
By farms in Bovingdon	69	9	3

In Temporals (Co. Hertford)—*continued*

	£	s.	d.
Customary fees in Gaddesden Parva	7	7	10
Customary fees in Frithsden	6	13	10
Rents of tenements in Berkhamsted	1	0	0
Fee farm rents in Aldbury	2	13	4
In Co. Oxon			
By rents and farms in Chesterton	27	13	2
By rents and farms in Ambrosden	31	5	10
In Co. Bucks			
By rents in Pitstone	16	2	6
Lands in the hands of the rector, and belonging to the college, in total 114 acres at the rate of sixpence per acre, are worth	2	17	0
By sale of the woods..	13	6	8
Fines for heriots and perquisites of courts	2	0	0
By fines and releases	2	0	0
Amount of Temporals	£319	19	8

In Spirituals	£	s.	d.
In Co. Hertford			
The rectory of Hemelhemstead	42	3	0
In Co. Oxon			
Rectory of Blackthorn, Oxon (Ambrosden)	30	1	8
Rectory of Chesterton	8	0	0
In Co. Bucks			
Rectory of Pitstone	15	8	6
Rectory of Ivinghoe	33	10	10
By fines and releases of the rectories	1	6	8
By returning their own tenths		13	8
Amount of Spirituals	131	4	4
Gross Amount	451	4	0
Deduct reprisals	31	1	8
Total Valuation	£420	2	4

This breakdown into detail gives a slightly different total from the annual value of £416 16s. 4d. returned to the Commissioners. Other authorities also display small discrepancies, but this fairly represents the worth of Ashridge, and places it in the rank of larger or wealthier monasteries.

The Bonhommes were not to prove martyrs to their faith. They were prepared to settle, and in common with most other such communities throughout the land, the rector and 16 brethren signed the Acknowledgement of Supremacy on 14 September 1534. Their names were Thomas Waterhouse, Thomas Hill, Elias Bernard, Michael Draper, John Hatfield, Robert Hichyn, Richard Gardyner, William Knighton, Richard Bedford, Roger Birchley, William Downham, Richard Saunders, John Axtyll, William Brooke, Joseph Stepneth, Richard Canan, and William Yonge.[28]

The end was not to be long delayed. The second Act suppressing the larger monasteries with an annual value above £200 became law five years later, and Ashridge was finally surrendered on 6 November 1539.

Newcome[29] gives the names of all to whom annual pensions were to be paid, the first portion of which was due in 1540:

To Thomas Waterhouse, rector, £100 p.a. and 50 loads of wood.

	£	s.	d.
To Thomas Hill	10	0	0
To Michael Draper	10	0	0
To John Hatfield	8	0	0
To Robert Hitchin	7	0	0
To Richard Saunders	5	6	8
To Richard Canan	6	0	0
To John Stepneth	8	0	0
To Richard Gardner	7	0	0
To William Knighton	6	0	0
To Richard Bedford	6	0	0
To Roger Birchley	6	0	0
To William Young	6	13	4
To William Downham	6	13	4
To William Brook	5	6	8
To Edward Peacock, novice	2	13	4
	£100	13	4

Two names are missing in this list from those who signed the Acknowledgement of Supremacy in 1534: Elias Bernard and John Axtyll, while the name of the novice, Edward Peacock, appears for the first time.

In many ways the final settlements made by the Commissioners were not ungenerous. Arrears of wages were paid and pensions were awarded for life: the death of a pensioner had to be reported to the bishop by the churchwardens of the parish in which he lived. The monks might supplement their pensions by holding other ecclesiastical appointments, and many of them were absorbed into the ranks of the parochial clergy. Not a great deal is known about how most of the Bonhommes fared after the closure, though many probably remained in the general vicinity. Thomas Waterhouse became rector of Quainton in Buckinghamshire.[30] He died in 1554 and directed in his will that he should be buried in the parish church of Hemel Hempstead. He bequeathed his monastic vestments between the churches of Quainton, Hemel Hempstead and Great Berkhamsted.[31]

William Downham, who was 34 years old at the Dissolution, took the degree of B.A. in 1541 and M.A. in 1543. He married and was rector of Datchworth, Herts, in 1552 (worth £14 13s. 4d. p.a.), and became chaplain to the Princess Elizabeth. He was eventually consecrated Bishop of Chester in 1561 and died in 1577.[32] The family of John Axtyll remained in the Hemel Hempstead area. One of his descendants, William Axtell, was town clerk of Berkhamsted in 1639; his son, Daniel Axtell, became an officer in Cromwell's army, and was Captain of the Guard at the trial of Charles I. In the revulsion of feeling which followed the king's execution, Axtell was tried and sentenced for recigide, and was hanged at Tyburn. Roger Birchley married and was rector of Ayot St. Peter, Herts (worth £7 0s. 0d. p.a.) in 1552.[33]

Let the final words on the closure of Ashridge be those of Henry Todd, who. had the advantage (which we have not) of access to the register of the college. He observed that someone, perhaps a brother, contemporary with Thomas Waterhouse, had recorded in the register in 1539, 'the final extinction of this noble house and the expulsion of the brethren its owners' in the words, *Hoc anno nobilis domus de Asscherugge destructa fuit, et fratres expulsi, in die Sancta Leonardi* ('in this year the noble house of Ashridge was destroyed and the brethren expelled on St. Leonard's Day'). Todd adds that there immediately follows an entry 'written with no small indignation', *Hoc anno decapitatus fuit ille eximius hereticus et proditor Thomas Cromwell, qui causa fuit destruccionis omnium domorum religiosorum in Anglia* ('in this year, 1540, was beheaded that extraordinary heretic and traitor, Thomas Cromwell, who was the cause of the destruction of all the religious houses in England').

* * * * *

The ultimate fate of the relic of the Holy Blood has always been a matter of conjecture. T. W. E. Roche said of Hailes that the local legend was that their portion of the relic was smuggled away to Burnham Abbey, Bucks, which Richard of Cornwall had founded, and there it was secretly buried within the walls, no one knows where.[34] It is interesting that Burnham today is the house of an Anglican Order of women known as the Sisters of the Precious Blood. Could the holy relic of Ashridge have been similarly removed and buried somewhere under oath of secrecy, or was it actually exhibited at St. Paul's Cross on 24 February 1538 when the Bishop of Rochester denounced it? The latter seems improbable, but such questions remain, though they are unlikely ever to be answered.

Chapter Seven

THE YOUNG TUDORS AND ASHRIDGE

1. Tormented Childhood

WITH THE CLOSING of the monastery doors Ashridge now entered upon a very different phase of its history, and this, for all its brevity, is compelling in its complexity. Within the next 10 years occurred the death of King Henry VIII, and in the following decade Ashridge was to witness something of the troubled fortunes of his three children as the reigns of Edward VI and of Queen Mary took their course. Although this chapter deals primarily with Elizabeth there was a close interaction of their lives up to 1558, when Elizabeth ascended the throne.

First, however, a final comment on the passing of the monasteries is appropriate. The closure followed a generally common pattern throughout the country. The outward signs had too frequently included the pointless spoiling of buildings and the plunder of such of the remaining contents that had not already been claimed for the state coffers or for the adornment of the houses of ambitious men. Wholesale and wanton destruction of books was common and many valuable libraries were dispersed and fine works of art desecrated. Ashridge seems largely to have escaped this, probably on account of the king's interest. The upheaval which the closures caused to society generally has often been exaggerated. The numbers of professed monks and canons had been falling steadily for a very long time. It has been estimated that the total number of those dispossessed at the Dissolution was about eight thousand.[1] Most of them received pensions and were able to take other ecclesiastical appointments if they wished, while the more aged returned to their families. A very large number of the lay workers and servants employed in household duties, in the kitchens, the farm estates, gardens and similar services would probably have found continuing employment as the new owners and tenants took possession and set up their establishments. At the beginning most of the religious houses and estates that fell into the hands of the Crown were leased. Baskerville asserts that out of almost one thousand six hundred grants of land during the reign of Henry VIII not more than one in 40 were outright gifts, and the eventual sale of monastic lands occurred quite gradually in the course of the next 100 years.[2] Ashridge falls into this pattern as it was to remain in Crown ownership for nearly forty years before Queen Elizabeth finally disposed of it.

The first tenant of Ashridge after the closure was John Norris, a gentleman farmer. He was granted custody of the house and former monastery, together with about one hundred and sixty acres of arable land, as well as the use of several woods in Letters Patent, dated 19 November 1541, for a term of 21 years at an annual rent of £6 0s. 10d., payable in two equal portions.[3] Another tenant farmer, Robert Eme, had earlier been granted a lease of and had occupied the Dairy House and cottages, barns and buildings, outside the gates of the monastery, and he also enjoyed a similar amount of arable and meadowland and rights in woods. He claimed that he held this by an agreement, bearing the college seal, made with the former rector, Thomas Waterhouse, dated 7 November 1536. The sequel is not difficult to imagine. It was not long before Robert Eme alleged that John Norris and his agent or partner, Oliver Louthe, used various dubious means to persuade him to sell his lease and rights. The case went before the High Court of the Exchequer Augmentations with counter-allegations that Eme had stolen from the monastery some old doors, and some lead, iron and glass. Eme denied this and said that Oliver Louthe had sold the things to him for five shillings. He went further and alleged that he had been physically assaulted by Louthe, and that he and Elizabeth, his wife, and his servants had been locked up in the monastery, 'whereby the said Elizabeth is likely by such durance of imprisonment to die'. Norris took advantage of his position and petitioned the king directly. Robert Eme protested his complete innocence, and both parties asked for costs and damages to be awarded.[4] Sadly, the final judgement is not recorded. From the style of the documents, Norris had the more accomplished lawyer, but it can only be presumed that some accommodation was reached as Robert Eme was shown as still having tenure of the Dairy House and the other lands in 1550 when Ashridge was conveyed to the Princess Elizabeth.

The exact conditions of John Norris's tenancy are not clear, but it is reasonable to suppose that in addition to the farming and grazing rights, they entailed a continuing care of the large range of former monastic buildings in such a way that the principal rooms at least could be occupied as required, for it was not long before the first royal visitor, the young Prince Edward, was to arrive.

* * * * *

The presence of royalty in residence at Ashridge was limited to a very short period of less than fifteen years, and was not even continuous during that time. Only the children of Henry VIII lived there, and indeed, with Hatfield, Hunsdon, Cheshunt, and Ware within easy distance there would have seemed to be no special pressure to keep Ashridge open, except perhaps that it was already destined to pass to Elizabeth under her father's will. The principal advantage in those days of still primitive sanitation was that it was always useful to have another house to go to when the time arrived for the present abode to be cleansed and sweetened of its malodours after too long an occupation by a large household. In the Hatfield Papers is a letter from John Lee to Sir Robert Cecil (1595) in which he recalls that, as a boy, he had seen Queen Elizabeth (then Princess) at his father's house 'where it pleased her highness to be lodged six and seven weeks together while her house at Ashridge, where her majesty usually lay, was aired and cleaned . . .'.[5]

For the royal children these were not especially happy times. Each had been deprived of the care of a natural mother, and the step-mothers changed with almost bewildering frequency. Mary and Elizabeth, deposed in turn from the expectations of succession, suffering the stigma of bastardy, and more often than not out of favour with their father, had little cause to look back on these years as their most joyous, and Mary felt the stigma more deeply than Elizabeth. Edward, succeeding to the throne before his tenth birthday, exchanged one form of loneliness for another under the deliberate restrictions of his Uncle Somerset's protectorship, and he was long prevented from personal contact with his sisters, especially with Elizabeth, whom he loved. Elizabeth herself, at first neglected, and later the target of suspicion and intrigue, was to be inevitably at odds with her sister Mary throughout most of the latter's reign. Such a background of early instability and unhappiness for the royal children needs to be understood in the light of the disastrous marriage record of their father.

Henry badly wanted a son to ensure the Tudor succession. He was six years younger than his queen, Catherine of Aragon, Four children had already been stillborn to her or had survived no more than a few weeks before a daughter, Mary, was born in 1516, and lived. After more miscarriages and yet another stillborn child it was plain that Catherine could bear no more children, and so the king was resolved on remarrying. The protracted negotiations for annulling his marriage in order to let him marry Anne Boleyn drove Henry to distraction. The political and moral implications were enormous, and as the arguments dragged on, with Henry becoming less sanguine of being able to secure his divorce, a break with the Vatican became inevitable. Catherine, stoutly refusing to acknowledge the validity of any of the stated grounds for a divorce, was banished, first to Ampthill, then to Kimbolton in Huntingdonshire. Here she was cut off from all friends sympathetic to her cause and was prevented from having her daughter Mary to live with her, lest together they should provide the spark for a rising against the monarch. At Kimbolton Catherine lived out her remaining years in quiet dignity as the Princess Dowager. When the annulment was finally pronounced, enabling the king to marry Anne Boleyn, it was the adolescent Mary who suffered more from the change than her mother. She had been a gay and lively child, but a very strict upbringing and a serious formal education had changed her. She was an accomplished girl, but for all her skill in conversing in Latin and playing the spinet, the Spanish influence in her rearing had taught her to avoid what might be thought frivolous, and she enjoyed few of the excitements and pleasures of a young girl growing up. At 17 she had become colourless and withdrawn. She was devoutly loyal to the Catholic faith, and she bitterly deplored Henry's attitude to her mother. Above all, with a fiercely youthful and immature pride, she deeply resented the woman who had supplanted her mother in her father's favour. Her cup of bitterness was to overflow when the verdict was delivered that, because the Princess Dowager had never been legally married, Mary, so far from being heir to the throne, was an illegitimate child.

Henry nervously awaited Anne Boleyn's next confinement after one male child had already been stillborn. When a daughter was born at Greenwich Palace in September 1533, his anguish and disappointment were intense. 'I can see well', Henry railed, 'that God does not want to give me male children', and his mind was quickly working out plans for a new marriage. Anne Boleyn suffered two more miscarriages, and with them she experienced the dreadful fear of failure, which only made her temper more irritable, and her behaviour more reckless. On the last occasion, when she found Henry making love to one of her ladies-in-waiting, Jane Seymour, Anne's rage was so furious that it brought on a premature labour and she was delivered of a dead boy. As Sir John Neale put it, 'she had miscarried of her saviour'. Charges of adultery with five men were brought against her, and she was condemned for high treason. She went to the scaffold in May 1536. Elizabeth, not quite three years old, remained in the care of the good Lady Bryan at Hatfield.

Henry's first queen, Catherine, had died earlier in the year, to his undoubted relief. Anne Boleyn had done her best to come to terms with Mary in her bereavement, but found her obstinate and resolutely determined to abandon neither her Catholic principles nor her faith in the rightness of her dead mother's cause. Anne's response to this rebuff, prompted partly by spite and partly by a frightening insight into the precariousness of her own position, was to order Mary to wait upon the new infant princess. Mary, already jealous of the newcomer who had supplanted her as heir to the throne, did not relish this, nor the scarcely-veiled reasons for such an appointment; nevertheless, after Anne's death, with a natural compassion for the motherless child, she found herself won over by the endearing ways of this lively small girl, so ready to show love to her elder sister. At heart this did not alter

Mary's conviction that she herself had been harshly treated and that she was little but a pawn on the losing side in a game she was only slowly beginning to comprehend. The result was the birth of a love-hate relationship between herself and Elizabeth which was to continue throughout the rest of her life.

Elizabeth had received little enough of her mother's time and attention and had so far spent most of her infant life at Hatfield, in far healthier surroundings than London, and where she was to remain for most of the next seven years. She is described as having reddish gold hair and a very white skin, with golden brown eyes and lashes so fair as to be almost invisible. She was a spirited child and very quick to learn. In the aftermath of Anne Boleyn's execution her position was now questionable. She was too young to feel any great emotion at the death of her mother, and afterwards she learned not to feel any particular shame at being the child of an adultress. It was probably a sign of the times that attitudes were changing, and as she grew older Elizabeth was not disturbed to the same extent by being pronounced illegitimate as was her sister Mary. It was sufficient for her that she was the daughter of the king.

Her governess, Lady Bryan, felt her own responsibilities deeply. Her small charge had outgrown the pretty clothes in which her mother had dressed her. Who now was going to provide for her? She hastened to write to Thomas Cromwell, the first Minister, asking for money for supplying new clothes: 'She hath neither gown, nor kirtle nor petticoat, nor no manner of linen . . . nor forsmocks, nor kerchiefs . . . I have driven it off as best I can, that by my troth I can drive it off no longer: beseeching you, my Lord, that you will see that her Grace hath that which is needful for her'. She also begged him that her young charge should not have to dine at the same table with the rest of the staff, as Sir John Shelton, then master of the Hatfield household, thought that she should, but that she 'should have a mess of meat at her own lodging . . .', and she adds, 'God knoweth my Lady hath great pain with her teeth, and they come very slowly forth'. Anxious that the king should be pleased with his young daughter, she concluded: 'For she is as toward a child and as gentle of conditions, as ever I know in my life . . .'.[6] The careful and sensible upbringing of Elizabeth by Lady Bryan, coupled, as it was, with a deprivation of luxuries and an absence of spoiling, must have played some part in developing the resilient spirit that was to stand her in good stead in the years ahead.

The king, meanwhile, in his fervour to beget a male heir, had lost no time in marrying the gentle Jane Seymour. Henry simply could not envisage a woman upon the throne of England and his preoccupation with having a son was beginning to assume obsessive dimensions. On 12 October 1537 at Hampton Court, Jane gave birth to the weakly infant Edward. Henry's pleasure was unbounded, though for Jane, alas! it was to be a different story. She had 'obeyed and served' her Lord, but her frail physique was not equal to the strain; within two weeks her strength had evaporated and she died. Henry was grief-stricken as he wrote, 'Divine Providence has mingled my joy with the bitterness of the death of her who brought me this happiness'. Though there were to be three more queens, the king was to have no more surviving children. He doted on the small boy, whose frail existence kept alive the hopes of a continuing Tudor dynasty, and at his christening at Greenwich the little Elizabeth performed her first public duty when she was allowed to carry the baptismal robe in the procession. Edward needed a mother and the king realised this; but Henry was also persuaded by his first Minister, Thomas Cromwell, that more than a wife and a mother for the heir of the throne was required. He ought to make a political marriage alliance which would thwart the Catholic claimants to the throne and, hopefully, strengthen his capacity to deal with France and Spain. Cromwell convinced him that Anne of Cleves, sister of the Duke of Cleves, a border state of some strategic value, would be the right choice for him. When Anne finally arrived, awkward and bereft of courtly graces, with no words of English, Henry's shock was ill-concealed. She certainly did not measure up to Holbein's flattering portrait which had preceded her. The king was left with little choice but to make the best of it and allow the arrangements for the wedding to his 'Flanders Mare' to proceed. Her married her at Greenwich in January 1540. Anne was without charm and unromantic, yet by most accounts she was amiable enough and intelligent, and she seems to have taken warmly to Elizabeth; but life with her held no excitement for Henry, and it became steadily more distasteful. He grew bored, and when his ever-roving eye hit on the pretty and vivacious Kathryn Howard, niece of Lord Norfolk, he was quickly captivated. He was resolved that this unsuitable marriage to Anne of Cleves should be annulled, but this time more decorously. A settlement was proposed and Anne was to have a generous pension, two manor houses for her residences, with suitable furnishings, and she was to be known as the king's sister. Anne accepted the situation with dignity and without hesitation. She rather enjoyed living in England, and was not a little relieved at this peaceable end to a strained relationship. One of the more homely conditions she insisted on was that she could continue to see Elizabeth, whom she loved, as often as she wished.

With this separation accomplished, the fate of Thomas Cromwell was sealed. He was already under an impending cloud for having brought about the king's marriage with Anne, and Henry had no further use for him; Cromwell's end came on 28 July 1540. If the king's conscience was in any way troubled at having consented to his death, it did not prevent him from choosing that very day to set out his wedding to Kathryn Howard, his 'rose without a thorn'. It was a marriage destined to be of brief durance. After a fairly rapturous year, there was as yet no sign of a child. Henry began to grow more moody, and the young queen, with a naive unconcern for the consequences, was ready for a liaison. The king set out in the summer of 1541 on a journey to the north, to Lincoln and to York, where five years earlier the people had revolted against his treatment of the monasteries.[7] Kathryn accompanied her husband, but almost under his nose was able to pursue a liaison with Thomas Culpeper. Unknown to her, information about this affair, and about earlier ones with Francis Derham and Manox before her marriage, reached the ears of Archbishop Cranmer. When the royal pair returned to London in the autumn, happy to be coming home, their arrival at Hampton Court was greeted with anxiety about the health of the young prince, who had a fever. It was decided that the fresher air of Hertfordshire would benefit him, and Edward was sent to Ashridge for a few weeks. So far as is known, he was the first of the royal residents.[8] Cranmer felt that the rumoured infidelities of the queen could no longer be kept from the king, and in sorrow he bore his fears to Henry by means of a paper, because he 'had not the heart to tell him by mouth'. Henry was quite shaken by this revelation and was incredulous, but the investigation which he ordered left no doubts. After the full weight of parliament and the process of law had been brought to bear Kathryn Howard went to the scaffold on 13 February 1542.

It was in this climate that the royal children were growing up, and it was understandable that their lives were confused by insecurity. The blow to the king's pride was severe. Four of his five marriages had failed. At the age of only 50 he now looked an old and very tired man, and the pains in his legs were getting worse. He endured his lonely widowerhood for a year, knowing that he ought to marry again for the sake of his children. His daughter Mary was now with him, and though he was fond of her, as he was of all his children, he could not understand her attitude or obstinacy in clinging to the Catholic faith.

Elizabeth, now 10 years old, was still living at Hatfield with her brother Edward. Neither had known much parental affection, and the king was too occupied to pay them much attention. While Mary had slowly come to regard her stepsister with more affection, Elizabeth and Edward, being near in age, developed a close and fond relationship. For a time they were all drawn together, though it was not to last. In 1543 all three were at Ashridge at the same time. Elizabeth and Edward had been moved there, and Mary was brought to join them, ostensibly for the sake of her health, and she remained throughout the autumn.[9]

In August the king held a Privy Council at Ashridge. War with France had broken out again. France was negotiating for the marriage of the Queen of Scotland to a French prince, and a union between these two countries was a serious threat to the king's aims of uniting Scotland with England. When the Emperor Charles V tried to bring England to his side in his campaign against France, Henry was ready to co-operate, with a sound reason. A small force under Sir John Wallop and Sir Thomas Seymour was sent to aid the emperor in the north of France. The Council dealt with a request for instructions from the force commanders and sent a reply:

> The King has seen their letters. They are to remain where they are 'in support of the Duke of Ascot and the Grete Master, and

> the Emperor of Holland, or the Prince of Holland, will come within 14 days to join you as you shall be able to asseige Laundersey or else to enter the enemy's country....' [The Council adds encouraging reports of progress in other places . . . and concludes with familiar greeting.] 'And thus fayre you hartly well' From Ashridge, the 27 August 1543.[10]

Whether Henry's presence at Ashridge coincided with that of any of his children it is not quite clear, but it seems unlikely that he spent much time with them. A short while before the hostilities broke out, he had married again. His new bride was the wealthy Katherine Parr, widowed twice already, 20 years younger than Henry, a complete contrast to Kathryn Howard. A graceful, quiet, but cheerful woman, well educated and endowed with a fund of human compassion, she had been courted by Thomas Seymour, but she could not refuse the king. She felt that she would be able to give Henry the warmth and kindness that his life had most lacked, and that she could create some kind of stability in his life. She calmed his temper and radiated the kind of cheerful goodwill and affection which Henry and his children all needed in their various ways.

Elizabeth was seldom allowed to remain for long at Court in her father's reign. This may have been a measure of prudence, as the Court was scarcely the place in which a young girl should be reared. She accepted that she had been supplanted as heir to the throne, and though she saw him but seldom she loved and admired her father; yet she was frequently hurt by his exclusion of her from his company, often for reasons she did not entirely understand. In the summer of 1543 she appears to have been out of favour again, and appealed to her new stepmother, to intercede for her so that she might return to Court. Nothing much seems to have happened, and almost a year passed in which she was not allowed to see either the king or the queen, before she once more implored Katherine Parr to intercede with her father: 'I well know', Elizabeth wrote to her in the elaborate, tortuous style which she was being taught, 'that the clemency of your Highness has had as much care and solicitude for my health as the King's majesty himself. By which thing I am not only bound to serve you, but also to revere you with filial love, since I understand that your most illustrious highness has not forgotten me every time you have written to the King's majesty . . . For heretofore I have not dared to write to him . . .'. This last sentence shows the anxiety of mind which coloured her relationship with her father. She continued, 'wherefore I now humbly pray your most excellent highness that, when you write to his majesty, you will condescend to recommend me to him, praying ever for his sweet benediction, and similarly entreating our Lord God to send him best success, and the obtaining of victory over his enemies, so that your highness and I may, as soon as possible, rejoice together with him on his happy return . . .'.[11]

Henry had recently left England to join his troops in the campaign against France, and was himself conducting the siege of Boulogne. In one of his rare personal letters (he seldom corresponded in his own hand) he wrote at some length to Queen Katherine, thanking her for her letters and for some venison she had sent, saying he 'would have written unto you again a letter with our own hand, but that we be so occupied, and have so much to do in forseeing and caring for everything myself . . .'. He reports that they had been detained because 'our provision of powder is not come out of Flanders as we thought it would'. They had, however, won most of the town; 'and this day we begin three batteries, and have three mines going, besides one which has done his execution in shaking and tearing off one of their greatest bulwarks. No more to you at this time, sweetheart, . . . saving we pray you to give in our name our hearty blessings to all our children . . .'.[12]

For Elizabeth, this last sentence conveyed the message she so much desired and the dark cloud was lifted.

In the autumn of 1544 she and her brother were again at Ashridge with their tutors and the faithful governess, Mrs. Ashley. Both children had been put under the discipline of a formal education at quite an early age. Little is known of their early studies, but Edward was being taught Latin at the age of six, and Elizabeth was already learning Latin and Greek with William Grindall. She was to show an aptitude for languages which astonished her teachers, and by the age of 12 she had also learned the principles of geography, mathematics and astronomy. Katherine Parr, who had shown more love to her than any of her family had previously done, with the exception of Anne of Cleves, took a very close interest in Elizabeth's education, and gave her an apartment at Whitehall so that she could be near. A close mutual affection developed. Elizabeth was by then a child of many accomplishments, of some beauty, and displaying very graceful manners, and, as Miss Strickland observed, 'she was also possessed of a wit and discretion to know when to employ it'.

Edward, though less quick than his sister, showed the same promise. His tutor, Dr. Richard Cox, reported proudly to Sir William Paget, one of the king's secretaries:

> *10 Dec. 1544.* From Ashridge
>
> He hath learnt the eight parts of speech and can decline any manner Latin noun and conjugate a verb perfectly . . .
>
> Everyday in mass he reads a portion of Solomon's Proverbs for the exercise of his reading . . . The Prince is a vessel apt to receive all goodness and learning, witty, sharp and pleasant.

The king was making an allowance of £20 a month from the Privy Purse for his children. It seems, however, that outside the royal entourage, the inhabitants of Ashridge were less than comfortable. Dr. Cox concludes his letter: 'I would God [it] might stand with his pleasure to appoint some certain sum monthly to be dealt among the miserable whereas the Prince's Grace doth sojourn'. He suggests that part of the allowance which the king bestowed monthly might 'be employed here until God send aid and provision otherways'.[13]

Elizabeth, in her joy at being again in favour, and in gratitude to her step-mother, decided to send a New Year gift to Katherine Parr. This took the form of a book, *The Mirror or Glasse of the Synneful Soul,*[14] somewhat dull and solemn in its content, but it was written on vellum in her own hand, and she described it as a translation 'out of French rhyme into English prose, joining the sentences together as well as my simple wit and small learning could extend themselves'. It was dedicated: 'To our most noble and vertuous Queene Katherin Elizabeth her humble daughter wisheth her perpetuall felecitie and everlasting joye', and it proceeds in a rather grown-up and obscure style that smacks more of the tutor than of the taught. It concludes:

> Praying god almighty the maker and creatoure
> of all things to guarante unto your highnesse
> the sam new yeres daye a lucky and

> prosperous yere with prosperous issue and
> continuance of many yeres in goo helthe
> and contynuall joye and all to his honoure praise and glory
> From Assherugge the last daye
> of the yere of our Lord
> God. 1544.

The handwriting is clear and well formed, though not yet the beautiful Italian script she was to be taught by Roger Ascham. The book is bound in canvas covered boards, embroidered in blue and silver silk. Both covers are decorated with an interlaced design in silver and gilt thread with corner motifs of pansies, or heartsease. In the centre of each cover are worked the initials 'K.P.', which the queen always preferred to use in her signature. At least four other books were made by Elizabeth in the next two or three years: for her father and stepmother, as well as one for her brother, Edward VI, in 1547. This first one was probably made 'under the supervision of her masters and governess to demonstrate their pupil's progress and industry to her cultivated and erudite stepmother, with whose encouragement she had begun to share lessons and tutors with her young brother, Edward. It is also the work of an exceptionally eager pupil'.[15]

It is difficult to believe, when handling this rather moving relic of the young princess, that it is the work of a schoolgirl of 11, albeit an unusually advanced one. Only the occasional alterations betray her immaturity, and it remains a remarkable reminder of a loving task which must have occupied most of her time during that autumn spent at Ashridge.

For the next two years Elizabeth saw little of Ashridge and spent most of her time at Hatfield with her brother. In November 1546 they were separated on the orders of the Council, with Edward going to Hertford and Elizabeth to Enfield. Both felt the separation keenly, and relied heavily on a fairly regular exchange of letters. A letter in Latin from Edward to his sister showed an awareness of his insecurity:

> 5 December 1546
>
> Change of place did not vex me so much, dearest sister, as your going from me . . . It is some comfort in my grief that my chamberlain tells me I may hope to visit you soon (if nothing happens to either of us in the meantime).[16]

1. Queen Elizabeth I as Princess (artist unknown).

2. Sir Thomas Egerton, Baron Ellesmere.

3. John William Egerton, 7th Earl of Bridgewater (by William Owen).

4. Ashridge, north front, 1780.

6. Ashridge Chapel, *c*.1820.

7. Adelbert, 3rd Earl Brownlow (by Frank Salisbury).

8. Adelaide, Countess Brownlow (by Frank Salisbury).

Letters from Elizabeth, preserved in the Harleian MSS., though undated, seem to belong to this period, showing in elegant terms her affection and her concern for her brother and his health.

> To my dearest brother the Prince.
>
> The return of this gentleman your servant (Deare Brother) and his desire to salute you from mee with more than his own words ministered the occasion of this ill-penned object to your princely view, which only tells you that I had rather be the messenger myself than to substitute any other to let you know how much I desire to see you till which happy time I live in hope.
>
> Y^r most loving sister, Elizabeth.[17]

Towards the end of 1546 Henry VIII was a desperately sick man, who really had to drive himself to receive state visitors and conduct affairs in Council. Finally his physicians insisted on him taking to his bed. He made a will, bequeathing the Crown to Edward, then, if there were no heirs, to Mary; and if she should have no heirs, to Elizabeth. If Elizabeth died without issue it was to go to one of the children of the two daughters of his sister, Mary. He named the members of the Council who were to direct the government during the minority of his son. Somehow he got through that Christmas, but his eyes, once so keen and merry, were now so bloodshot that he could scarcely see, and his body was a misery to him. He fought to live up to the end, but early in the morning of 28 January 1547 he died.

2. Edward and Elizabeth

Edward and Elizabeth were now brought together momentarily at Enfield to hear the news of their father's death from Lord Hertford, which caused them inconsolable grief and tears. Hertford's immediate purpose was to secure the person of the new king, and to ensure the safety of Elizabeth. He arranged for Edward, not yet ten years old, to be taken to the safety of the Tower of London, where the Council gathered to pay him homage. This grasping, ambitious man was quite determined to rule the young king. From the beginning he had dominated the Council of guardians whom King Henry had appointed, and he persuaded them to let him assume the title of Protector, with power to act independently of their advice. One of his first acts was to instruct his young nephew to create him Duke of Somerset. At the same time that Hertford was made Duke of Somerset his brother, Thomas Seymour, was made Lord Seymour of Sudely and Lord High Admiral. In character vain and selfish, Seymour nevertheless had a handsome figure and with his charm of manner and high spirits he always had a way with the ladies. He was intensely jealous of his brother's importance as Protector, a position which he felt should be shared between them. If he could not rule the king, at least he could set out to ingratiate himself with the boy, which he did, often providing him liberally with pocket-money. Seymour was also ambitious for a good marriage and hopefully he set his cap at Elizabeth, but the Council would not hear of such a match. He therefore returned to wooing again the widowed queen, whom he had courted before her marriage to King Henry, and he and Katherine Parr were married secretly. It was hardly a sensible thing to do so soon after Henry's death, and he was obliged to play out an absurd farce of seeking support and approval from the young king and from his own brother, the Protector, for his suit to a woman who was already his wife.

After her father's death Elizabeth went to live with Katherine Parr, and so Thomas Seymour was now brought into close contact with the young girl he had thought to marry. This had all the makings of a dangerous situation. From an early date he made a practice of visiting her in her bedroom first thing in the morning, and much boisterous frolicking would ensue, which on the face of it was innocent enough. Indeed the Dowager Queen entered into the fun of this romping with Elizabeth, but there is little doubt that Elizabeth was attracted by the attentions paid to her by a man 20 years her senior. Eventually tongues began to wag, and the gossip began to make Katherine jealous. She was herself pregnant by then and thought it would be prudent to send Elizabeth away. Soon after Whitsun in 1548 Elizabeth returned to Cheshunt.

In September Katherine Parr died in childbirth, and Elizabeth lost her good friend and wise counsellor. Kate Ashley, Elizabeth's governess, who was fascinated by Seymour's charm but lacked much sense of caution, began match-making, remarking to Elizabeth that the man who had earlier sought her as a wife was now free. Elizabeth demurred at this, but was not slow to blush every time Kate Ashley returned to the theme. Seymour was showing great interest in the estates that Elizabeth was to receive under her father's will, and he quizzed her cofferer, Thomas Parry,[18] many times about her financial expectations, and visited Elizabeth often at Ashridge. Towards the end of the year Elizabeth seemed to be showing signs of interest in Kate Ashley's machinations, but, having already learned the importance of caution, she refused to commit herself.

All this time Seymour continued to intrigue behind his brother's back with the young king in an endeavour to have himself appointed as governor of the king's person. Although this move failed, he did not cease to plot and scheme to oust his brother from power. When he attempted to build up a party and a following among the noblemen and gentry in the western counties, the Council thought that he had gone too far. It was beginning to look too much like a planned *coup d'etat* and the Council became suspicious. His intrigue to marry Elizabeth brought matters to a head, and in January 1549 he was arrested and put in the Tower. Kate Ashley and Parry were also taken for questioning, and Sir Reginald Tyrwhitt was despatched to Cheshunt to try to prise the truth about Seymour's plotting out of Elizabeth. He learnt nothing and found her common sense and wit more than a match for him. He had her moved to Hatfield for easier questioning, but she maintained an obstinate silence. When she was told that rumours were circulating that she was with child by Seymour, she wrote a spirited letter of denial to the Protector: 'My Lord, these are shameful slanders for the which, besides the great desire I have to see the King's majesty, I shall desire your Lordship that I may come to Court that I may show myself as I am'.

In the Tower, first Parry and then Mrs. Ashley broke under questioning, and admitted the frequent visits of Seymour to their mistress at Ashridge, but this was not enough for the Council, who wanted evidence of an actual plot by Seymour against the State. Elizabeth continued to deny that Ashley or Parry had urged her to plot with Seymour, and a stalemate had been reached. She refused to accept Lady Tyrwhitt as a governess in place of Mrs. Ashley, and she wrote direct to the Protector with some courage, reminding him that she was the king's sister, and that it was his and the Council's duty to safeguard her honour. Mrs. Ashley was released but forbidden to return to her mistress. Thomas Seymour, counting unwisely, as it happened, on the support of the king, scornfully refused to answer the Council on all but three of the many charges against him. As a result parliament approved a bill of attainder brought against him, though without hearing his defence, and he was executed on 20 March 1549. When told of his death, Elizabeth is reputed to have remarked, 'this day died a man with much wit and very little wisdom'.

It is clear that she had suffered great emotional distress as a result of these events and for a few months she was quite seriously ill at Hatfield. Although in slightly better odour with the Council now, she remained a virtual prisoner in disgrace and was still forbidden to see her brother, and Edward, caught between his natural ties of affection towards her and the jealous controls of those in the Council who manipulated his actions, could do little for her. Gradually she was able to resume her studies, seeking in them to wipe out the memory of an unhappy affair. She was greatly helped in this by her new tutor, Roger Ascham, who had been appointed after William Grindall had died of the plague the previous year while still a young man. Ascham was acquainted with the princess because Grindall had been one of his own students at Cambridge, and he had guided him in his teaching, and Elizabeth had already corresponded with him in Latin. It is mostly from Ascham's letters that the details of her education come, and from his book, *The Scholemaster.* He could not sing her praises loud enough, and he clearly took pride in her application and achievement. As he wrote in 1550 to his friend John Sturm, the Protestant Rector of Strasburg University, 'numberless honourable ladies of the present time surpass the daughters of Sir Thomas More in every kind of learning. But among them all, my illustrious mistress the Lady Elizabeth shines like a star, excelling them more by the splendour of her virtues and her learning, than by the glory of her royal birth . . .

'For two years she pursued the study of Greek and Latin under my tuition; but the foundations of her knowledge in both languages were laid by the diligent instruction of William Grindall, my late beloved friend and for seven years my pupil in classical learning at Cambridge . . . The Lady Elizabeth has accomplished her sixteenth year; and so much solidarity of understanding, such courtesy united with dignity, have never been observed at so early an age. She has the most ardent love of true religion and of the best kind of literature. French and Italian she speaks like English; Latin with fluency, propriety and judgement; she also spoke Greek with me, frequently, willingly and moderately well . . . Nothing can be more elegant than her handwriting, whether in the Greek or Roman character. In music she is very skillful, but does not greatly delight. With respect to personal decoration, she greatly prefers a simple elegance to show and splendour . . .'[19] Ascham's influence did much to restore her confidence, and even when he resigned his post to return to Cambridge he continued to take an interest in her studies long after her accession to the throne.

Early in 1550 the question of Elizabeth's estates was finally settled and Edward formally conveyed Ashridge to his sister:

> *17 March 1550.* In fulfilment of the will of Henry VIII.
>
> Grant to the King's sister Elizabeth of . . . the rents of the free and customary tenants of Little Gaddesden and Frithsden amounting to £6 10s. 10½d. of the late College of Asserudge, Bucks, and the messuage or capital mansion of Assherudge, the site of the same, the tenement called lez Dairy House, and the lands called Hodenhall alias Hunden hall Park in Edlesborough, Bucks, in tenure of Robert Eme, which belonged to the said college . . . and grant of all lands and liberties pertaining to the premises in . . . Asheridge.[20]

The whole of the grants mentioned in this document, including Ashridge, were stated to have 'a clear year value of £3106 13s. 1¾d.'. Additional lands were conveyed in a grant, dated 24 April 1551, consisting of 'the manors of Berkhamsted, Hemel Hempstead (which belonged to the late College of Bonhommes), the mill of Hemel Hempstead, and the manor of Redbourne, with two mills, le Corne Mill and le Malte Mill, and other lands'.[21]

Elizabeth, still not fully recovered in health, wrote to her brother on 15 July 1550, sending him her portrait (which he had requested) remarking, 'For the face I grant I might well blush to offer, but the mind I shall never be ashamed to present'. It was a serious letter, prudent in expression, expressing the hope of seeing him, but acknowledging that the time may not have come for this. 'I see not as yet the time agreeing thereunto'. A few weeks later she was preparing to move again to Ashridge, which was now her own possession. Thomas Parry, writing on her behalf to Sir William Cecil, whom Elizabeth had come to respect as a friend, tells him, 'I had forgotten to say to you that her Grace commanded me to say to you, for the excuse of her hand, that it is not now as good as she trusts it shall be; her Grace's unhealth hath made it weaker, and so unsteady, and that is the cause . . . She removes not to Ashridge these ten or twelve days yet, for the unreadiness of things there; but then, God willing, she will be there'. Apparently things were made ready more quickly, for after only seven days Thomas Parry writes again to Cecil from Ashridge, with a request from Elizabeth for the preferment of one of her old servants, John Reynon, to the parsonage of East Harptree in Somerset.

In March 1551 Edward received her with a great show of affection for his 'sweet sister Temperance', so that when she returned from court she could feel with some satisfaction that her reputation had been retrieved. Elizabeth spent the following year quietly either at Hatfield or Ashridge, and kept up a regular correspondence with Edward. There is a letter to him from Ashridge dated 20 September 1551, congratulating him on his recovery from a serious illness.[22] Edward's gradually failing health did not prevent him from keeping up the daily Chronicle he had started at the age of twelve. Two unrelated entries for January 1552 are noted:

> *16th.* Sir William Pickering delivered a token to the Lady Elizabeth —a fair diamond.
>
> *22nd.* The Duke of Somerset had his head cut off upon Tower Hill between eight and nine o'clock in the morning.

The Duke of Somerset had dominated the king ever since his accession, but he had displeased the Council and parliament by various actions, and was displaced as Protector in 1549, though later he was given back a seat on the Council. He was supplanted by the Duke of Northumberland, but for the king this was merely the substitution of one form of domination for another. Elizabeth kept very much in the background. She went to Ashridge during the summer, from which there is a letter from her to Lord Darcy, the Lord Chamberlain, appealing for help in getting her kinsman Cary a pardon for debt:

> *16th July 1552.* Ashridge
>
> . . . I do . . . commend unto you the safety and cure of a poor man, my friend, that most part of his life has served my kin, a poor man full of children, but evermore of honesty much commendable, which without your aid is utterly incurable. He became surety for Sir John Butler, deceased, in ten pounds to one Dormer of London, deceased, for silks, and the principal debtor being not sued this poor bearer was compelled to pay of his own proper goods to the executors. And that notwithstanding, he is outlawed, and then in danger of his own goods, as you know, so he and his [are] utterly undone forever.
>
> If therefore it may please you to get him his pardon . . . as all his goods is not able to relieve him, and to bear this burden, I shall account this among the rest of your benefits, worthy of my recompense therefor . . . Your loving friend, Elizabeth.[23]

By Christmas, Edward was markedly worse with a fearsome cough. He was now completely in the control of Northumberland, who had set out deliberately to undermine the boy's confidence in Elizabeth. By keeping him estranged from both his sisters, he managed to persuade the king to alter the succession in favour of his own daughter-in-law, Lady Jane Grey, in spite of the provisions made in Henry VIII's will. At the same time he was planning to get Elizabeth married to some Protestant prince who would take her out of the country, and so eliminate from the scene one who would certainly stand up for her rights to the succession. He even tried bribing her with offers of money and lands to abandon her hereditary claims, but Elizabeth would have nothing to do with any of these designs. The young king held out until May, but the tuberculosis which gripped him was advancing too quickly, and he died at Greenwich on 6 July 1553.

3. Elizabeth and Mary

An unhappy reign had ended. Northumberland still hoped to gain custody of the two princesses until Jane Grey had been proclaimed queen, but Mary received advice of his intentions while on her way to London. She diverted with her small retinue to Framlingham in Suffolk, where, displaying something of her father's spirit, and counting on strong support in East Anglia, she hoisted her standard and proclaimed her accession. Elizabeth had also received a friendly warning, possibly from Cecil, and remained at Hatfield. Within 10 days Mary's supporters were strong enough to defeat Northumberland. The conspiracy collapsed and he was sent to the Tower. On 29 July Mary came to London with an army. Elizabeth wrote to congratulate her sister upon her succession, and in a display of loyalty met Mary at Wanstead on the following day, and the two sisters rode together into the City. The people of London rejoiced because they had no sympathy with Northumberland's rash conspiracy, and for a brief moment conflicts of religion were forgotten in the celebrations that followed. The contrasts between the two daughters of Henry VIII did not go unremarked. Mary, at 37, short and thin, had lost the good looks of her youth. Elizabeth, just 20, was radiant; her vitality, her good looks, her red hair, a fine skin and beautiful hands seemed to fire the people, and she reminded them of her father.

The problem facing Mary at the onset of her reign was how, as a dedicated Catholic, she was to rule a country which had been adjusting to the Reformation for the past 20 years. Her faith had sustained her in adversity all this time, and she was passionately resolved on bringing her country again within the embrace of Rome. In no time at all the Mass was again being said in some London churches, provoking some rioting, and some Catholic bishops were reinstated. When the Mass was reintroduced at Court, Elizabeth pointedly did not attend. Mary's initial goodwill towards her sister began to turn to resentment and suspicion. It was clear to Mary that her new position as queen required that she should marry, but when it was suggested that she should marry Edward Courtenay, she rejected the idea. Nor was it certain that Courtenay, so much younger, aimed so high. Mary turned for advice, as she always did, to her cousin Charles V, the Holy Roman Emperor, whose ambassador, Simon Renard, became a more important confidant at Court than her own English councillors. Charles wanted her to marry his son Philip, then king of Spain, because this would strengthen his hand against France. When Mary agreed to the proposal this provoked a wave of unpopularity among the people, which was not to be easily calmed.

In the meantime Mary's relationship with Elizabeth was rapidly deteriorating. Elizabeth, realising her sister's coldness, decided to give way, and attended her first Mass, though without conviction. Mary was sceptical of her action, and so was Renard. Charles V went further and even urged Mary to find a pretext for confining Elizabeth in the Tower. When parliament met, Mary proceeded to sweep away most of the religious innovations of her brother's reign, though not without opposition. She also caused to be repealed the Act which had nullified the marriage of her mother, Catherine of Aragon, thus removing the clauses against her own legitimacy. Significantly the Council had not repealed the clauses affecting the legitimacy of Elizabeth. This did not satisfy Mary. If Elizabeth was illegitimate in law, she was still legally next in succession to the throne, and it was this provision that Mary wished to remove. Here she encountered her greatest opposition. She was advised that parliament would certainly not consent to alter the succession, and that if she wished to make a foreign marriage, the people would only be reconciled to such a course if there was a firm assurance that the Crown would not pass at her death to a foreigner.

This was the very last advice that Mary wished to receive, and all the heat of her bitterness was turned towards Elizabeth, with Simon Renard glad to assist in fanning the flames. It was a major failing on the part of Mary that she unable to override the past in adapting to her new position as queen. She blamed Anne Boleyn for all the troubles of the past, and was sure that Elizabeth would be no better. Elizabeth's so-called conversion was all hypocrisy, and all her friends were heretics. If, as was now openly suggested, Elizabeth were to marry Edward Courtenay, her claim to the throne would be greatly reinforced, and Mary was quite determined that Elizabeth should not succeed. She deliberately set out to diminish Elizabeth's status at Court. Elizabeth, reading the danger signs, asked leave to withdraw from Court, and in December 1553, she retired to Ashridge. Renard was consulted about this and agreed that it would be a good thing for her to go, provided that she was carefully watched, and so queen's representatives were added to the Ashridge household to report on her actions. On her journey, Elizabeth sent back to her sister asking for copes and chasubles and other items required for the ritual of the Mass. Mary sent these to her, but remained untrusting and unconvinced of her motives. Elizabeth was probably only trying to create a good impression.

As Mary relied on the counsel of Renard, it was natural that Elizabeth should be drawn to friendship with the French ambassador, Antoine de Noailles. He was convinced that if Elizabeth and Courtenay married they could provoke such an uprising in the south-west that would overthrow the queen and the Spanish influence. Opposition in London was rising steadily and unrest was in the wind everywhere. What was in doubt, however, was whether Courtenay had any enthusiasm for the marriage, and surely Elizabeth would not be so rash as to take part in a conspiracy which could only have one ending if it failed.

On her return to Ashridge Elizabeth put in hand some fortifications of the house and gathered a small armed force within the walls. Miss Strickland gives as one reason that this may have been for defence against partisans of the deposed Lady Jane Grey. The Spanish faction, however, were quick to interpret it as a defiance of the queen. In January a rebellion broke out in Kent, led by Sir Thomas Wyatt, son of the poet-courtier of Henry VIII. Its object was to break the Spanish match and to set Elizabeth and Courtenay upon the throne. The rebellion failed, largely through faint-heartedness on the part of Courtenay. It was quickly crushed and Wyatt was sent to the Tower. Immediately the trouble broke out Mary wrote to Elizabeth requiring her to come to Court, but Elizabeth replied excusing herself on the grounds of poor health, being 'troubled with such a cold and headache that I have never felt the like'. At this point a series of mishaps followed. Government agents discovered a letter from Wyatt to Elizabeth advising her to move from Ashridge to her house at Donington Hall, Berkshire, further away from London, where she could defend herself if necessary. Another mischance was when agents intercepted a courier of the French ambassador and found a copy of the letter from Elizabeth to the queen, from which it was incorrectly assumed that she was in regular contact with de Noailles. Lord Chancellor Gardiner was sure his suspicions about Elizabeth had been confirmed, and Mary reacted vigorously. She sent her personal physicians, Dr. Owen and

Dr. Wendy, to Ashridge to see how ill Elizabeth was, followed by a commission of three councillors attended by a strong escort of soldiers, who were to bring her to Court if she was able to travel. The Commission consisted of Lord William Howard, a great-uncle of the princess, Sir Edward Hastings, and Sir Thomas Cornwallis. The doctors found that Elizabeth was certainly ill, but thought that she would be able to travel, and so Lord William Howard reported to the queen:

> *From Ashridge, the 11th February, at four o'clock in the afternoon.*
>
> . . . We found her Grace very willing and conformable, save only that 'she much feared her weakness to be so great' that she should not be able to travel, and to endure the journey without peril of life, and therefore desired some longer respite until she had better recovered her strength: but in conclusion, upon the persuasion as much of us, as of her own Council and servants . . . she is resolved to remove hence tomorrow towards your Highness, with such journeys as by a paper, here enclosed, your highness shall percieve . . .[24]

The plan of her progress, so enclosed, was to make the journey of just under 30 miles by easy stages of five to eight miles a day only. Travelling in the queen's litter, she reached Redbourn on the first night. The second night she passed at Sir Ralph Dowlett's house at St. Albans; the third at Mr. Dod's at Mimms, and then to Mr. Cholmeley's house at Highgate. Here she must have been really ill and remained nearly a week. The French ambassador's report to his king, dated 21 February, stated that 'the princess is lying ill about seven or eight miles from hence, so swollen and disfigured that her death is expected'. Preceded by such reports and by rumours, now that she had been poisoned, then that she was enceinte, Elizabeth reached the City on the 22nd and Westminster on the following day. The London she saw presented a horrifying spectacle in the wake of the executions following the rebellion, as the heads of traitors, brave men no less, were exhibited on public buildings. The princess's reluctance to come to London was understandable enough.

For three weeks Elizabeth was lodged at Court, but was not allowed to see her sister, or receive visitors. The question to be answered was whether she had played any part in Wyatt's plans. Examined by Bishop Gardiner, who advised her to throw herself on the queen's mercy, Elizabeth denied any knowledge of the plot, saying that she would not ask for mercy for a misdeed she had not committed. The queen and parliament were just then due to move to Oxford, so that a decision had to be taken about Elizabeth's custody during the queen's absence. Finally, though not unanimously, the Council decided that she must be kept in the Tower. Elizabeth could scarcely credit the news when it was broken to her, and in great alarm, and seeking to delay her fate, she begged to be allowed to write to the queen, protesting her innocence. ' I have heard in my time', she wrote on 16 March, 'of many cast away for want of coming of their Prince . . . I humbly crave to speak to your Highness . . . And as for the traitor Wyatt', she ended, 'he might peradventure write me a letter, but on my faith I never received any from him. And as for the copy of the letter sent to the French King, I pray God confound me eternally if I ever sent him word, message, token, or letter, by any means, and to this truth I will stand in till my death'.

Mary was not moved by this appeal, and on Palm Sunday, 18 March, travelling by barge, Elizabeth entered the Tower by what is now called Traitor's Gate, speaking the oft-quoted words, 'Here landeth as true a subject, being prisoner, as ever landed at these stairs; and before Thee, O God, I speak it, having none other friends but Thee alone'. She was lodged in the Bell Tower. Gardiner and nine of his councillors continued to examine Elizabeth to try to extract a confession from her, but they achieved no success. In the hope of further revelations. Wyatt's execution was postponed to 11 April, but proof could not be obtained. The evidence was not sufficient to warrant keeping Elizabeth in prison any longer, though Renard continued to urge that every security must be employed before Philip II of Spain arrived in England for the marriage. Wyatt was reported to have cleared Elizabeth of any implication before his death. Public opinion was firmly on her side, but if she could not be condemned, equally she could scarcely be released to cause embarrassment at Court. It was therefore decided that she should be handed over to the custody of Sir Henry Bedingfield and be kept for a period at Woodstock in Oxfordshire, which was rather further away from London than Ashridge.

The wedding of Mary to Philip of Spain took place in July 1554, without much enthusiasm on the part of the people. It was to give Mary confidence, however, to signal England's formal return to the Catholic fold by the admission of the papal legate, Cardinal Pole. Then, within a few months, began a shocking sequence of persecution and punishment by burning of martyrs, as if this was the way to enforce conformity. She followed her own foreign sympathies at the expense of the national interest, and permitted excesses both in the persecution of heretics and the removal of political as well as of religious opponents.

In the midst of this Mary now believed herself to be with child, and to have an heir would crown all her desires. As the signs developed, Elizabeth, in her plight at Woodstock, found an unexpected ally in King Philip, because Mary was obliged to consider the question of succession afresh in case she should die in childbirth. She was shrewd enough to see that if she were to die the people were likely to give vent to their hatred of Philip and his Spanish followers. The release of Elizabeth would be the guarantee of their lives, and so at the end of April she was brought back to Hampton Court. Meantime, while the persecutions progressed, Mary's pregnancy did not. Whatever disorder had produced the symptoms, she had to accept with despair that she was not carrying a child, and in August Philip left her to return to Spain. Mary was very much in love, and very lonely, as she tried to convince herself that her husband would soon return. The two sisters were drawn together for a time, but as the months dragged on Mary's spirits grew lower. Elizabeth had even made a complete set of baby clothes for the hoped-for arrival. These were still in the house at Ashridge when Lord Chancellor Ellesmere purchased the estate in 1604 and were preserved in the possession of the Brownlow family until the sale of Ashridge in the 1920s.

In October 1555 Elizabeth returned to Hatfield, to be reunited with her beloved Kate Ashley and the rest of her household, and Roger Ascham was permitted to resume his readings with her. Early in the following year the question of a new lease of Ashridge arose, and in an indenture dated 13 March 1556, 'upon dyvers causes and good considerations'

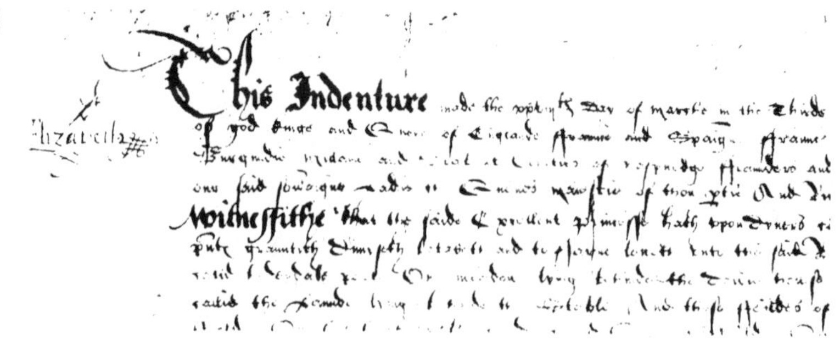

Fig. 2. Detail from lease of Ashridge, 1556

the princess granted a lease for 21 years to Richard Combe, gentleman, of Hemel Hempstead. It included all the lands, both arable and pasture, and all the woods until lately in the occupation of John Norris and Oliver Louthe, and also the oversight and custody of the college or monastery of Ashridge, with all the houses, barns, stables, the dovecote, orchards and gardens within its precincts. The agreed rent was £6 0s. 10d. per year to be paid in two equal instalments, identical with the rent paid by John Norris for the past 15 years.[25]

Whether Elizabeth had decided by then that she would not again reside at Ashridge is not certain. Her last memories of its pleasant surroundings, as she was borne away sick in the queen's litter on a cold February day two years before, to face imprisonment in the Tower, can hardly have been happy ones. The decision may have been made later, but at all events, so far as known, Ashridge did not again receive Elizabeth, and within two years she had ascended the throne.

After an absence of a year and a half, Philip made a brief return to England in March 1557. Once again he was trying to arrange a marriage for Elizabeth and again she flatly rejected the idea. He also wanted the English to support him in his war against France. Receiving an assurance of aid, Philip departed. The promised expedition, however, was mounted rather half-heartedly and Calais fell. With this news added to her agony of unrequited love, Mary became more despairing than ever. Again she thought that she was going to have a child, and again it proved to be but an illusion. Hardly any of her good intentions had come to fruition, and much blood had been spilled in the attempt. Unpopular with her people and deserted by her husband, she now became very ill. When finally she was compelled to recognise Elizabeth's right to the succession it was as if a knife was being turned in her wounds. The unhappy queen died at Greenwich on 17 November 1558.

At Hatfield, Elizabeth, walking in the park on a late autumn morning, quietly received the news that she was queen, and fell on her knees in thanks to God.

Chapter Eight

THE LORD CHANCELLOR

A SURVEY OF THE VALUE of Ashridge was made in about 1570 under a commission appointed by the Court of the Exchequer and it suggests that plans were then being considered for its exchange or disposal. The valuation, calculated on the value of the materials only, 'as if all the several things should presently be pulled asunder, taken down, and then sold', showed that the worth of the mansion and other premises, the barns, stables, dove-houses, and the timber in the woods was £1,189 19s. 10d.[1] In the meantime Richard Combe continued quietly to enjoy his lease until 1572, when it was assigned to William Gorge, one of the queen's gentlemen pensioners, at the same rent.[2] He held it for only three years, and the queen then granted it to John Dudley and John Ayscough and their heirs, under Letters Patent dated 29 January 1575. This seems to be the time when Queen Elizabeth finally yielded up her interest in the manor of Ashridge. Dudley and Ayscough were merely agents and only two weeks later they granted the lease by deed, dated 12 February 1575 to Henry, Lord Cheney and Jane, his wife. Lord Cheney died without issue and the manor of Ashridge came to Lady Cheney. In 1590, by Letters Patent dated 21 July, the queen granted to Lady Cheney the adjacent manors of Little Gaddesden and Frithsden. Lady Cheney, with Sir John Crofts and his wife, sold all these manors by indenture dated 27 November 1602 to Ralph Marshall and his heirs. Marshall appears to have been only a speculator, for only a few weeks later on 7 March 1603 he conveyed the estates to Randolph Crew and Thomas Chamberlain. A year later Crew, Chamberlain and Richard Cartwright conveyed them to Sir Thomas Egerton, Baron Ellesmere, and Sir John Egerton, his son, on 21 October 1604.[3]

In such a way Ashridge passed into the ownership of the Egerton family, whose principal residence it was to remain for almost two hundred and fifty years.

* * * * *

Thomas Egerton was born in 1540, a few months after the College of Bonhommes had been forced to close its doors. He was the son of Sir Richard Egerton, baronet, of Ridley in Cheshire, by Alice Sparke, an unmarried maid who was employed in the Manor House of Dodleston, close by Ridley. The Egertons of Ridley had a distinguished family record of military service stretching back over many years, and they were respected in the county. In Elizabethan times the stigma of illegitimacy varied according to the family circumstances, and if a wealthy man acknowledged his indiscretion by giving the child of his amour his family name, there was a very good chance that the child would suffer little in later life. This certainly seems to have been the case with young Thomas Egerton, the future Lord Chancellor of England. Far from abandoning the mother and boy, the lusty Sir Richard provided well for them; he even had a second son by the same mistress, to say nothing of one by another later, before he married. Thomas was brought up as a full member of the family. From school he entered Brasenose College, Oxford, at the age of 17, and after three years he went to Lincoln's Inn to serve an apprenticeship in the law. He made remarkably rapid progress, demonstrating not only a clear knowledge of the law but a skilful ability in presenting and arguing his case, and his reputation grew quickly. On one occasion, when he was defending in an important action brought by the Crown in the presence of Queen Elizabeth, she is said to have exclaimed, 'Never again shall this man plead against me!' It was not long before he was made Queen's Counsel, and by the early age of 41 he was Solicitor-General. He sat in the House of Commons as M.P. for Cheshire from 1584 to 1587.

As Solicitor-General he was involved in the trial of Mary, Queen of Scots, and was one of the signatories to the House of Commons petition praying that she should be executed. Always a kindly man in his private life, nothing was allowed to interfere with his interpretation of what was his public duty.

In 1592 he was made Attorney-General, and two years later he was knighted and made Master of the Rolls, with the additional office of Chamberlain of Chester. The boy from Cheshire had climbed far in his 50 years, and while he owed nothing of his earlier success to favouritism, there is no doubt that the queen thought well of one of the the few ministers who was equable in manner and who was always courteous and sympathetic in his dealings with his ageing monarch. Unlike many of his contemporaries, he was not a self-seeking man. Egerton combined prudence with caution in all that he engaged in. He was attentive to the queen because he admired her, rather than for motives of self-advancement. He believed himself capable of the highest office, but took the view that this would happen to him in due course, not that he should strive to make it happen. He was a rare figure who appeared to be interested only in serving his country.

Like most men in a similar position he prudently invested any profits from his office in the acquisition of land, and gradually bought estates in Lancashire, Cheshire, Shropshire and Northamptonshire, as he did later in the counties of Buckingham, Bedford and Hertford. It was at about this time, too, that Richard Brownlow, also engaged in the law as a Prothonotary (principal clerk) in the Court of Common Pleas, an office he was to hold for 47 years, took the first steps to acquiring lands in Lincolnshire that were destined to become linked with those of Thomas Egerton in the common ownership of one of his descendants some two hundred and fifty years later.

In 1596 Egerton was promoted to become Lord Keeper of the Seal. (His secretary for the next five years was the poet, John Donne.) This was nearly the equivalent of being Lord Chancellor, since the Lord Keeper, even if he were not a peer, always presided over the House of Lords in the absence of the Lord Chancellor. There is a portrait of him at Brasenose College, Oxford, and a similar contemporary portrait in the possession of Lord Brownlow at Belton House shows him as a serious dignified person, with a neat appearance and an impressive bearing. Thomas Fuller, the 17th-century cleric, whose book *The Worthies of London* appeared in 1662, describes him admiringly: '. . . surely all Christendom afforded not a person which carried more gravity in his countenance and behaviour than Sir Thomas Egerton, insomuch that many have gone to the Chancery on purpose only to see his venerable garb (happy they who had no other business) and were highly pleased at so acceptable a spectacle. Yet his outward case is nothing in comparison with his inward qualities, quick wit, solid judgement, ready utterance'.

In the closing years of Elizabeth's reign the Attorney-General was greatly concerned by the quarrel of his friend, the impetuous young Lord Essex, with the queen, and did all he could to persuade him to heal the breach. Essex would not yield his position. He was sent to Ireland, where he proved to be inefficient, and when eventually he quitted his command as Lord Deputy and came back to England without authority, presuming on his position as her former favourite, the rage of the queen was immense. She would not go so far as to have him tried for high treason, which his action deserved, but while her advisers sorted out the legal position she consented to Essex being committed to the custody of the Lord Keeper at his home in York House in the Strand. This state lasted a whole year. If anyone could have won over this rash young man it was the elder statesman, whose friendship he enjoyed and in whose house he lived, but it was not to be so. Essex was released, but was forbidden to go to Court. He believed his enemies at Court to be responsible for his position and that they were wrongly advising the queen. Essex and his followers plotted to raise a force sufficient to capture the Court, the Tower, and the City of London, and to change the government by bringing James VI of Scotland to the throne. Forewarned, the Council summoned Essex to appear before them, but he refused to do so. When Lord Egerton and three Councillors went to Essex's house to fetch him in the name of the queen, they were taken hostage and kept prisoners. Essex then fell back on the other part of his plan, having lost the element of surprise in his plot to take the Court. He and his followers counted on raising enough support in the City of London, but he had miscalculated his popularity with the citizens, and the attempt had to be abandoned. Returning to his house he found that his principal hostage, the Lord Keeper, had been able to escape. All that was left was for him to surrender. He faced trial for treason, was found guilty, and, arrogant to the last, was led out to execution on 25 February 1601. As Francis Henry Egerton later wrote in his life of Thomas Egerton, Essex was a man who 'through the centuries had excited both admiration and pity'.

Sir Thomas Egerton was married three times. His eldest son Thomas, by his first wife, saw military service under Lord Essex and was knighted for valour at the capture of Cadiz, but he died in battle in Ireland in 1599 to the great sorrow of his father. Already in mourning for the death of his second wife, Elizabeth, who had died a few weeks earlier after only 15 months of marriage, his grief was so profound and prolonged that even his friends thought it excessive, and the queen herself had to intervene to make him come to terms with reality. Naturally there was no lack of ladies anxious and prepared to marry an ageing widower who had both wealth and position, but when in 1600 he married the widowed Alice, Countess Dowager of Derby, some twenty years his junior, a cultured woman and a patroness of Edmund Spenser (as she was later to be of Milton), this amiable man could not have anticipated the dance into which she was to lead him. She henpecked him without mercy, and the great and successful lawyer, whose life till then had been so even and comfortable, simply lacked the spirit and the experience of women to assert himself. Among papers found after his death was the sad admission, 'I thanke God I never desired long life, nor had less cause to desire it than synce my last marriage, for before I was never acquainted with such tempests and storms'.[4]

The countess spent money liberally and dominated everything in their lives, brooking no opposition. She was an elegant and charming hostess for their several residences, of which Ashridge was but one, but in any extended argument Thomas found it easier to give in than submit to her 'cursed railinge and bitter tongue'. Within two years of their marriage she contrived that her daughter, Lady Frances, should marry Egerton's only surviving son and heir in order to ensure that the Egerton fortune should remain within the family. John, the future Earl of Bridgewater, showed much more spirit than his father in dealing with his stepmother, while the sweet-tempered Frances proved to be a constant source of comfort to her unhappy stepfather.

When Queen Elizabeth paid a three-day visit to the Egertons at their home at Harefield, Middlesex, in 1602, it cost the Lord Keeper over £2,000—rather more than a quarter of his annual income. For the queen, however, it required a very great effort of will and physical strength to sustain a long visit like this, even to an old friend in whose company she could relax. She was in her seventieth year and was beginning to show real signs of infirmity. Forty-four years on the throne of England had taken their toll. Christmas of that year passed with gaiety and the usual enjoyments, but within a few weeks she lay on her death-bed at Richmond. As there was no obvious and settled heir to the throne it fell to the Lord Keeper to ascertain her intentions about the succession. The queen, confirming popular opinion in the matter, declared that her successor should be her nearest kinsman, James, King of Scotland.

James I ascended the throne of England on 24 March 1603. One of his early acts was to raise Sir Thomas Egerton to the peerage, creating him a baron. He took the title Ellesmere from the manor in Shropshire which he had recently purchased from the Earl of Derby, and he adopted the motto *Sic Donec* (thus until).[5] Almost simultaneously the king appointed him to be Lord Chancellor. This meant giving up the rather profitable post of Master of the Rolls and that of Chamberlain of Chester, as a later reference will show. From the point of Egerton's appointment as Chancellor we see a rather different man emerging. His loyalty to the Crown had been born of long service, but his total respect for its authority led him to support the king in a policy of diminishing the power of parliament. Whereas Elizabeth had always recognised parliament's right to the final decisions on legislation and taxes, retaining only the issues of high state policy in her own control, James I saw parliament only as an instrument of his own will. The result was that the Lord Chancellor forfeited the respect of parliament, who regarded him as the mouthpiece of a king, of whose policies they did not generally have any great opinion. It was a sad and rather pathetic change, as if he lacked confidence in himself and feared to be dismissed.

He found the time in a busy life to assume the duties of Lord Lieutenant of Buckingham which he performed for nine years from 1607 to 1616, and he was elected Chancellor of

Oxford University in 1610, an office he retained until only a few weeks before his death. Throughout his life he enjoyed the friendship of many famous men, but none more so than Francis Bacon, whose fine intellect compelled his admiration. Bacon followed him in office, first as Attorney-General, and eventually as Lord Chancellor.

It was not until he had held his office for nine years that accumulating doubts as to the propriety of many of the king's actions at last led Lord Ellesmere to show the signs of independent judgement again. When the monarch attempted to cheat justice by promising a pardon to the Earl and Countess of Somerset for plotting the murder of Sir Thomas Overbury if they were found guilty, because they knew too much that was damaging to the king's reputation, the Lord Chancellor flatly refused to sign the pardon warrant. He was now 74 years old, tired in spirit as well as in body. He would have liked to retire and he probably felt that a stand on principle could scarcely make much difference to his future now. The king, however, appeared to bear him no ill will for his refusal, and even pressed him not to push the matter of retirement. In 1616 he again requested to be allowed to resign his offices owing to his great age and its accompanying infirmities; his spirit was heavy, he said, and his memory lost so that he had difficulty in judging things, and he had difficulty in hearing. The king finally consented in a letter from Newmarket dated 9 February, and later in the year, on 7 November 1616, created him Viscount Brackley. This was rather a disappointment as he had hoped for an earldom, and he held on to his positions to the end in the hope of improving his status, though more for the sake of his family and future generations than for himself. Finally, bedridden and feeble, he relinquished all his offices: a week later, on 10 March 1617, he died at York House, and was later buried at Dodleston in Cheshire. Somewhat cynically, it would seem, the king sent a message of comfort to him on his deathbed through Lord Buckingham and Sir Francis Bacon, that he was to have the desired earldom forthwith and a pension of £3,000 a year; but the old man shook his head in refusal, saying that 'all these things were to him but vanities'.[6]

Three years after his appointment as Lord Chancellor he had been taking stock of his financial position. He had been obliged to spend a lot of money in the recent years; his lifestyle had been changed and he must have felt that it was time that the king was quietly acquainted of the position. The appeal[7] merits reproduction, at least in part:

> Most Gracious Soveraign,
>
> I leave others, that have learned to price and value their own worthiness and services, to plead desertes. In my selfe I find nothing valuable but honest care and diligence, and sincere fidelitie. And in this when I have done all I can, I am but *servus inutilis* [a useless servant] and therefore condempne myself as one that meriteth nothinge, yet when I see . . . many plentifully watered with the gracious streames of the royal fountayne of your bountie I have presumed (for which I pray pardon) to offer to your princely view this vile scrowle inclosed . . . God bless your Majestie, longe and longe to raigne over us.
>
> Your majesties most humble, duetifull and loyalle servant,
>
> Thomas Egerton, Chancellor.
>
> 16th July 1606.

The enclosed scroll or petition ran as follows:

> Most sacred Soveraigne,
>
> Experience teacheth, he is not worthy to be remembered that remembreth not himself.
>
> I have served as Keeper of the Great Seale, and Chancellor, tenne years or more. I have served the State many yeares before.
>
> Your majestie was pleased (and I humbly obeyed) that I should leave and yelde uppe the office of Maister of the Rolls (wherein I had an estate for my lyfe) and the office of Chamberlain of Chester, which I had enjoyed by the space of eleven yeares: both which offices are of verie good value.
>
> It cost me above £1000 for the late Earle of Essex' entertaynment, whilst he remaynde in my house by the late Queen's Commande.
>
> In this great place, wherein I now serve, I spend a 1000 marks yerelye more than the annualle proffits of the office discharged.
>
> I never made profette of denizens or church-livings as most of my predecessors did . . .
>
> My predecessor's fortunes, and the rewardes they receyved (which their heyres injoye) for lesser services and shorter tyme, putte me in remembrance of myself. And I wysh my state were such as I needed not to be a remembrancer in this kinde.

That the appeal bore some small fruit at least is shown in a warrant of 1606, signed by King James, enabling Lord Ellesmere to hold land to the annual value of 200 marks, upon his surrender of the offices of Masters of the Rolls and Chamberlain of the County Palatine of Chester.[8]

Accounts for the year 1603[9] suggest that Sir Thomas Egerton must have been in occupation of Ashridge before the estate was formally conveyed to him in 1604, even allowing for the old calendar. Todd took his details from manuscripts he was able to examine at Cleveland House:

From the 4 of Feb 1603 to the 11.	£	s.	d.
Larder	14	4	8
Buttery	0	47	0
Pantry and Pastry	0	26	8
Sellor [cellar]	0	26	4
Woodyard and Colehouse	3	17	2
Spycery	0	10	4
Chaundry	0	17	8
Rewards	0	5	6
Stable	0	56	5
Extraord. bylles	0	23	5

The expenses rose for the following week, which is annotated 'My Lady came this weeke upon Thursday supper':

From the 11 of Feb to the 18	£	s.	d.
Larder	16	8	7
Buttry	0	51	4
Pantry and Pastry	0	34	0
Wood and Colehouse	5	5	6
Spycery	0	8	11
Chaundry	0	22	10
Rewards	0	14	4
Stable	3	7	0
Extraord. bylles	0	62	7

Extensive repairs and some additions to the house were set in hand almost at once. Between 1604 and 1607 many persons 'did gratify my Lord Chancellor with carriage' of the necessary timber and stone, including Sir Edmund Ashfield, who had been one of the commissioners at the Inquisition of 1575. Planning and new designs were quickly effected so that by the end of 1607 and through 1608 new furniture and furnishings were beginning to arrive. Examples of his purchases included:[10]

	£	s.	d.
For two suits of tapestry hangings for the purple bed-chamber, and the withdrawing chamber to it	132	15	0
For canvas and cord to pack them in, and portage to Ashridge	0	37	2
For the Lady Francis's nursery [wife of his son, Sir John Egerton] 3 beds of mingled coloured carroll, furnished with feather beds and bolsters, pillows, mattresses, etc.	33	6	0
For the Great Chamber. Paid for 8 pieces of hangings, 5 Flemish ells and half deep, in the whole 247 Flemish ells and half at 10s.	123	15	0
For a handbell for the Chapel		8	0
15 May 1607. For 2 bedds of blew and white carroll (and furnishings), and a bed for the chambermaid	33	6	0
Paid to Rees Ellison the upholsterer	12	10	0

Later accounts[11] show payments made on behalf of his granddaughters and include:

6 May 1615		
For the pare of hose for Mrs Bouth sent to her to Ashridge	4	4
For 3 thousand pins sent thither also	3	0
For a payre of shoes sent also thither	2	0
Some (*sic*) total ..	9	4

Other payments for Mrs. Bouth included:

2 Octob. 1615. For a black wrought holland wastecoat for her..	34	0
For a black beaver hat and embroidered band and new trimminge her old hat	56	0

And for Mrs. Francis Egerton:

To Mr. Newport for teachinge her to play on the lute for 7 months, from the first of May 1615, etc at 20s the month	7	0	0
Disbursed for Mrs. Francis and her sisters: viz. delivered to Mrs. Heard by the ladye Francis her direction to be paid to one who teacheth Mrs. Francis and her sisters to singe, for 6 months from the first of May, 1615 etc., at 40s the month	12	0	0
Delivered more by the lady Frauncis' direction to one to teache them to daunce for a month	3	0	0

The Lord Chancellor spent much money on adding to and refurbishing Ashridge, which was his favourite country residence. Although he had purchased Harefield, in Middlesex, jointly with his third wife Alice, it was always regarded as hers. At Ashridge he could get some peace. It was a refuge where he could 'pass the time as a poor hermit in the desert, here among the woods, not altogether idle nor void of care'.[12] Moreover, it held associations with the late queen, and contained relics such as her bed and a case with a pair of her gloves and stockings, as well as a complete toilet set and the set of baby linen she had worked for the child that her sister, Queen Mary, was never to bear.

The career of Lord Ellesmere contrasts strangely with that of other great predecessors in his office. Compared with Wolsey and Cromwell the power and authority he wielded as Lord Chancellor was almost as nothing. Admittedly the nature of government had changed, but he saw himself neither as a man of action nor as an initiator of policies. His main legal contribution was a notable codification of the Poor Laws, completed in 1601. A man of great industry and compassion, he was content to limit his vision and his action to the judicial duties of his office, becoming under James I more an instrument of his master's will rather than an unbiased adviser, but regaining in the last years something of that independence of mind and judgement on which his great reputation had been built.

Chapter Nine

THE EARLS OF BRIDGEWATER (1617–1701)

THE HEIR TO ASHRIDGE was Lord Ellesmere's only surviving son, John, Viscount Brackley, who was 38 years old when his father died. Like his elder brother Thomas he had seen military service in Ireland, where he had been knighted. In 1602 he married Lady Frances Stanley,[1] daughter of the widowed Dowager Countess of Derby, who, only two years earlier, had become his father's third bride. James I had made him a Knight of the Bath at his coronation. On succeeding to his father's title and estate, John Egerton's overriding ambition was to gain the earldom which had been offered to his father as he lay dying, but rejected. He lost no time in trying to bring this about. Not wishing to approach the king directly (who might put him off with a few fine words), he sought the help of George Villiers, Duke of Buckingham, who professed himself willing to aid him. Buckingham indicated that a sizeable payment would be required; while £20,000 is said to have been involved it may well have been more. The king approved the earldom, according to the Rev. Francis Egerton, 'out of respect for the memory of Thomas Egerton and in recognition of his services'. Because the Court had temporarily moved to Ireland a formal investiture could not be arranged for some time, but so anxious was the new earl (possibly spurred on by his mother-in-law) for the title that he begged Buckingham to urge the king to dispense with the ceremony and simply to issue the necessary patent. James I surprisingly consented to this break with tradition, to the disapproval of Lord Keeper Bacon. By the end of May, only a little more than two months since the death of his father, John Egerton assumed the dignity and title of the Earl of Bridgewater and took his seat in the House of

Lords. The Egerton family had formerly owned the manor of Bridgewater, Somerset (now spelt Bridgwater).[2]

In that same year he was nominated to the Council of Wales and the Marches and over the course of the following years he was active in the House, serving on various commissions, including the Poor Law Commission. He was advanced to President of the Council of Wales in 1631, with responsibility over 16 Welsh and border counties, although he was not ceremonially installed until 1634. His entry into Ludlow Castle was a solemn affair, attended by a large gathering of local nobility and gentry, and to mark the occasion he arranged a number of spectacular entertainments concluding with a great masque in honour of the Dowager Countess, the head of the family. The theme for the masque was supposed to have been provided by an episode involving three of his children, Lord Brackley, the Hon. Thomas Egerton, and their sister, Lady Alice. They were returning from visiting some relatives in Herefordshire when the young lady became lost for a short time in Haywood forest.[3] This 'experience' is said to have furnished the theme for a masque with words by John Milton to music written by Henry Lawes, probably the best-known composer of the day, who had taught the Earl's children. *Comus* received its first performance on Michaelmas night, 29 September 1634, with the young Egertons playing leading roles. Great sadness affected the family a year later when the Earl's wife, the beloved Lady Frances, died at the age of fifty-two. In 33 years of happy marriage she had borne him no less than 15 children, four sons and eleven daughters, of whom two boys and two girls had died young. As her memorial in Little Gaddesden church records, 'seven of her daughters she married richly and honourably . . . she died religiously on the 11th March 1635, and she reigns triumphantly for ever'. The following year her mother, the Dowager Countess of Derby, was laid to rest. This remarkable woman, who in earlier years had made the life of Lord Chancellor Ellesmere so miserable with 'her cursed railinge', had mellowed much with advancing years. She had been sorely tried by a scandal affecting her eldest daughter, Anne, who made a disastrous second marriage to a depraved scoundrel, Lord Audley, the 2nd Earl Castlehaven, but her resolute character had prevailed over this setback to her pride, and she died both loved and honoured by the very large family over which she had presided.

A rather lonely widower, the Earl now found much comfort at Ashridge in his fine library, mostly a legacy from his father. He had no wish to become embroiled in politics, and his financial affairs were beginning to worry him. Some of his investments had not been very successful and great caution and prudence were called for at a time when the country was drifting fast towards the Civil War. The king was making constant demands for money, and it was embarrassing to have to tell His Majesty that he could no longer help him. The king responded by removing him from the Presidency of the Council of Wales. As things were to turn out, this was to his ultimate advantage since it could not then be alleged against him that he was actively aiding the royalist cause. The impending Civil War called for certain precautionary measures. Thomas Williams, the Earl's steward, who regularly wrote to his master on estate matters during his absences in London, reported to him on 4 March 1641 that he had ready '81 muskets, 24 pikes and 3 half-pikes'. A few months later he was reporting that 'the work on the Cloisters pool is finished and looks very neat'. They had been gravelling the garden walks and 'hay will be dear'.[4]

As the Civil War developed almost the whole of eastern England, from Hampshire to Kent in the south right up through Hertfordshire and Essex to Bradford and Hull in the north, was held by the parliamentary forces. Raids and incursions into bordering counties by the troops of both sides were common, and in 1643 Ashridge suffered an assault by royalist troops plundering in Hertfordshire. The Earl was living at his London house in the Barbican at the time, and he took his complaint to parliament, as the *House of Lords Calendar* for 1643[5] shows:

> *June 13.* Petition of the Earl of Bridgewater complains that soldiers under Capt. Washington and others entered his park and house at Ashridge on Saturday last, beat down the ceilings, heaved down the doors, though open to them, searched his evidence rooms and studies, took away plate, arms and household stuff, killed not only male deers but does ready to fawn, and fawns that could hardly stand, and turned the game as much as possible over the

country; he forbears to mention losses formerly sustained by the taking of forty-four valuable horses, but prays for reparation for these and protection from future losses.

The Lords made an Order granting protection and also ordered that the officers concerned should be sent for to answer the charge, but this did not prevent a further raid on Ashridge a few days later.

June 27. Information of John Morgan that on Saturday the 17th, Capt. Washington and Capt. Burre came to Ashridge with troopers and demanded the keys of the granary from Thomas Williams, the steward, and took away eight horses and sent for horses and carts to carry away the grain.

Annexed:

1. Information [of Thomas Williams] that when Capt. Washington came to Ashridge informant showed him the orders of the House and that on reading them Capt. Washington was very angry, saying that he was accused of plundering and stealing.
2. Information of same that Nathaniel Hole, quartermaster to Major Fountain, came with twenty soldiers and cried pish at their Lordship's orders, and offered to lay wagers that it was gained for £5 of John Brown, and took away what little was left of the oats and peas in the granary, and two horses not fit for any service.

On this additional evidence their Lordships made further orders for the protection of the house and park, and for the offenders to be brought before them. Not many months later the earl was required by the House to declare his own position, whether he supported the king or parliament. After some delays and evasions he could no longer avoid the issue and, though still a royalist at heart, he reluctantly signed the Parliamentary Covenant.[6]

The next few years saw his health gradually decline and he lived quietly at Ashridge in the company of his daughter Alice just long enough to survive the tragedy of the execution of Charles I, the king he had served until the Civil War. He died on 4 December 1649, and was buried beside his wife at Little Gaddesden. His memorial records that 'his deportment was graceful, his discourse elegant . . . he was a profound scholar, an able statesman, and a good christian . . . a loyal subject to his Sovereign in those worst of times when it was accounted treason not to be a traitor'. Three years later the Lady Alice married Richard Vaughan, 2nd Earl Carberry, a talented and wealthy landowner in Wales, who at the Restoration became the first Lord President of Wales since Lord Bridgewater was deposed. So she came again to Ludlow Castle, as her mother had done 18 years before.

* * * * *

The 2nd Earl, John, the eldest surviving son, was married to Elizabeth, daughter of the Duke of Newcastle. As a strong monarchist, he was content during the years of Cromwell's protectorate to lead a quiet life in the country without drawing attention to himself. There were other good reasons also for wishing to avoid too much public appearance. His father had left him heavy debts of more than £80,000, and he had incurred others of his own. He was being pressed for payment and was, in fact, an extremely worried man, as letters to his agent reveal:

> *11 Feb. 1649.* Just now came here Mr. Ireton, and desired to speake with me, when I came to him he served me with this letter to appeare in Chancery tomorrow, but withall told me that upon what had passed between him and you, he was contented to stay prosecution for a weeke or ten dayes if I pleased . . . just as he was going downe staires from me he met Bowes coming up and served him with this writ with the same conditionall termes he had used to you; I thought fit to delay no time but to send them both to you immediately, and the rather than you might be acquainted with them before the meeting tomorrow morning. With my hearty thankes to you for the daily great paines you take for my sake, I rest.
>
> Your very loving friend,
> J. Bridgewater

Many of the Earl's letters have survived[7] in his firm hand with a distinguished signature, from which it is evident how much reliance he placed on John Halsey, his friend and agent, for advice in personal and estate affairs. The above letter is dated shortly before he assumed the earldom. From the following, it seems that the pressure was getting much worse:

> The receipt of your letter this night hath very much contented me, to hear that the conclusion is made with Cockman, and I hope that I may by some meanes be enabled to keepe day with him, that so the trouble of him may be taken off . . . I shall be very glad when the rest of his debt is payed. But it hath also raised very great trouble in my mind, to think in how great danger I am of falling

into the hands of fiends incarnate. I shall take as much care as I know how to take, I will speake with no strangers but such as I am before sufficiently informed of; my dayes of hunting the weather itself forceth not to be constant, and I have ever a watchfull eye upon any new face that happens to come into the field, yet for a single footman to arrest me I should think it very strange, for (as I think) none but some worthy Catchpole or other, either Sergeant or Bayley is of sufficient authority to do such a business . . . yet knowing how many are violently bent upon the desire of my misery, and that though one be but now spoken of, yet many more may be procured, make me value the information, and earnestly desire to heare from you as soone as possible you can, what can be further learnt of these threats, which very much molest me, for I must confess I do so much detest a Monkish and imprisoned life, that were not my Wife and Children concerned in my life, I should be willing to chuse death before it . . . I do earnestly desire that you would advise and settle some way how I may answer my suits . . .

To my very Loving and much
respected Friend, Mr. John Halsey.
Ashridge, 11 Feb. 1650. J. Bridgewater

For a time at least he had other troubles to contend with also. On account of his monarchist views he was briefly under the suspicion of the Council of State in 1651 and was arrested for examination, but he was bailed after a few days on a bond of £10,000 and two sureties of £5,000 'not to do anything prejudicial to the present government'.[8] Always a very methodical man, he used this period of withdrawal from public life to make a review of his household arrangements at Ashridge. The careful and precise instructions which he drew up for every department of his establishment left none in doubt about the smooth manner in which he expected the household to function. The discipline was rigid and the standards expected were high; provided that every employee played his part, the efficiency he demanded would be achieved. Those who did not measure up to these requirements were to be discharged. The following extracts[9] will show how one 17th-century nobleman ordered his household affairs:

June 24th 1652

These are the Orders which I require and command to be observed by all the servants in my family in their several and respective degrees

J. Bridgewater

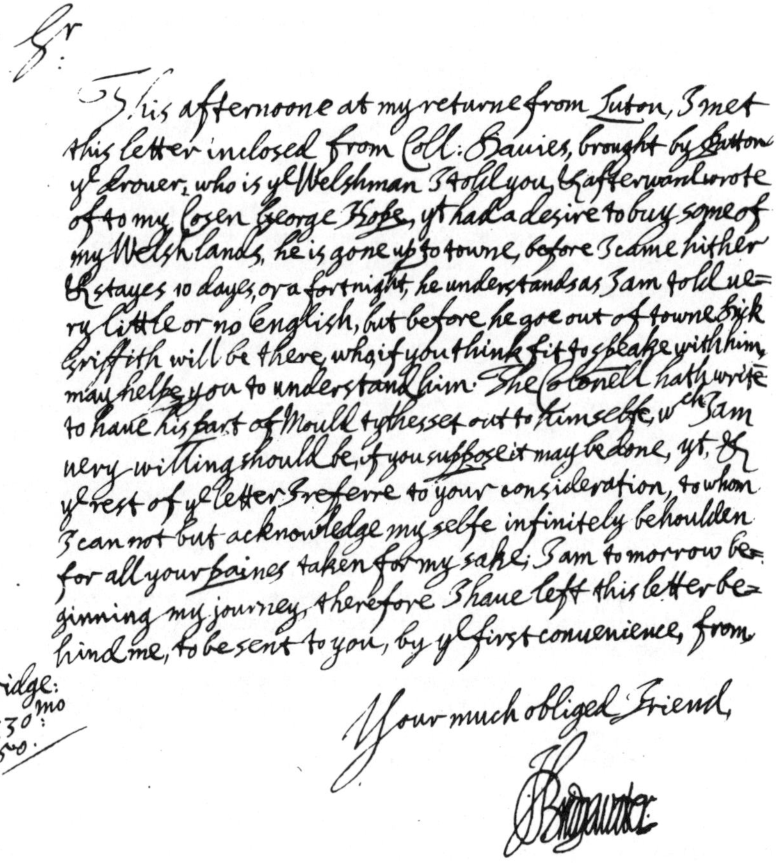

Sr:

This afternoone at my returne from Luton, I met
this letter inclosed from Coll: Dauies, brought by Sutton
ye drouer, who is ye Welshman I told you, & afterwards wrote
of to my Cosen George Hope, yt had a desire to buy some of
my Welsh lands, he is gone up to towne, before I came hither
& stayes 10 dayes, or a fortnight, he understands as I am told very little or no English, but before he goe out of towne Sir R
Griffith will be there, who if you think fit to speake with him,
may helpe you to understand him. The Colonell hath writē
to haue his part of Moull tythes set out to himselfe, wch I am
very willing should be, if you suppose it may be done, yt, &
ye rest of ye letter I referre to your consideration, to whom
I can not but acknowledge my selfe infinitely behoulden
for all your paines taken for my sake; I am to morrow beginning my journey, therefore I haue left this letter behind me, to be sent to you, by ye first conuenience, from

ridge:
30: mo
1650.

Your much obliged Friend,

J Bridgewater

Fig. 3. Letter of John, 2nd Earl of Bridgewater to John Halsey, 1650

FIRST. All the servants in the house at the ringing of the bell, or other warnings given, are immediately to repair to the morning or evening prayers or sermons, either in the Chapel or such place as I shall appoint, and thither to come with reverence; and there to continue with devout behaviour: and not to absent themselves unless with leave obtained upon some special and urgent occasion.

2. All, both gentlemen and yeomen, are in a willing and decent manner to bring up the first course to the Table, and because the attendance of the gentlemen cannot afterwards be spared from thence, during the meal the yeomen are afterwards to bring up the second course, and the fruit. And all take care not to use any uncivil, careless, slighting, or unseemly demeanour, in their attendance at the Table, and particularly to show respect and courtesy up to strangers.
3. All are diligently to attend to their service at the Table, without gazing about . . . or listening too earnestly to what is being said . . .
4. All are to take notice that the meat taken from the table is to be delivered into the Clerk of the Kitchen's hands again, in the kitchen, without any embezzling or taking away any part of it, that so much care may be taken that the meat provided may suffice the family.
5. None is to carry out of the dining room any napkin, spoon, knife, glass, or anything else but by the . . . appointment of the Butler, that so nothing of that nature may be set in windows, or by-corners, there to advantage breaking, stealing, or being purloined away . . .
6. Civil and sober demeanour is to be used by all the servants, one among another at their meals . . . and all unseemly and rude deportment to be avoided both in words and actions; and none are to rise from the Table until Thanks be first given to God.

The opening commands are given in detail, subject only to a modernisation of the spelling; but since it would be tedious to reproduce them all at length those which follow have been condensed in order to convey their scope and intention:

None is to be lodged in the House except those allowed on the check-roll of servants, and no household servant may keep within the house, without permission, a horse, hawk or dogs. All quarrelling, brawling and fighting among the servants is to be avoided within the house or abroad.

All are to obey the Steward, 'who is by me authorised for the governing of the whole family', and the Gentleman Usher 'who is to direct in matters of attendance'; and all footmen and stable workers are to obey the Master of the Horse.

If anyone is found to be a notorious swearer or blasphemer, a common drunkard, or haunter of alehouses, or a misleader or debaucher of his fellows by instigating them to disobey these orders, he is liable after warning to be dismissed; 'for I will not suffer so great a blemish to the reputation of myself and my whole family to continue in my house'. If they are to continue in his service all are to endeavour to live virtuously.

The *Steward* must maintain a check-roll of all employees and their wages, the list to be approved by the Earl lest 'unnecessary expenses may arise'. He must ensure the observance of the rules with impartiality and good example 'that all good servants may willingly love him' and others less good be compelled 'to fear and obey him'. He must keep an inventory of all household goods, see the bills are paid, check the kitchen accounts, confer daily with the Clerk of the Kitchen and the caterers about a suitable and sufficient diet, and by his example encourage them to be thrifty. Lastly, he must have a constant care that God be duly served and the household well and orderly guided so that 'neither myself nor my wife be molested or disquieted'.

The Gentleman of the Horse must keep a perfect list of all the horses, know them by their names and colour, and keep the stables in good order.

The *Gentleman Usher* must observe the hours for prayers at 11.30 a.m. and 6.30 p.m. daily, and on Sundays at 10 a.m. and 4.30 p.m.; be ready to bring strangers (visitors) to his lordship or his wife but taking care 'that access be not so far to us that we be troubled with those that we desire not to admit'. He must keep a list of servants appointed for daily attendance, and see that the Yeoman Usher lights the lights as appropriate. There are suitable orders for the Yeoman Usher.

The *Clerk of the Kitchen* is charged to see that all provisions are good and the prices reasonable, and to see that no meat is embezzled, that all is kept clean and neat, and that no kitchen utensils are lost or spoilt.

The *Butler* must inspect all his vessels for leakages. He must give courteous entertainment to visitors directed to him by his lordship or his wife. There must be no banqueting in his office. The bins for bread must be kept clean and sweet 'that there be not spoil made by rats or mice'.

Orders are made for the *Wardrobe Keeper* and the *Usher of the Hall.* No gaming is permitted in the Hall, but shuffle board is excepted. After meals none are permitted to stay drinking in the Hall. All the broken meat left over is to be gathered up and carried to the gate for distribution to the Poor.

The *Porter* is to open the gate from 6–7 a.m. to 9 p.m. in winter, from 5 a.m. to 10 p.m. in summer. He must ensure that no 'household stuff, plate, meat or drink' be carried out of the house by any servant to strangers. He must ring the bell at times for prayers and keep the gates closed while the family is at prayers or meals; have a care against fire; search the court for strangers and not open the gates at night 'because the safety of the family depends very much on his care'.

These instructions served to guide the household for some twenty years, but with a constant need for a careful watch on his finances, and because he frequently had to be away from Ashridge to carry out his duties in London, the earl found it necessary to add a supplement to his directions.

In 1670 he added special injunctions to the clerk of the kitchen and the cook against wastage in the kitchen, with special mention of butter 'which hath hitherto been too little considered, and too little valued, and too much wasted'. They must keep the kitchen doors shut during the preparation of meat until dinner is ended to avoid 'slovenly accidents' to the meat, such as contamination by the taking of tobacco, or by 'other disorders'. Servants must keep their appointed places at table and not 'have so much pride as to exalt themselves from the table in the hall to the table in the parlour'. If they are rebellious about these orders they risk being 'expelled my family'.

Then there were 'Memorials for Bulmer [his Steward] to put into execution when he should be gone to London', dated 17 October 1673:

> No others are permitted to eat of his meat but his own and his sons' servants; for it is not fit strangers should be admitted to meals, where there is no house kept. This injunction, rigorously observed, will stop what has been 'so very expensive to me'. No strong beer, ale or wine is to be spent in his absence and strangers must not expect to be entertained while he is away, much less must it be wasted on the servants.
>
> Sundays, which have been days not only of great expense but of the greatest disorder, are to be kept the most private of all days, and are to be employed in service to God, not debauchery abroad, much less at home.
>
> The Grooms must keep to their duties and not frequent ale houses, nor keep their horses at the door of one, while they make themselves drunk and give their horses colds.
>
> If on the other hand his eldest son, Brackley, or his other sons are at home they may have whatever wine and strong beer they may call for, but no other expense of this kind is to be permitted, except by their direction.

Such a close direction of household duties was not a new feature of life in great houses, though it was not common. The practice had its origin in monastic life, and there is evidence that the earl's grandfather, Lord Ellesmere, had organised his own establishment on similar lines.[10]

Oliver Cromwell died in 1658 and when Charles II was summoned back from exile in Holland and restored to the throne two years later, the 2nd Earl of Bridgewater (his affairs now being in much better order) again emerged into public life. Curiously, the first evidence which survives is not a public appointment but a Royal Warrant, dated 20 September 1660, which required the earl to take measures to preserve the game and drive out the poachers from the woods around Ashridge:

> . . . We are informed that our game of hare, pheasant, partridge, heron and other wild fowl about Ashridge . . . is much destroyed by divers disorderly persons, with greyhounds, mongrels, setting dogs, guns, trammels, tunnels, nets and other devices: for the preservation hereof and that our game may be better preserved for our sport and recreation . . . we do hereby will and command you to have especial care that no person or persons do hereafter use any of these unlawful means, or engines . . . within ten miles compass of Ashridge . . .[11]

The warrant authorised him to appoint such deputies as were necessary, and required all mayors, sheriffs, justices, constables and so on, to aid and assist him. Undoubtedly the king, always with an eye to his own pleasures, believed in putting first things first. That the earl must be presumed to have been on good terms with his monarch may be gathered from a letter dated 27 March 1661 to his friend John Halsey: '. . . I hope that this letter may come time enough to let you know the King has promised to Christen my child on Saterday next at which . . . you shall be very welcome'.[12]

In 1662 the earl was appointed, together with the Bishop of London and the Lord Chancellor, to manage the conference of the two Houses of Parliament on the Bill of Uniformity. The following year he was elected High Steward of Oxford University. Within a month his happiness was suddenly shattered by the death of his beloved wife, Elizabeth. The circumstances were indeed very sad. On 12 June Lord Bridgewater received and accepted a challenge to a duel from the Earl of Middlesex over some contentious action. The king heard of it and endeavoured to get them to settle the dispute peaceably. Middlesex, however, was obdurate, and both men were therefore ordered into custody, Lord Bridgewater being placed under the supervision of Black Rod. The Lady Elizabeth, being pregnant at the time, insisted on accompanying her husband to London and had the misfortune to die in childbirth on 14 June, in Black Rod's house at Westminster. They had been happily married for 23 years and she had borne him five sons. A sincerely religious woman, and a model of piety, her memorial in Little Gaddesden church records that 'her death was as religious as her life was virtuous: on 14th June 1663 . . . she exchanged her earthly coronet for an heavenly crown'.

The day after the duel the earl was released to his house in the Barbican, and shortly after both lords were reprimanded, and Middlesex was ordered to make an apology. Although he remained a member of the Privy Council throughout the reign of Charles II, the earl was never really prominent in state affairs. In 1667 he was given the task of enquiring into the application of several sums of money granted to the king for maintaining the war against Holland, and in the following year he became a Commissioner for Trade and Plantations. In some way his report must have upset the king, for Pepys lamented in his diary about 'the ruinous condition we are in, the King being going to put out of the Council so many able men such as . . . my Lord Bridgewater . . . only the Duke of York do endeavour to hinder it'.[13] And so, we may suppose, the duke succeeded. It was inevitable, however, as less and less use was made of his obvious ability by the king, that the earl should have been drawn more into county affairs. He served as Lord Lieutenant of Buckinghamshire from 1660–1686, of Chester and Lancashire, where he had estates, for six years from 1670, and of Hertfordshire from 1681 until his death. In Buckinghamshire the Lord Lieutenant, a rigid churchman and strict disciplinarian, gained a reputation for the severity with which he upheld the Act of Uniformity in cases of unlawful assembly, and the leaders of the Dissenters, particularly the Quakers, had cause to fear the harshness of some of his sentences.

That indefatigable traveller, Thomas Baskerville, accompanied by Mr. John Hyde (the Lord Chancellor) visited Ashridge in September 1681, where earlier his old friend Richard Blower had been Master of the Horse to the earl. He has left a picture of what he found:

> I went thither purposely to see him and this ancient house, grown more famous in the country by the present Lord's great housekeeping, for which to help it he hath here a park for fallow and another for red deer, and in them especially near his house some lofty groves of trees and so thickset together that the like is scarce anywhere to be seen . . . and doubtless were it not for these trees this would in winter time be a very sharp cold place, standing as it doth so high and open to all the northern storms . . . Here are squirrels in plenty which leap and dance from tree to tree.
>
> As to the fabric or form of the house within the gate-houses, for it hath one fair gate-house which gives entrance through a large court on the northern side of the house to the hall to which they ascend by steps on a terrace walk which leads to the hall, and another gate-house which leads to the stables . . . The hall is a noble room . . . Here is a fine garden about the house, and the place took its name from a ridge of ashes, one of which being grown tall and bulky my Lord cut down and made a fair shuffle-board table in his hall . . .[14]

The 2nd Earl died on 26 October 1686. Against this event he had methodically and piously prepared the wording of his memorial, which is on the wall over the main doorway of Little Gaddesden church. This records his lasting grief over the death of his wife Elizabeth, after which 'he did sorrowfully wear out 23 years 4 months and 12 days, humbly submitting to and waiting on the pleasure of the Almighty'. Sir Henry Chauncy, who knew him well, described him as 'a person of middling stature, somewhat corpulent, had black hair, a round visage adorned with a modest and grave aspect . . . he was a learned man, delighted much in his library, and was endowed with all the rare accomplishments of virtue and goodness; very temperate in eating and drinking; spoke sparingly but always pertinently . . . he was most devout in his acts of religion and firm to the Church of England . . . remarkable for hospitality to his neighbours, his charity to the poor, his liberality to strangers . . .[15]

In his will the earl left his Cheshire estates of Tatton and Worsley to his younger sons. Sir Thomas Egerton received the Tatton estate, and Sir William Egerton received Worsley. When William died without sons, Worsley reverted to the main line of the family. This event was to prove of the greatest significance, because it was the successful development of a canal system to distribute coal from the Worsley mines that enabled Francis Egerton, the 3rd Duke of Bridgewater, to build up his great wealth in the following century.

John, Viscount Brackley, who succeeded as 3rd Earl, was 40 years old and had already decided on a political career. A year before his father's death he successfully contested an election at Aylesbury and entered parliament as a Whig M.P. When he moved into the Upper House it was not long before he was sworn a member of the Privy Council, and he immediately followed his father as Lord Lieutenant of Buckinghamshire. James II had just come to the throne and changes were ahead. Under Charles II, who had dispensed with parliament, the government of the country rested on a convenient working arrangement between the Court and a largely Tory and Cavalier majority in the House of Lords. When James II became king he summoned parliament together and outlined to them his policies. Initially they voted him the huge sums of money he demanded to raise an army to crush the rebellion of Monmouth. When this had been successfully accomplished James felt ready to advance his ambition of making England a Roman Catholic country again, with himself as supreme monarch. The large new army he had raised was officered mainly by newly commissioned Catholics. The king's aim was to keep these forces in being, as well as to restore the Catholic peers to the House of Lords. When his Council strongly resisted this move, its leader, Lord Halifax, was dismissed. James declared to parliament that the militia had been useless in the recent rebellion: what the country needed was a strong standing army under Catholic officers. Parliament, staunchly Cavalier in spirit, was shaken by the proposal. As Sir Winston Churchill wrote: 'Its most hideous nightmare was a standing army; its dearest treasure was the established Church'. The Lords, too, were opposed, and 'here', he continues, 'Devonshire, the hardy Whig; Halifax, the renowned ex-minister; Bridgewater and Nottingham, actually members of the Privy Council; and, above all, Henry Compton, the Bishop of London, asserted the rights of the nation'.[16] The king recognised the serious obstacles to his plan and dismissed parliament, which did not meet again during his reign. Gradually he alienated his best friends and supporters, and in 1687 he removed Lord Bridgewater from the post of Lord Lieutenant of Buckinghamshire. When, in 1689, the king was eventually forced to flee the country, it was reported that 'there is great joy in Bucks. Lord Bridgewater is reinstated'.[17]

He became a Commissioner for Trade and Plantations before becoming head of the Admiralty in 1699. He served as Speaker of the House of Lords, and was made one of the Lords Justices of the Realm to govern the country during the absence of King William III in Holland during the summer of 1700. His career seemed to be set on an extremely favourable course when he died suddenly on 19 March 1701, at the early age of fifty-four. Described by his friend Chauncy as a man 'of a sweet and pleasant countenance and comely presence', and by Macaulay as a nobleman of very fair character and of some experience in business, the third John Egerton had made more impression in a short time on public life than any of his predecessors since his great-grandfather, the Lord Chancellor.

His family life had twice been marred by great sadness. His first wife Elizabeth, daughter of James Cranfield, 1st Earl of Middlesex, had died before she was twenty-two. He chose as his second wife Jane (sometimes Anne), daughter of Charles Powlett, 1st Duke of Bolton, whose father, the Marquis of Winchester, was the premier Marquis of England. The Duke of Bolton, a clever, avaricious and successful man, was once described by Bishop Burnet as 'the great riddle of his age'. He was certainly eccentric: whether he was actually insane or merely odd in his behaviour has never been really established, but something of this eccentricity seems to have been inherited by future generations of Egertons. His daughter bore Lord Bridgewater six sons and two daughters. Only six months after he had succeeded to the earldom two sons, Charles, the eldest, and Thomas, the third son, perished tragically in a fire at Bridgewater House, which was said to have been caused by the carelessness of their drunken tutor.

> *11 April 1687.* The 11th about eleven at night, hapned a sad fire in the Earl of Bridgewater's house in the Barbican: it burned but a small part of his house, yet it burnt two of his Lordships sons, the eldest and another, it beginning in their room.[18]

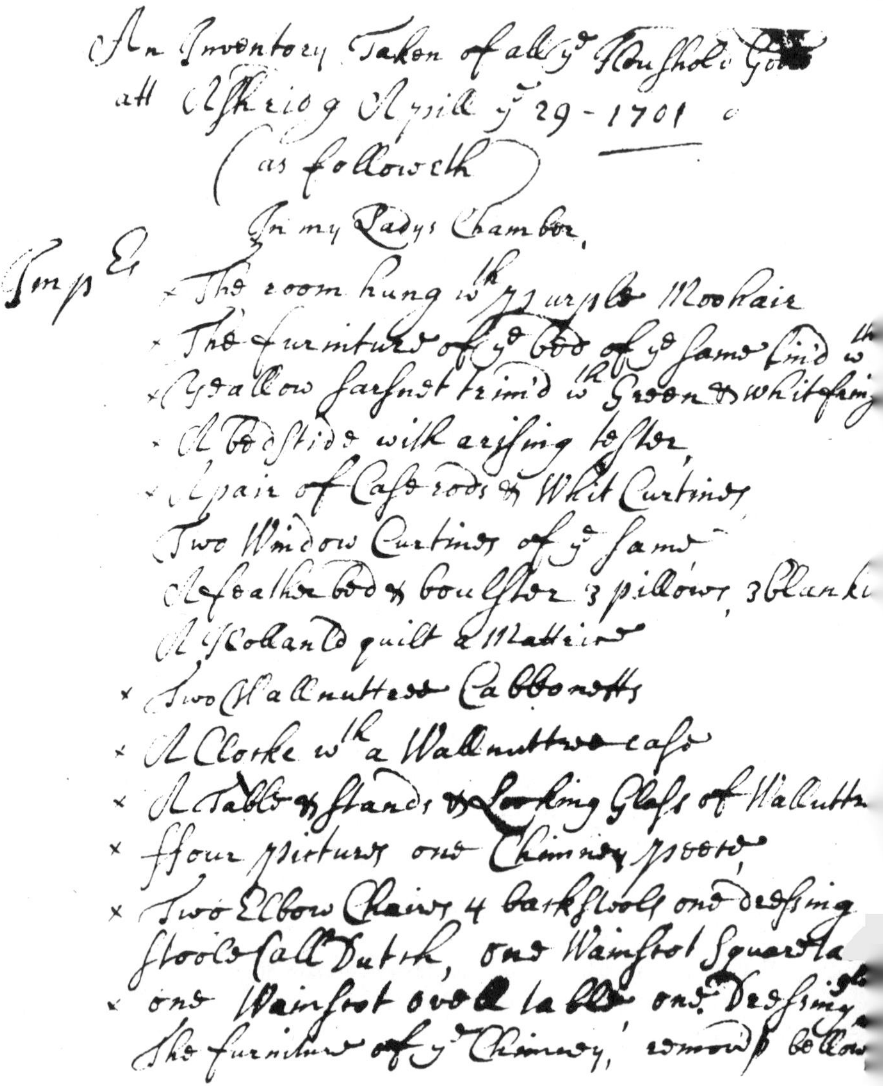

An Inventory Taken of all ye Houshold Goo
att Ashridg Aprill ye 29 - 1701
(as followeth)

In my Ladys Chamber

Imps
× The room hung wth purple Moohair
× The furniture of ye bed of ye same lind wth
× yeallow sarsnet trim'd wth Green & whit fring
× A bedstide with arising tester
× A pair of Castrods & Whit Curtinds
Two Window Curtinds of ye same
A featherbed & boulster 3 pillows, 3 blank
A Hollond quilt & Mattris
× Two Wallnuttree Cabbonetts
× A Clocke wth a Wallnuttree case
× A Table & stands & Looking Glass of Wallnutt
× ffour pictures one Chimney board
× Two Elbow Chairs 4 backstools one dressing
stools call Dutch, one Wainscot Square ta
× one Wainscot ovall table one Dressing gla
The furniture of ye Chimney, romaine bellow

Fig. 4. First page of an Inventory of Ashridge, 1701

A Note of my Lady's Cloaths.

A Velvet Gowne and Petticoate.
A Tabby Gowne and two rich Petticoates.
A Cloath Gowne and Petticoate
A Crape Gowne and Petticoate
A Short black Petticoate, A black velvet Petticoate.
A black velvet Lining for a Mantow
A Rich Indian Dark Mantow
A Rich black Petticoate, A Rich White Indian Mantow, &
A Rich black Petticoate, A Cloath Mantow & Petticoate.
A Indian black & White Mantow & Petticoate; A Indian blue Mantow,
and Petticoate, a Rich Silke Mantow & Petticoate; an Orange
Petticoate with Silver futtings, A Yellow Petticoate wth black &
Silver Lace, A Short velvet Petticoate with Silver Lace.
A Stuff Night Gowne, A Dust Gowne, 2 quilted petticoats
2 fflowred holland Petticoats, 2 Dimity Petticoates.
A Muslin Petticoate, 2 Quilted Wastcoates, A White Sattin Wastcoat
3 Flannin Petticoats & linings to them, A Gold & Silver Stuffe
Gowne & Petticoate. A thick Night Gowne.

A Note of the Linnen.

Sixteene Shifts 16 Handkerchiefs 4 laced Handkerchiefs
4 Suits of laced Night Cloaths 6 fflourisht Night Rails,
One Point Night Rail, 1 laced Cushion Cloath, One of Point.
One Plaine Cushion Cloath. Six paire of Stockings thred
& Cotton. 8 Damask Towells 4 Damask Napkins, 2 Muslin Aprons.
5 Shift Laces, 5 Night Smock Laces, 2 Stript Muslin Cushion Cloaths
A flowred Apron, 6 plaine holland pinners.

Fig. 5. The wardrobe of Anne, 3rd Countess of Bridgewater, 1693

So runs the laconic account of the journal of Nathaniel Luttrell. These unfortunate children were buried in the family vault at Little Gaddesden church in the same urn. Of their other children, Sçroop, the eldest, was to succeed his father in due course. The next boy, Henry, became Bishop of Hereford, and was the grandfather of the 7th and 8th Earls of Bridgewater.

Few records of Ashridge House have survived from this period, but two of interest have recently come to light,[19] being the contents of the wardrobe of Anne, Countess Bridgewater, the 3rd Earl's second wife (Fig.5) and an inventory of the household goods (Fig.4) taken on 29 April 1701, just five weeks after the earl had died. The value of the household inventory lies in its naming and description of the functions of the various rooms and offices, enabling a picture to be gained of a house of which no actual plan has been found. There is space for only a few examples.

My Lady's Chamber was hung with purple mohair, and her bed was furnished with the same, lined with yellow sarsenet (silk) trimmed with a green and white fringe: all the furniture was of walnut. In the Wainscot Dining Room there were 28 pictures, a map of England, two oval tables, two sideboards and 18 cane-bottom chairs. The Great Dining Room appears to have been used only for sitting in, as it contained no tables in it. A room was still preserved as My Lord Chancellor's Room, containing in addition to the bed and furnishings seven pieces of tapestry hangings, two elbow chairs, four back stools, 'suitable to the bed', a table, a looking-glass inlaid with silver, a pair of dogs, a fire shovel, tongs and a pair of bellows. The King's Bedchamber and dressing room were appropriately furnished: a bedroom above it was hung with gilt leather, having bed furnishings of 'sad coloured watered harrateen' (a dark or dull cloth).

The Great Hall held two long tables and '24 silver pieces belonging to the tables'. On the walls the guest would have been able to admire, if such were his taste, four pictures of horses, two of mares, five pictures of hounds, 24 stags' heads and 10 bucks' heads, but he might have been left wondering at the presence of 47 water buckets. In the Cedar Gallery were hanging 32 pictures of relations, and 25 more pictures, three black sconces and a large looking-glass adorned the Great Stairhead.

There was a fully furnished bedroom and a little room adjacent over the chapel, which had been built as recently as 1699 and was entered from the cloisters. At its opening on 27 August 1699 the sermon was preached by the Rev. George Burghope, rector of Little Gaddesden.[20] The chapel had three window curtains and 10 quilted cushions of red baize. The pulpit cloth, communion cloth, and cover for the reading desk were of crimson velvet with a gold fringe. The 41 prayer books, three bibles, 34 psalm books and a book of homilies suggest a modest sized congregation of family, guests and household servants, for whom the gloom of dark afternoons would have been relieved by the lights from 16 little brass candlesticks and two brass sconces over the chimney-piece. The kitchen ('Ye Kitching') contained 10 spits and 11 trivets, and an array of pots, pans and cutlery. It also held 18 muskets, 12 headpieces and two halberds, so that nothing was left to chance.

The complete inventory describes the contents of about ninety rooms and indicates a mansion of considerable size, including two lodges. White Lodge was then the name of the old monastic gate-house and stood a little to the north of the present main entrance. Red Lodge, at the western end, still remains, though it has been greatly modified and enlarged in recent years. Unlike many inventories of houses taken on the death of the owner, no valuations are attached to this one.

Of such then was the nature of the house which Scroop Egerton, Viscount Brackley, the eldest of the surviving sons of the 3rd Earl, inherited from his father at the age of nineteen.

Chapter Ten

THE DUKES OF BRIDGEWATER (1701–1748)

SCROOP EGERTON owed his name to his maternal grandfather, Emmanuel Scroop, Earl of Sunderland, one of whose illegitimate daughters, Mary, inherited a large part of her father's great wealth and became the wife of the Duke of Bolton. Scroop's mother, the widowed Lady Bridgewater, was very anxious for him to make a good marriage and was more than pleased when the young man fell passionately in love with the beautiful daughter of England's most renowned general, John Churchill, Earl of Marlborough and his wife, the former Sarah Jennings. Elizabeth Churchill, not yet 16, and the only daughter left unmarried, was the apple of her parents' eyes and there was some natural reluctance at the thought of parting with one whose engaging company gave them so much pleasure. The match was an attractive one, however, and Scroop was an ardent and persistent lover. The Churchill star, moreover, was rising high, and before the wedding took place in 1703 Elizabeth's father had been elevated to the rank of Duke of Marlborough. The Duchess enjoyed the close friendship and confidence of Queen Anne, who signified her approval of the match with a wedding present of £5,000 to the charming young bride. Duchess Sarah had already established a dominant position at Court. The weak queen ('Mrs. Morley') had come to rely so completely on her favourite 'Mrs. Freeman' that little took place in matters requiring the royal favour which had not either been manipulated by the Duchess or had received her support.

In such 'fortunate' circumstances Scroop Egerton began his married life. His wife, Elizabeth, became a Lady of the Queen's Bedchamber, and he received the appointment of Master of the Horse to Prince George of Denmark, husband of the queen.

Slow and cautious in contrast to his lively young wife, Scroop seems to have been a man of evident good nature. He had no political ambitions such as his father had, but appeared content to set his sights on a comfortable life of service at Court. His real ambition was to elevate the family name by becoming a Duke, like his wife's father, and he felt sure that the influential support of his new parents-in-law was going to help him to gain his objective. However, as time went on, powerful forces began to assert themselves against the Marlboroughs. The failure of the Whig government to achieve peace with France, in spite of Marlborough's great victories, led to a strong Tory reaction. Not only they, but the public at large wanted an end to war. The Whigs were toppled, and the Duke of Marlborough fell from favour. The military campaign was halted, and a campaign of reproach and unjustifiable vilification began against him. The queen quarrelled with the duchess, and when she transferred her allegiance to a new favourite, Abigail Masham, Sarah's dominating hold was finally broken. Marlborough, rather than endure the insults and disgrace, thought it best to go into voluntary exile in Europe. In 1712 he and his wife made various pilgrimages to Aix and Frankfurt, but finally settled in Antwerp. Scroop's prospects of advancement seemed now to be vastly diminished, if not at an end. In 1714 fate dealt a cruel blow both to him and to the exiled Marlboroughs. The gay and lovely Elizabeth fell ill and died of smallpox. She was only 25, and Scroop was left with a son, John (fated to die at the age of 15) and a daughter, Anne. Another son, Charles, had died in infancy. The Duke of Marlborough received the news of his beloved daughter's death in his Antwerp home with such shock that he fainted, and in falling he struck his head on the mantlepiece. His fortunes, however, were about to change abruptly for the better as the Tory ministers at home fell out among themselves and the ailing queen was near to death. The Marlboroughs felt that they could now reasonably return to England, and the duke was received cordially by King George I. He was reinstated in his appointment as Captain-General and given a seat in the Cabinet. Sarah, too, was well received and, in characteristic fashion, she set about arranging suitable positions at Court for her relatives, though 'she thought it a pity that the widower Bridgewater was such a manifest fool that she could get him nothing better than Chamberlain to the Princess of Wales', later to become Queen Caroline.[1] Three years later Scroop became a Lord of The Bedchamber to the king. He may have been a dull kind of fellow, but he seems always to have been able to remain quietly and unostentatiously in favour at Court. He was probably a great deal more single-minded in purpose than was obvious, as his quiet wooing of the king was eventually rewarded, and on 18 June 1720 he realised his ambition when he was created Marquis of Brackley and the first Duke of Bridgewater. In spite of his wealth and estates he had inherited his father's debts and it was now more than ever necessary that he should make a wealthy second marriage. This, he reasoned, would be an easier and more certain way than risky financial speculation of ensuring the additional funds necessary to maintain the type of establishment and level of entertainment appropriate to his new eminence. Scroop also had to consider seriously the question of the succession, as he had no son. John, his first born, had been a sickly youth and had died in 1719 at the age of 15 while at school at Eton. If a second marriage should prove not to be blessed with male issue then all his achievement of the dukedom would be in vain. He therefore devised a scheme by which the patent should be so worded as to permit his brother's children to benefit. Surprising as it may seem to us today, this proposed variation appears to have been accepted, and the legal and administrative fees for the modification would have amounted to only 300 guineas. When his brother, Dr. Henry Egerton, Bishop of Hereford, was invited to pay this sum, either he was dubious of the plan or else was unduly mean, and he declined to do so; presumably Scroop felt that he could not afford the expense either. As a consequence, though not for some years to come, the dukedom was eventually to be extinguished.

When the Duchess of Marlborough returned to England there was much to occupy her mind. Blenheim was unfinished and the costs were mounting extravagantly. The duke's health was declining after two strokes and he needed her attention; there was also her very large family with all their problems. In 1716 she took her granddaughter, the motherless Lady Anne Egerton (Scroop's daughter by his first wife) to live with her, because she felt that at Ashridge the girl was being 'very ill looked after'. This arrangement appeared to work very well for some years until Anne was approaching marriageable age, when in 1722 her father took as his second wife Lady Rachel Russell, daughter of the second Duke of Bedford, thereby joining two very large estates. Scroop had already begun to estrange himself from the Duchess of Marlborough. After the death of the duke in 1720 he had been disappointed by the provisions of the duke's will, so much so that he had even absented himself from the funeral. Shortly after his marriage he commanded his daughter to come to Ashridge to wish him and his new bride well. Sarah perceived in this a plan for Anne to be kept and married to the young 3rd Duke of Bedford, Wriothesly Russell, and she was determined to prevent it. She composed a reply for Anne to send: 'My Grandmama hopes you will excuse her for not sending me now. I have had so great a cold and pain in my ear that my head is now wrapt up in Flanel . . . My Lady Dutches is in a melancholly condition which makes her unwilling to part with me'.[2]

This reply infuriated Scroop, who at 11 o'clock at night went immediately to Marlborough House 'with a candle and lantern before him, a footman's coat upon him for fear of catching cold, and the air of being quite mad', and he demanded his daughter. Eventually he went away but returned the next morning before anyone was up, still furious, and through the servants exchanged bitter reproaches with the duchess, who was still in bed, until Sarah agreed. 'He would not go into any room, tho' he was desired to do it, but walked about in the Hall like a madman, with the most ill natur'd countenance that was ever seen in any human creature'. At last the Lady Anne came down, dressed, and he took her away in a coach.[3] Sarah was much pained by this episode, as she had brought up Anne almost as her own daughter, and she could not bear ingratitude. A year or more later she wrote to Anne reproaching her for having neglected to visit her, and indicating that the proposed marriage was certainly not to her liking. Scroop obtained the letter and instructed the messenger who carried it to convey a message to her Grace: 'I have commanded my daughter never to go to her, nor to write or send any message, nor to receive any from her . . .'[4] The outraged duchess thereupon took a portrait of the young girl and blackened the face, writing underneath it,

'She is blacker within', and hung the frame in her sitting room for all her visitors to see.[5] Anne, however, did marry the youthful Duke of Bedford, though it was not a successful match. He gambled wildly and they quarrelled. His health was indifferent, which made him moody and subject to fits of sudden anger. He was advised to go abroad in the hope that his health would benefit, but he died in Spain in 1732, only seven years after the wedding. The young widow later made a much more suitable choice by marrying the Earl of Jersey, and she lived until 1762.

The marriage of the Duke of Bridgewater to Lady Rachel Russell resulted in eight children, including three sons: Charles, who died at the age of five from smallpox, after inoculation; John, who was to die before he was 21; and Francis, who seemed the least likely to (but did) achieve great renown. Scroop continued to enjoy the favour of George I, and then of his rather more attractive son, George II, and without becoming involved too much in public affairs he led the kind of life, between town and country, that was expected of a man of his position. Until about 1740 he kept up the fine collection of coins that had been started by his grandfather (the famous Bridgewater collection last changed hands at Sotheby's in 1972). He had time to worry about his health, and while he was at Ashridge he maintained a correspondence on his ills with his physician, the eminent Sir Hans Sloan, as two letters, both from 1733, show:[6]

> I am much better, but I mend slowly, the bitters gave me a good stomack and I went once a day. I used in morning to drink water-gruel with currants, but for ten days I took ½ pt of cow's milk with a little water in it and took my bitters at noon and went once a day. Last Sunday in ye afternoon I took ¼ of a pint of Asses Milk with ye same powder my son takes, the next morning I was more bound and could not do anything . . . I went ye next morning with great difficulty finding myself much bound and my head aking . . . [there follows a recital of other variations tried]. . . . with your assistance I hope to be well soon and am Sir,
>
> Yr obedient humble servant,
>
> Bridgewater
>
> [P.S.] Company is just go [*sic*] from me and I have time only to say I am better since dinner and my head well.

July 9th, 1733

The Bitter Drink has had a very good effect on me. I was very well friday and saturday last, but on sunday and this morning the least motion put me into a sweat, since my breakfast I am pretty well and intend about 6 of ye clock to ride out for an hour to see what effect that will have. I try what I can not to get cold, but my pores are so open that it is a difficult matter. I am, etc. . . .

Lady Bridgewater too relied on the renowned physician's advice, even when she was away.[7]

30th June 1732

I have been a fortnight today here and have not been free from either a pain in my back or the lower part of my belly. I have had very little Gravell come away my first week. I could get no rest, which made me so dispirited that I went to a Doctor here . . . he sent me Matthew's Pill. I took it two nights in which I rested pretty well. I have taken nothing else but your prescription which I have followed exactly . . . About a week since I found one of my legs felt sore, and it grows more so every day, it is swelld a little and pitts. I have been able to walk very little yet but if I was I should be glad to know it if would be proper to do so, if you will send me your directions I will follow em, who am,

Your most obliged,
humble servant,
R. Bridgewater.

* * * * *

The real Industrial Revolution was still a generation away, but new ideas and inventions were constantly being introduced and there was no shortage of wealth or will to foster greater trade both at home and abroad. Facility of transport was still a major limiting factor. The conventional means of carrying goods was either by sea or by pack-horse: wheeled traffic for heavy goods was exceptional because of the abysmal state of the roads. Scroop, who had travelled quite widely in Europe, and had seen how the French had developed their canals, was shrewd enough to see that not only industrial Lancashire, but he personally, would considerably benefit if the coal from his waterlogged Worsley mines could be carried on its journey to Manchester by a waterway from Worsley to the River Irwell near Barton. An Act of Parliament to make the Worsley brook navigable was obtained in 1737, and while Scroop has been credited with promoting it[8] it seems unlikely because his name headed the list of Commissioners appointed to arbitrate between the landowners and other interests, and it would scarcely have been proper for a promoter to be an arbitrator. However, nothing came of the scheme, and the Act lapsed.[9] Twenty years later Scroop's son, poring through the family papers and visiting his estates, could not have failed to have been moved by his father's close involvements to realise that the project was worth re-examination.

Scroop died at the age of 63 on 11 January 1745, and was buried in the family vault at Little Gaddesden church, where curiously there is no memorial to him. His widow had shown little concern over the upbringing of their children—perhaps resenting such an obligation, in the way of fashionable 18th-century ladies, as an intrusion upon her pleasures. If her husband's health had been better in his last years he might have prevailed on her to take more interest, but, truth to tell, he entertained no high expectations that either son would outlive him by many years. He must have reflected with some sadness on the waste of all his efforts to elevate his family's position as he saw the chances that the Dukedom would survive and with them his hopes of founding a great dynasty slipping away.

John, the elder surviving son, was 17 when he inherited the dukedom from his father. Francis, born on 21 May 1736, was not yet nine. Their mother, flaunting convention, waited less than a year before she became the wife of Sir Richard Lyttleton, Master of the Jewel Office, a man more than twenty years her junior. If the Duchess of Bridgewater ever held any real hopes that John, the brighter and seemingly the more robust of the two boys, might survive to manhood, these were to be dashed when he fell victim to smallpox and died on 26 February 1748 at the age of twenty. The prospect of the line continuing now seemed bleak indeed; but fortune had by no means yet abandoned the Egertons, as the following chapter shows.

Chapter Eleven

THE CANAL DUKE (1748-1803)

FEW SONS OF THE NOBILITY can have had a more inauspicious start to life than Francis Egerton. He shared with his brother the indifferent health and weakly constitution that seems to have dogged most of the Bridgewater progeny through the ages. His mother was not in the least bit interested in him: he was, in fact, an irritation to her. She placed him early on in the care not of a governess, but of lesser members of her household staff, who, disliking his proclivity for getting into mischief, left him very much to his own devices. He was delicate and backward, and, because he was neglected, he was badly behaved and awkward of manner. When his father died he was sent away to a boarding school at Markyate, Herts.[1] His mother, too much bound up in her own social pleasures and greatly ignorant of the needs of small children, considered Francis to be a near imbecile, and as such quite unfitted to inherit the title. At one time she even seriously contemplated action to have the inheritance set aside on the grounds that he was mentally deficient. Francis fared little better at the hands of his stepfather, whose outward charm belied a private tyranny and harsh discipline in his own home that was to make the boy fear and detest him. These two were the pair of whom Horace Walpole, not unknown for his shallow judgements, was later to write to a friend: 'You will be happy too in Sir Richard Lyttleton and his Duchess; they are the best humoured people in the world'.[2]

Francis Egerton came into the family estate as the 3rd Duke of Bridgewater at the age of eleven. It is fortunate that not long after he was to come under the influence of three practical and sensible men: Samuel Egerton of Tatton, Cheshire, his cousin and co-guardian with his mother, who showed him much kindness. His uncle, the 4th Duke of Bedford, with whom the boy would spend some holidays from school, stoutly defended his interests against the indifference of his mother and step-father, and was the prime mover in sending Francis on the Grand Tour of Europe. Granville Gower, Lord Trentham, who was married to Lady Louisa Egerton, Francis's eldest sister, was to have a good effect on him all his life; sharing an enthusiasm for the development of canals, he remained one of the few really close friends that the duke was to make.

The extremely unhappy Francis presented his relations with a problem. He had received no proper education and appeared to be woefully ignorant. In an attempt to remedy this defect they decided to send him to Eton. Samuel Egerton undertook to supervise this and it was to him that Francis's tutor, Robert Purt, was to report in June 1749: 'You, Sir, who are not unacquainted with the disadvantages under which his Grace had labour'd will not expect any account of a great progress made in so short a time as we have been at Eton . . . I have procur'd him a place in the school where he will have an opportunity of conversing with manly boys, by which means he will, I hope, become so himself, and wear off any childish bashfulness which may otherwise stick by him'.[3]

The Eton experience, which lasted until 1752, achieved no miracles. He was neither a very willing pupil, nor an able one, but he was certainly not mentally deficient. His health improved a little, and he grew into a tall young man, though not physically strong, but he appeared to have acquired few of the social graces desirable in a young nobleman. In a final attempt to bring the boy out into manhood his guardians decided to send him on the Grand Tour of Europe. He was placed in the care of Robert Wood, a distinguished archaeologist, writer and scholar, but also a man of the world, in the hope that exposure to the experience of travel amid cultural surroundings might succeed in implanting in this awkward youth some interest in the arts and a sense of the civilities of life, as well as a taste of its pleasures. In France they visited Paris, where Francis found fencing lessons more to his liking than dancing classes, and then went south to Lyons where he attended the Academy for a while. A brief excursion into Switzerland was followed by a return to the south of France where they visited the docks and works of the Languedoc canal. The French had much earlier recognised the importance of canals for linking the major river systems. The Languedoc canal, completed in 1681, traversed the country from the Bay of Biscay to the Mediterranean. The sight of it and of the technical problems involved must have recalled to Francis his father's interest in a canal scheme from Worsley. A journey along the line of the canal to Bordeaux, lasting two weeks, probably clarified in his mind that his interests were of a practical, rather than an academic, nature. During a further stay in Lyons he attended a course which included some science and engineering, and he started to learn Italian prior to visiting Rome. Before they were able to leave he was again taken ill, but eventually they reached the Holy City. Here he made the acquaintance of many of the cardinals and ambassadors and enjoyed a cheerful social life in the company of other young Englishmen. He enjoyed entertaining his friends lavishly and was not infrequently the worse for drink, which was something totally unsuited to his state of health. He suffered a very serious relapse, causing his tutor considerable anxiety, but after a lengthy convalescence he recovered and Wood was able to report to the Duke of Bedford that his charge was now,'thoroughly persuaded of the necessity of great temperance . . . the physician has been very explicit with him'. The experience of Rome appeared to have been of a good effect. In another letter, dated 9 January 1755, Robert Wood was able to report to the Duke of Bedford with more confidence perhaps than he knew:

> I shall take it upon me to promise that extravagance will never be his Vice. He is indeed going on so well at present that it would be dangerous to wish the least alteration in his pleasures: tho' he seems quite determined against the expense of building [at Ashridge], yet he has a great desire of furnishing one room of the old Convent with pictures of the best masters now here. I have not hesitated in lending £400, all the money I had to command, for that purpose.[4]

This was the modest beginning of the great Bridgewater Collection, and a few years later, even when his finances were being most stretched by the demands of his canal project, he would not sell his pictures to help raise money.

The young man who returned home at the end of 1755 at the age of 19 was a very different person from the ill-mannered youth who had rather reluctantly left England two years earlier. His health had improved remarkably, and he had acquired some of the social graces which were lacking earlier. Under the warm and cultivated influence of Robert Wood a much more confident and civilised person had emerged, though still shy in manner, especially towards women. He indulged in most of the fashionable pursuits of a young man about town. He became ardently absorbed in horse-racing, keeping a house and stables at Newmarket, and even riding occasionally as a jockey, though he lacked the physical stamina for much success. He gambled both on horses and at cards, although never to the point of extreme foolishness. The old Egerton sense of caution in expenditure never deserted him, which was as well, since he was far from rich. The many estates that he had inherited were heavily encumbranced with mortgages, and Francis had to be careful. This fact, as much as any other, may have inspired a determination and desire to amass and keep great wealth in his later days. His dalliance with women seldom attracted great notice: he was still too lacking in social polish to achieve the kind of reputation that gladdened the hearts of the scandal-mongers. His name had been linked in a Manchester newspaper, shortly after his return to England, with Miss Jane Revell, a wealthy heiress, and it was predicted that a marriage could shortly be expected to take place. For some reason the duke did not pursue the engagement seriously, and the young lady bestowed her heart and her fortune on another. The other match which attracted London's attention, and which came closer to succeeding, was in 1758, when he fell in love with the recently-widowed Duchess of Hamilton. A few years earlier two beautiful but portionless sisters, Elizabeth and Maria Gunning from Ireland, had captivated society with their good looks, their charm and graceful manners; and, not surprisingly, they had made good marriages, Elizabeth gaining for herself as husband the Duke of Hamilton, and Maria marrying the Earl of Coventry. When the Duke of Hamilton suddenly died his widow, Elizabeth, returned to the London scene and Francis immediately fell under her spell, pursuing her with something of the impetuosity with which his father had wooed Elizabeth Churchill. Francis pressed her for an immediate engagement, and was accepted; but what promised to have been a hopeful union foundered, mainly on account of the duke's concern about an affair which Maria was having with Lord Bolingbroke. The Duchess of Hamilton, affronted at criticism of her sister, refused to understand Francis's point of view, and decided that she preferred instead her cousin, Colonel John Campbell, heir of the Duke of Argyll, and she broke off the engagement. Her shy and rather plain suitor lacked the glamour of his rival. As a face-saving gesture it was given out that the duke had made the break because the duchess would not cease to associate with her sister, the Countess of Coventry, of whose lax conduct he disapproved. According to Lord Ellesmere 'family tradition' held that it was really Francis who had broken off the engagement.[5] The duchess lost little time in marrying her cousin.

On 4 March 1759 the duke gave a great ball at his London house, and thereafter began to withdraw from the social round. The gossips were convinced that disappointment over his matrimonial adventures was causing him to shun society, but the true reason was quite different. Since 1757, when he became 21, he had had full control of his estates. He was already acquainted with John Gilbert, who was to play such a prominent part in his future affairs, and he was already deeply involved in plans for making a canal to carry coal from his mines at Worsley. A week before the ball his first Canal Bill had had its third reading in parliament and on 23 March it received the Royal Assent. He now intended to concentrate his mind and energy on his all-absorbing project. Henceforth he was to be found more where the work was to be done and his less frequent presence in London was mainly for the purpose of lobbying parliamentary support for the canal. He had found a serious purpose for his life and was determined to fulfil it, particularly as it promised, if successful, to bring him much needed wealth. Ultimately he was to achieve very considerable wealth, but not before he had endured many years of acute financial worry and had incurred business debts of such dimensions as he could scarcely have imagined in those early days.

The time was propitious for enterprising young men. England in 1759 was financially more stable than she had been for many a year. This was the year in which James Watt set up a workshop in Glasgow and Matthew Boulton succeeded to his father's business in Birmingham; Josiah Wedgewood arrived in Burslem, Staffordshire, and Richard Arkwright was ready with a mechanical process of cotton spinning to be introduced at Bolton in the following year. Industry and invention were on the move, not least in the Midlands and in the north-west. Manchester had a population of 20,000 and was growing: Liverpool was even larger. The advance of industry, however, was being impeded on almost every front by the absence of good roads and the high cost of transport. Wheeled transport for goods was almost impossible owing to the dreadful state of the roads in most of Lancashire, most of which were passable only by pack-horse. The prospect was not much better for passengers. Arthur Young's advice was to the point: 'Let me seriously caution all travellers who may accidentally purpose to travel this terrible country to avoid it as they would the devil . . . They will meet here with ruts, which I have accidentally measured, four feet deep and floating with mud, only from a wet summer. What, therefore, must it be after a winter?'[6]

The difficulty was that the demand for coal was greater in winter than in summer. If it was sent from Worsley to Manchester the high costs made it almost prohibitive for the inhabitants, for included in them were the horse transport from the mine to the stream; the high charges of the Mersey and Irwell Navigation Company for carriage in boats; and the cost of unloading it again for carriage by horse into the city. The duke's problem was that the coal on the Worsley estate was not yielding much profit. If it could be transported by water all the way it could be marketed cheaply in Manchester. Herein lay the solution and with it the prospect of a very profitable enterprise. Put very simply, a pack-horse could carry at most two hundredweight; a carthorse might pull one ton, but one horse could pull up to 30 tons on water. The first canal in England to employ a lock had been made near Exeter as early as the 16th century, and while it was common to use navigable rivers, often improved by cuts, for the transport of goods, the canal era proper did not begin in England until the 18th century. As early as 1720 there had been a scheme to use the River Irwell from Manchester to Liverpool by contriving locks and weirs, but it was abandoned as being too difficult to control the extremes of flood or drought. Scroop Egerton's project for joining Worsley to Manchester and the Irwell in 1737 has already been mentioned. It is probably less well known that his father, the 3rd Earl of Bridgewater, had introduced a Bill into the House of Lords in 1688 for joining the Thames and the Severn, roughly from Oxford to Bristol. 'Many lords and gentlemen were ingaged in it . . . but some foolish Discourses at coffee houses laid asleep that great design as being a thing impossible and impracticable'.[7] There is no reason to believe that the 3rd Earl was seriously interested in canals as such; he was probably merely lending his name and position to further a business venture. In 1755 an Act had been secured for improving the Sankey Brook at St. Helen's, Lancashire, and this short stretch was completed in 1757.

Lord Gower, the duke's brother-in-law, had put forward an ambitious scheme for connecting the Mersey, Trent and Severn rivers by canals so that the ports of Liverpool, Hull and Bristol could be linked together. His agent was Thomas Gilbert, who also worked for the duke, and who eventually became his chief legal agent. Thomas Gilbert had been educated for the Bar and was later M.P. for Newcastle and Lichfield, in Staffordshire. His younger brother, John, born in 1724, had received only a village school education in Farley, where the family home was. At the age of 12 or 13 John was apprenticed to Matthew Boulton senior, a millwright and father of the famous engineer, and he came to be very well regarded by his employer. 'Notwithstanding his early disadvantages he possessed talents which, matured by age and experience, could not fail of recommending him to notice'. At the age of 19 his father died, and John had to leave the employ of Matthew Boulton to look after the small family estate, which included a lime works. He joined the duke's service about ten years later in 1753 and assisted his elder brother. Two or three years later Thomas Gilbert asked John to inspect and report on the collieries at Worsley, where some improvements were being contemplated.

'After viewing the works it immediately recurred to him that if the coals on that part of the estate could be brought to market in such a populous town as Manchester, and for the supply of the numerous works in its vicinity, the colliery, which, in the state it was at the time of his inspection, yielded little profit, would become extremely valuable. It is said that he secluded himself altogether for two days at the *Bull* inn, at Manchester, to consider how this might be done by water-carriage, as that by land was very expensive, and on account of the badness of the roads, very inconvenient and almost impracticable'.[8]

Having worked out his scheme he communicated it to the duke, who was in complete accord, and John Gilbert was appointed to be his agent for the canal project. In June 1757, Gilbert moved with his family to Worsley and so began a partnership and close friendship between the two men that was to last until Gilbert's death in 1797.

The preliminaries to securing assent for the duke's Canal Act included two petitions to the House of Commons from 'the gentlemen, traders and manufacturers' of Manchester, Salford and smaller adjacent towns and villages, supporting the advantages of the proposed canal. Opposition came from the Mersey and Irwell Navigation Company and landowners, but since not the least of the benefits promised was that coal would be delivered in Salford at fourpence per hundredweight as against the prevailing rate of sevenpence or eightpence, it is not surprising that this was a powerful argument, and the Act was passed in March 1759.

The account from which the foregoing quotation about John Gilbert is taken also states that an initial tunnel for extracting surplus water from the colliery was planned and executed entirely by Gilbert; and that he, being acquainted with James Brindley, and knowing him to be an ingenious millwright, sought his assistance in this quite hazardous undertaking, and introduced him to the duke. The duke was probably aware of Brindley's work, since he was at that time engaged in surveying for Lord Gower a canal to link the Mersey with the Trent. Whatever may have been the precise sequence of events, it is clear from the duke's account books at Northampton that James Brindley had joined him by July 1759.

Brindley was 41 years old at the time. He was born near Buxton, Derbyshire, and had been apprenticed to Abraham Bennett, a millwright in Macclesfield. Bennett and his men had been ineffectual teachers, leaving the young apprentice a great deal on his own, and Brindley had been obliged to find out much for himself. Fortunately he possessed an abiding sense of curiosity about how things worked, and he was blessed with a determination to triumph over difficulties. He was thorough in everything that he undertook and he developed a quite remarkable mechanical skill and ingenuity. Some historians (Francis Henry Egerton among them) have described him as illiterate, but this seems scarcely probable: he could read and write, perhaps not fluently, and if his spelling was rather crudely phonetic, he could keep reasonable working accounts. Brindley's apprenticeship and later work had made him familiar with the construction of machinery for water- and windmills, and events were to provide him with ample scope for his ingenuity. Work must have started very soon after July 1759, as the first two stretches amounting to about three miles had been cut before the end of the year. It was then decided that the original route sanctioned by the Act would need to be altered in order to carry the canal on a longer stretch of level water following natural contours, thereby avoiding the need for a number of expensive locks. Brindley was sent to London in January 1760 to present and justify to the parliamentary committee the new route, which involved carrying the canal across the River Irwell by means of an aqueduct. This revolutionary conception of an aqueduct was greeted by conventional engineers with derision. One such consultant is said to have joked with the duke: 'I have often heard of castles in the air, but never before saw where any of them was to be erected'. The parliamentary committee was equally critical and dubious, but Brindley was quite undaunted and patiently explained his intention to use arches to carry the aqueduct, carving a model in demonstration from a cheese he had purchased. Asked how he would prevent the water from spilling out of the canal, he gave a simple demonstration of the method of 'puddling' clay to provide a lining. The second Canal Act was passed in March 1760, and within only 15 months the remarkable aqueduct at Barton was completed, carrying the canal over the Irwell at a height of 39 feet. The critics had been confounded; the 'castle in the air' had become not only a reality, but one of the wonders of the countryside to be visited and marvelled at.

Towards the end of the same year the duke petitioned parliament for an extension of the canal from near Stretford to Runcorn on the Mersey estuary. Opposition was again encountered, but arguments were sustained that the Mersey and Irwell were 'very imperfect, expensive and precarious', and that the Navigation Company had failed to build a single wharf in the 26 miles between Manchester and Warrington. By March 1762 the duke's third Canal Act had received Royal Assent. The enormous building activity was beginning to affect the look of Worsley, which Josiah Wedgewood was to describe as having 'the appearance of a considerable seaport town'. The small army of workmen that had been gathered included miners, bricklayers, labourers, blacksmiths, masons and boatbuilders. Typical daily rates of pay in 1760[9] were:

Bricklayer	18d.	Labourer	16d.
Boatbuilder	32d.	Miner	16d.
Blacksmith	16d.	Mason	18d.

As the work proceeded it began to receive wide acclaim. *The Annual Register* for 1763 recorded with suitable pride: 'It is with great pleasure that we can, at the head of our article of projects for this year, set one, which is an honour to our country, and indeed one of the greatest works of our age. It is that stupendous undertaking of an inland navigation begun and directed by His Grace the Duke of Bridgewater'.

Progress was impeded by delays in completing land purchases and by the often outrageous claims for compensation of owners. All was not yet plain sailing by any means, and the financial problems of the duke became more serious. The improvement in his coal-mining profits and the growing revenues from the Worsley to Manchester section of the canal were certainly not sufficient to meet the whole cost of capital investment needed. The canal debt already exceeded £60,000, and the duke was hard put to borrow sufficient money. Eventually Child's Bank lent him £25,000 on the security of the completed Worsley to Manchester canal, to which the duke sought to add by means of loans of any small amounts which he or John Gilbert were able to procure, even from local tenants. The duke reduced his personal expenditure, by no means extravagant, to a mere £400 a year. He never enjoyed the reputation of being a well-dressed man, but rather the reverse, and he preferred stumping around his construction sites in old clothes, smoking his pipe. An extract from his accounts[10] of the time, kept by John Gilbert, shows that expenditure on clothes ranked very low on the duke's mode of living at that time:

28 Oct 1766	£	s.	d.
Paid Mr. Hindley the Mercer for gray cloth for his Grace's clothes	3	14	0
Baxter the Taylor for making and trimming and for repairing waistcoats		5	1

It stood to reason also that he had neither the time nor the resources to do much repairing or building at Ashridge. Provided that the rents came in and the farms could be kept going and the timber looked after, maintenance of the deteriorating buildings that his father had enjoyed would have to wait until the time was much more propitious. When he visited the place he stayed in the White Lodge rather than in the cold and uncomfortable rooms of the main house. Two further extracts from the Worsley accounts of the same date are of interest:

	£	s.	d.
Paid William Rallif for 19 oxen which he bought for his Grace and were sent to Ashridge	131	3	11
Richard Howard for shoeing the oxen		19	6
Richard Hinal for taking the above oxen to Ashridge..	6	12	7
do. his wages for 20 days at 1s. 4d.	1	6	8
Paid James Williamson expenses to and from Ashridge and making drains there for 71 days	8	3	0

In another endeavour to increase the canal revenue from navigation it was decided to introduce a passenger service. It took until 1769 before the necessary boats had been designed and built, but once the service started it proved to be both popular and successful. Apart from the initial novelty it was a clean and relatively comfortable way of travelling. Two classes of travel were offered, and as the service was extended dining and refreshment facilities were introduced, which were claimed to be as good as any offered by the best London hotels. Special landing stages were made for passengers; that at Worsley may still be seen. A short time later a service of packet boats was sailing every weekday from Manchester to Runcorn and between Worsley and Manchester. The yearly receipts from fares rose steadily from £1,326 in 1781 to over £4,700 by 1801.

In 1772 James Brindley died at the age of fifty-six. His fame as an engineer rests on a period of achievement lasting less than fifteen years, during which he had specialised in the building of canals, working not only for the Duke of Bridgewater, but for other owners and developers in the Midlands and the north-west, and on recognition of the brilliance of some of the inventions he devised to overcome his problems, such as his remarkable hydraulic cranes. As Hugh Malet puts it, 'His greatest achievement lay in spreading the canal idea'.[11] Brindley's employment by the duke, it has to be remembered, was not permanent, but on an 'as required' basis. In the initial stages, lasting about three years, planning and surveying seem to have occupied about two-thirds of his time, as extracts from the duke's accounts show:[12]

	£	s.	d.
2nd Jan. 1763			
Paid Mr. Brindley for 101 weeks between 1 July 1759 and 24 July 1762 at 12s per week	60	12	0
28 Oct 1766			
Paid Mr. Brindley for 250 days and ½ attending to this Grace's work from 24 Aug 1764 to 7 Dec 1765 ..	175	7	0
Paid do. for Turnpike and expenses at different times by his Grace's directions for levelling and surveying the intended navigation to Stockport	105	0	0

The national reputation of Brindley has rested very much on the account of Samuel Smiles in his *Lives of the Engineers.* More recent evidence shows that Smiles failed to examine the account books of the duke, or was not shown them, and he deduced incorrectly that Brindley was a full-time employee whose wages had not been regularly paid. In the Day Book of the duke appears a note written by William Strachan, dated 27 March 1924: 'Smiles came to the Bridgewater offices, Hulme, before publication of the Brindley volume, in quest of information. He was referred to the Muniment Keeper, who was apparently unaware of the existence of this book, and of many things actually in his own custody, which would have thrown much light on the making of the canal. Incidentally, it shows that Brindley was fairly well paid, contrary to Samuel Smiles'.[13] F. H. Egerton, who had spent long weeks in the company of his cousin the duke seeking material for his biography, wrote a spirited defence of his character after his death in his *Letter . . . upon Inland Navigation.* He was loud in praise of his character: 'he was an enemy of show . . . and quite free of ostentation'; and he was emphatic that the duke alone had conceived the

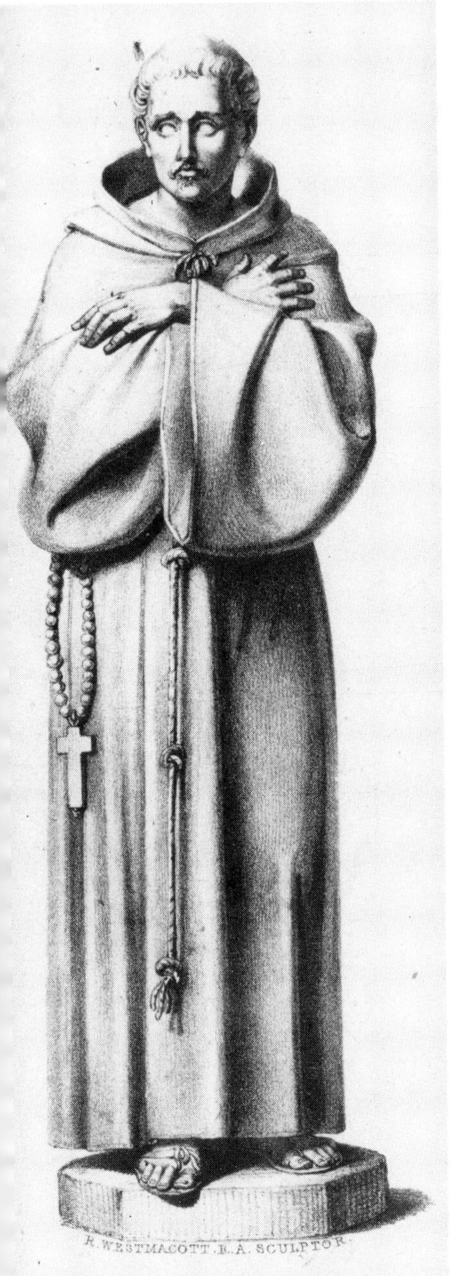

1. A Bonhomme of Ashridge.

2. Thomas Waterhouse, the last Rector.

4. Edward, the Black Prince.

WESTMACOTT. R.A. SCULPTOR

R. WESTMACOTT, R.A. SCULPTOR.

3. Edmund, Earl of Cornwall.

5. Plan of Ashridge House, 1762 (enlarged from an Estate map by George Grey).

6. Francis, 3rd Duke of Bridgewater.

7. The front of Ashridge, 1800.

8. Francis Henry Egerton, 8th and last Earl of Bridgewater.

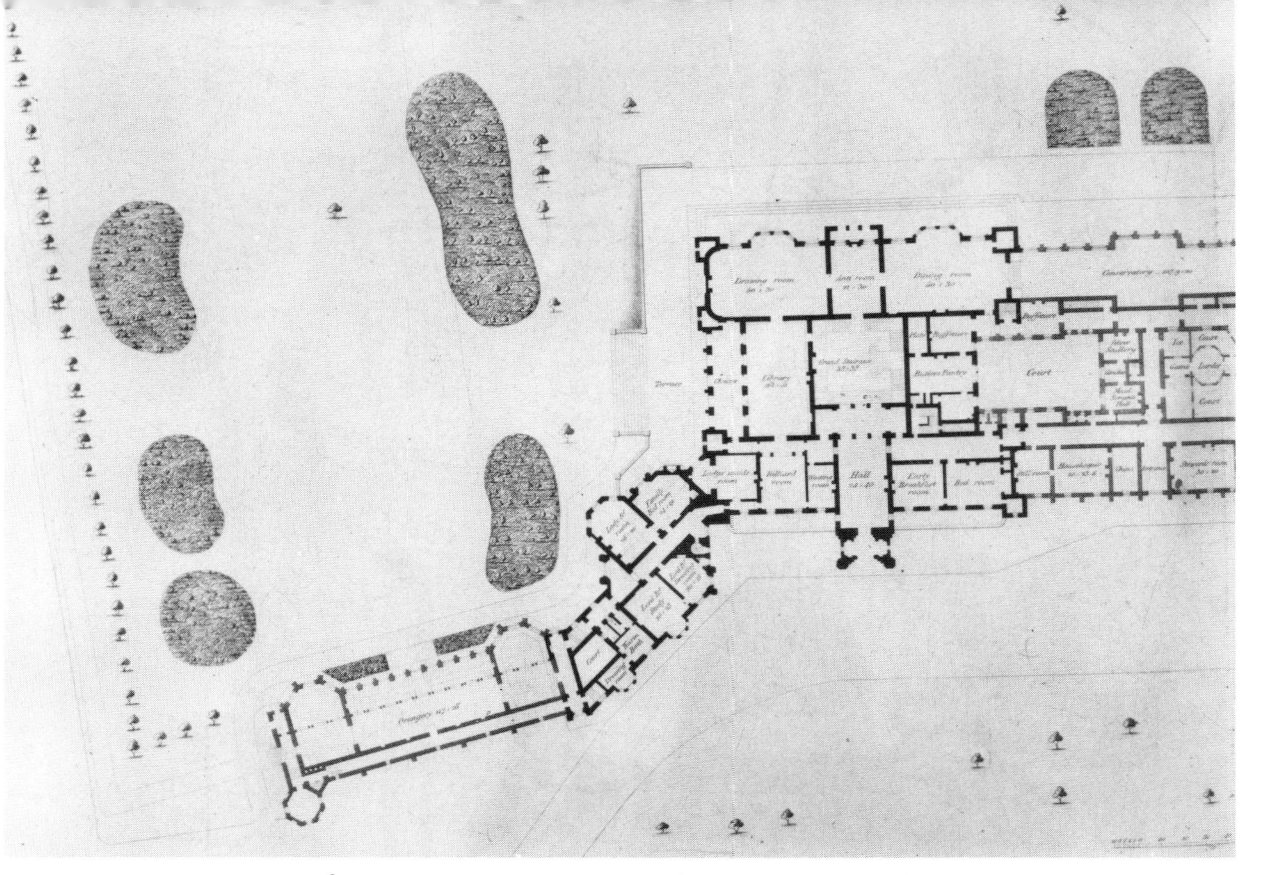

9. Plan of the Mansion, *c.*1818 (from Todd's *History*).

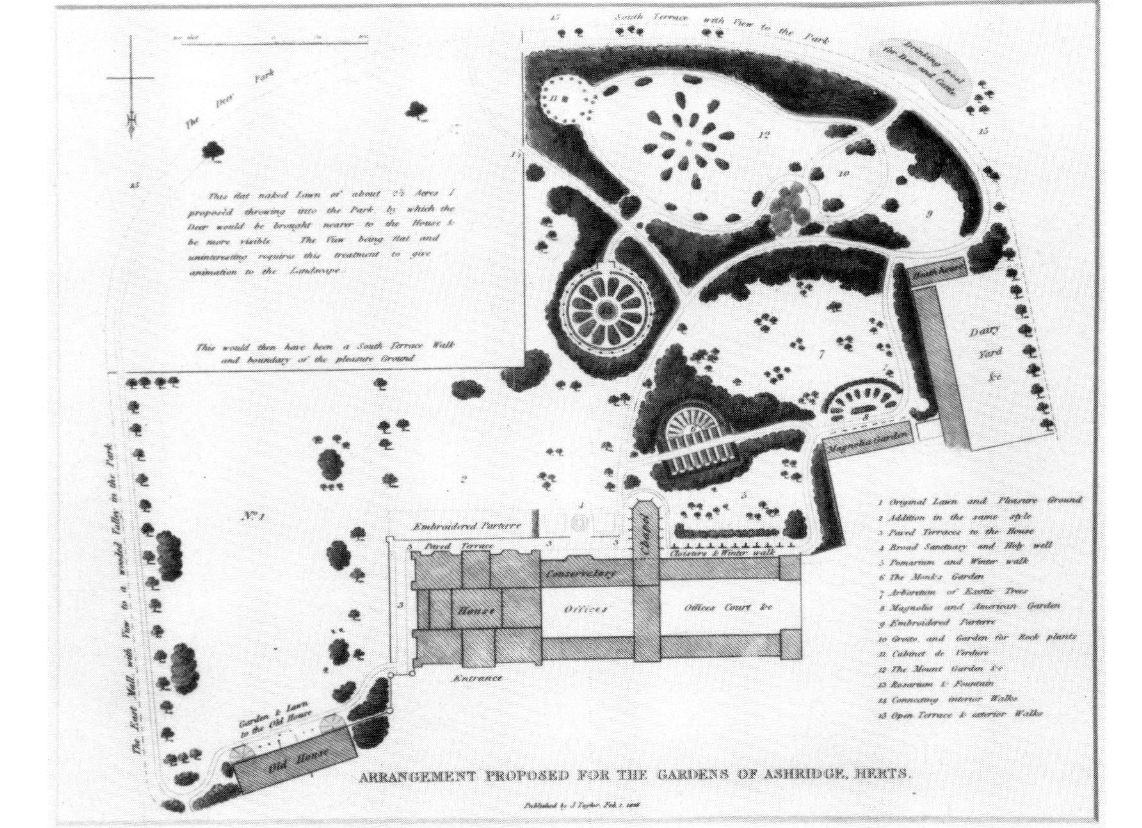

ARRANGEMENT PROPOSED FOR THE GARDENS OF ASHRIDGE, HERTS.

Published by J. Taylor, Feb. 1. 1816

11. Victorian Drawing Room.

13. The Orangery *c*.1900.

15. Aerial view, *c.* 1950.

16. The Lazell Building from Coronation Walk.

17. Lazell Building: from cow-barn into modern foyer.

18. The western arch, Red Lodge and the Brew House tower.

19. The Quadrangle.

20. The Chapel Organ.

idea of the canal. While he praised the ingenuity and invention of Brindley, he felt that the duke had received too little recognition, and Brindley too much.[14] One result of this hitherto incorrect assessment of Brindley was that the important contribution of John Gilbert was overshadowed. As one writer concluded, 'he was so probably so modest and unassuming that he did not lay claim to the honour which belonged to him with respect to the Duke of Bridgewater's canals and collieries . . .'.[15] Gilbert, with his engineering training, fulfilled the combined role of co-ordinator, surveyor, designer, director of operations and general manager. In an era just beginning to accept the idea of a meritocracy he became one of the earliest salaried professional managers in industry.

* * * * *

The final stage in the completion of the canal from Lymm was to link it with the Trent and Mersey Canal at Preston Brook, and carry it from there to the Mersey estuary at Runcorn. Brindley had been succeeded by his brother-in-law, Hugh Henshall, for this part of the canal. Stiff and prolonged opposition to the route came from one of the more powerful landowners, Sir Robert Brook of Norton Priory, and delays were occasioned while he petitioned parliament; but eventually he conceded, and the last link to the Mersey was finally accomplished in 1776. Seventeen years of dogged effort had been needed. Only the unshakeable faith of the principal characters, the duke, Thomas Gilbert, his legal agent, James Brindley, and John Gilbert, had enabled seemingly insuperable legal, technical and financial difficulties to be overcome, and the Bridgewater Canal was at last a reality. The great venture achieved far more than the provision of an easy outlet for coal from the Worsley mines at half its previous price. The route between Manchester and Liverpool had been made navigable by boat, and the benefits in terms of reduced freight charges, in the increased speed and in the regularity of transportation, held implications for the industries of Lancashire and Cheshire that were profound. In turn opportunities for employment increased rapidly as industry sought outlets for mass production, with a resulting improvement in the general lot and prosperity of the people.

A fourth and last Canal Act of 1795 enabled the duke to extend the system westwards from Worsley to Leigh, a short length of about five miles, in order to provide a link with the Leeds and Liverpool Canal.

When the main canal was finished in 1776, the duke turned his attention to Worsley and began a series of improvements to the collieries there and at nearby Walkden. Quite the most remarkable of these was a series of underground canals, for the design of which John Gilbert has been credited. Their purpose was to enable coal to be taken from the seams in baskets to boats at three different levels. The wooden boats were then moved to positions beneath specially made shafts, and the coal was hoisted up and loaded into larger boats at the main canal level. The entrances to the canal, cut into the sandstone face of the mine, are still to be seen at Worsley, and a commemorative plaque on a nearby bridge records that in all 46 miles of underground canals were constructed. For general haulage horses provided the main motive power, but some sail was employed on the Bridgewater Canal. Experiments were tried with steam propulsion of boats on the main canal, but were abandoned, as this form produced no increase in the speed of travel and led to other operating and maintenance problems.

As his enterprise began to succeed the duke was relieved of the necessity of spending so much time at Worsley and his visits became less frequent. He would remain only for two or three weeks at a time, leaving the general running of his affairs there in the very able hands of John Gilbert, whom he respected as an administrator and now valued as an old friend. He nevertheless enjoyed visiting the construction sites, and even had his coach mounted on a boat to enable him to carry out inspections more easily. His ability to move about freely, talking to employees, lost him no respect. On one occasion he found that workmen had not returned to work at one o'clock after the lunchtime break. Enquiring the reason, he was told that they had not heard the single stroke of the clock. The duke thereupon arranged with a local clockmaker to alter the clock so that it struck 13 at one o'clock and the men would have no excuse for future lateness. He was recognised as a strict employer, but always a just one; far from being parsimonious, he was capable of generosity in cases of need. The scale of his operations was so great that he was one of the largest employers in the country. He believed in a care for his workforce and built houses on a huge scale for his employees at Worsley, and let them at low rents. His colliers were tenants at will, circumstances which operated as 'encouragements to good conduct'. A Report of the Betterment of the Poor Society in 1798 described how he established shops and a small market where the workers could purchase necessaries; at the end of the month the storekeepers took their monthly bills to the colliery agents, who deducted the amounts from the wages due (colliers were paid monthly). The agents paid the storekeepers and paid the balance to the workers. Debts at public houses were not allowed to be brought in; and the butchers and traders, being also tenants of the duke, dared not be exorbitant in their prices, or fraudulent in their weights.

When the Loyalty Loan was launched in 1796 the duke invested £100,000 in the fund. What his true annual income was at this time is difficult to assess accurately, although one estimate placed it as high as £80,000—a far cry from the £400 a year expenditure to which he had limited himself in the 'sixties. Another source suggests that he was eventually paying £110,000 a year in income tax. The peak of the success of his shrewd management of his affairs was not realised until after his death in 1803. A summary of His Grace's 'Navigation, Colliery, Lime and Farm concerns in Lancashire and Cheshire from midsummer 1759 to Jan 1806'[16] shows that 'the utmost accumulated debt' at 14 January 1786 was £345,805 18s. 3d., and that the whole of the principal had been repaid by the year 1805. Total profits on the four main activities continued to rise as follows:

Year	Profits exclusive of difference in Stock £				Profits from Estate	Annual Profits
	Navigation	Colliery	Lime	Farm		
1806	38,870	13,436	747	642	13,438	£53,697
1836	58,737	19,943	199	2,014	20,962	£104,117

* * * * *

The duke was by nature a shy and solitary man rather than a recluse. Although his name was linked in one magazine with a certain not very successful actress, Miss Langtree, whom he was alleged to have set up in a quiet house on his estate for a time, he was genuinely more at ease in the company of men, and he shied away from that of women. His sister, Louisa, married to Lord Gower, died in 1761, a loss which he felt sadly. The duke had little liking for Lord Gower's second wife, Lady Susannah Stewart, nor she for him, but he continued to rely heavily on the friendship of his brother-in-law, with whom he could share his concern about business interests, the threat posed by the talk of new railways ('those demned tram-roads') or the wickedness of the French.

Lady Gower, humourless and rather strait-laced, never seemed to be able to regard the duke with any favour: she considered that he was eccentric and most certainly her inferior in situation and understanding. Years after, and by now the Marchioness of Stafford, she confided in letters of 1783 to her adored son, Granville Leveson Gower:[17]

> . . . *Decr ye 1st.* His Grace of Bridgewater is with us, not less positive nor less prejudiced than usual. It is a great disadvantage to live with our Inferiors either in Situation or Understanding. Self-Sufficiency is the natural consequence, with many attendant evils; but his Want of Religion makes him an Object of Pity. I do not mean that he does not believe in God, but there he is with the Gout and a Disorder in his stomach, and Death and Immortality never occupy either his Thoughts or Words, and he Swears!. . .
>
> *Decr ye 3rd.* . . . You will be amused when I tell you that Susan got up this morning early enough to be at the Duke of Bridgewater's *déjeuner* before his Departure, and to see him safe into his Carriage at eight o'clock. She was the only Person in the Family that pay'd him this Proof of Affection . . .

On the other hand, in another letter to her son she wrote in kindly terms about the duke's only surviving sister, the unmarried Lady Caroline Egerton:

> *Trentham, 12 Sept. 1791*
> . . . Lady Caroline was, for a week before her Death, expected to expire daily. She died last Thursday about one o'clock and has left many poor People, as well as a great number of friends to lament her death . . . She has left a great Deal in Charity and many legacies.
>
> You will be surprised when I tell you that you are in her will. Her goodness to me and my Children was quite unexpected. She

> has left each of you £500, and to me all her books, therefore you will have a tolerable library of modern books when I am gone.

Lady Caroline Egerton's Charity is still remembered in Little Gaddesden today, and though now combined with others, it continues to provide a small annual sum of money for disbursement.

Much of her Ladyship's spiky and rather contemptuous opinion of the duke can perhaps be attributed to the knowledge that her own son would not benefit under the duke's will. Instead a major portion of his fortune would go to her stepson, George Granville Leveson Gower, Lord Trentham, the son of Louisa, and Francis Egerton's nephew. The duke always showed a great fondness for his nephew, and it was Trentham who by his own fashionable dalliance with the collection of pictures and works of art, was to arouse his uncle's interest in acquiring a collection of his own. The duke enjoyed the company of this young man, who having started an art collection liked nothing more than to shop among the salerooms for bargains. This appealed to the duke and they would dine two or three times a week together. In spite of having made the Grand Tour in his youth, when he purchased some fine pictures, the duke had never since shown much enthusiasm for the visual arts, 'but as in other directions he was fully alive to any chance which fortune might throw his way'. His biggest *coup* was undoubtedly the acquisition of part of the Orléans Collection under the guidance of Michael Bryan, a well-known art dealer and expert, who negotiated the purchase. This collection had been started in the time of Louis XV and had been regularly added to. The Duc d'Orléans, being in need of money, decided to sell his pictures, and the collection of mainly French and Italian masterpieces eventually arrived in London between 1790 and 1795. They were purchased by a consortium of the Duke of Bridgewater, Lord Gower, Lord Trentham, and the Earl of Carlisle. Each proceeded to make a selection for their personal galleries, and the remainder not chosen were put up for sale by private treaty. This sale realised £41,000, which was only £2,000 less than the group had paid for the entire collection.[18]

The duke's acquisitions for Bridgewater House included Raphaels, Titians, Tintorettos, many of the Dutch School, and many by English artists, such as Turner (of whom he was a patron), Gainsborough, and Reynolds. At the time of his death his pictures were said to be worth £150,000. James Lewis, the architect who had worked on his house, Woolmers, near Hertford, was engaged to build a gallery on to the side of Bridgewater House, for which he received £1,500.[19] That his primary interest in pictures was that of a businessman making a good investment is rather borne out by the neglected condition of those remaining at Ashridge in the last decade of the 18th century. As the duke's successor at Ashridge, his cousin, John William Egerton, was to recall in a letter dated 23 March 1821 to the Rev. Philip Bliss at Oxford: 'There was not a picture which for its intrinsick value was worth five shillings. The Duke never thought about them till I suggested the probability of a picture of one of his ancestors being sold for half a crown, and when he heard of its gracing the taproom in an alehouse, he would give Two Guineas to have it back again, and then he desired me to look them over, and if there were any that were so badly decayed that they could not be brought away, they had better be burned, than to go into the sale. A very few therefore to escape worse went into the fire . . .'.[20]

The 7th Earl's recollection of these events in the closing years of the century is of interest in other respects also, showing clearly that the duke had already decided that there was no possibility of repairing the old buildings of Ashridge, and touching on the disposal of the library. He tells his correspondent in the same letter: 'The Duke of Bridgewater had talked to me of pulling down Ashridge, apprehensive as was said to him of its falling, but his doubt was what to do with the books, for he knew the library was extremely good, tho' not aware of a more modern idea of the value of many of the books. The moving them to Cleveland Court [i.e., Bridgewater House], having known Mr. Todd for several years, I mentioned him as a person who would have pleasure in having them packed, sent and placed there. The sale of such furniture as was then intended to be sold was ordered . . . As to the books they were all packed by Mr. Todd, and when upon arranging them in Cleveland Court, it was found that there were many valuable duplicates and triplicates, it was suggested as a proper thing that they should find their way into the world, and went to the hammer at, I think, Mr. King's . . .'.

Among the rare books in the library were the Ellesmere Chaucer manuscript of *The Canterbury Tales,* a fine collection of Bibles, four Shakespeare folios, and various quartos, and the manuscript of Milton's *Comus.* Auction sales took place at Ashridge in 1800 and 1802, the first conducted by Mr. Ellis of Whitechapel, London, and the second by Mr. Gilham.[21] The first included furniture, household items, timber, and the remaining pictures that had not been removed. The second was of building materials, paving stone, lead, iron and so on. In the hall all the paving (two lots of 650 square feet) went for £18. Two oak tables, one 25ft. by 3ft. 6ins., and one 45ft. by 3ft. 6ins., fetched £1 12s. 0d. and £4 1s. 0d. respectively. Nine paintings on canvas were sold for 16s.; 34 other paintings on wood and canvas went for 4s. only! The turret clock brought in £20, and two bells, sold at £5 10s. 0d. per cwt., fetched £23 7s. 6d. Much of the stone was removed to Berkhamsted for onward transmission to its new destinations by the new Grand Junction canal. The final demolition of the old buildings was not completed until 1804–5, just after the duke's death.

* * * * *

The duke was beginning to tidy up his affairs. One curious direction in which this took him, according to a contemporary, Isaac D'Israeli, father of the later prime minister, concerned the family papers: 'The late Duke of Bridgewater, I am informed, burnt many of the numerous family papers, and bricked up a quantity which, opened after his death, were found to have perished. It is said he declared that he did not choose that his ancestors should be traced back to a person of a mean trade, which it seems might possibly have been. The loss now cannot be appreciated; but unquestionably stores of history, and, perhaps of literature, were sacrificed. Milton's manuscript of *Comus* was published from the Bridgewater Collection, for it had escaped the bricking up!'[22] Was it eccentricity or mistaken pride which prompted such an action—or both?

In his last years the duke aged quickly. His great corpulence and slow gait made him look older than he was. Joseph Farington noted in his *Diary* for 13 January 1803, only a few weeks before his death, that the duke's habits were 'to rise between 8 and 9, and to dine at 5 o'clock, from which time till

10 o'clock he remains at the dinner table, and though slowly, must drink a bottle of wine a day. Port is his wine . . . Though the Duke turned his attention to pictures lately it has become a passion which his friends are glad of, as it causes him to take the exercise of walking much about his galleries and rooms. He goes to bed about 11 or 12'.[23]

This was perhaps not an unexpected picture of the closing days in the life of an elderly bachelor, reflecting in the solitude of his large mansion on the accomplishment of his youthful dream, the struggles involved, and on the satisfaction and wealth it had finally brought to him, yet wondering whether the arrangements he had devised for perpetuating the benefits of his life's labour were secure. The duke took the greatest care and advice in the drafting of his will, which ran to 66 pages of type. Anxious to ensure that the public should enjoy and benefit from the use of the canal for as long as possible, he placed its administration and that of his collieries in the hands of a Trust. He could not feel sure that his successors would show the same concern for the future good management of these enterprises as he did, and he so devised matters that they should enjoy the income but take no part in their direction.

In general terms he left to his nephew, George Granville Leveson Gower (later the Duke of Sutherland) his estates in Lancashire and Cheshire, including Worsley; Brackley, in Northamptonshire, and Bridgewater House in London with its valuable collection of pictures and silver, with remainder to his second son, Lord Francis Gower (later 1st Earl Ellesmere), who was required to, and did eventually, assume the name of Egerton. Specific legacies were £40,000 to his cousin, the Rev. Francis Egerton, and £10,000 each to his nieces, Lady Louisa Macdonald, the Countess of Carlisle, and Lady Ann Vernon, with £50,000 to the three Trustees of the Canal Estates. The remainder, worth in all about two million pounds, he left to his cousin, General John William Egerton. This included his estates in Shropshire, Hertfordshire and Buckinghamshire, together with liquid assets of about £600,000. A codocil provided for legacies of one year's wages 'to each of my domestic servants who shall be in my service at the time of my death, and who shall have lived with me one year and less than two years', and two years' wages for any who had been with

			£	s	d
03	Brought forward		827	15	6
Aug 2[illegible]	Mr. Henry Siffen — his Bill	86. 5. 9			
	wages	27. 17. 9			
	mourning	20. –. –			
	One years wages as a legacy	80. –. –			
	Gift	20. –. –	234	3	6
	Thomas Stedman for wages	18. 4. 11			
	allowance for boots &c	2. 15. –			
	two years wages as a legacy	36. –. –	56	19	11
	Do. for wages due to his brother		3	18	7
24	Mr. James Hall for expences attending the probate of the Dukes Will and stamp duty for the administration		1080	17	6
25	Mr. Thomas Holmes coachmaker his Bill		228	3	–
	Duty paid on legacies to the servants		37	4	3
26	Mr. Pheasant Marriot in part of the purchase money for his estate at Little Gaddesden purchased by the Duke of Bridgewater		500		
	Carried forward		2.969	1	9

Fig. 6. Extract from accounts of the executors of the 3rd Duke of Bridgewater

him for longer than two years. And so, among the final payments made by his executors were:[24]

		£	s.	d.
To.	John Chennels for wages	12	2	11
	do. for pumping the Cellar	4	14	0
	two years wages as legacy	36	0	0
	Eleanor Lamb for wages	7	16	6
	do. for mourning	10	0	0
	one years wages as legacy	8	0	0
	Mr. John Woodman for mourning	30	0	0
	two years salary as legacy	244	0	0

The duke would have been bitterly disappointed in the subsequent performance of the Bridgewater Canal Trust that he set up. The Trustees consisted of Sir Archibald Macdonald of the Treasury; Edward Harcourt, Bishop of Carlisle (and later Archbishop of York); and his agent, Robert Haldane Bradshaw. The first two were married to nieces of the testator; Bradshaw, the most important, enjoyed the full confidence of the duke who, as time would show, made the mistake of conferring almost unlimited powers on him. The profits of the undertaking rose steeply, but the Trust, particularly Bradshaw, failed in the duke's intentions by pursuing a policy of maximum current profit regardless of long-term investment, mainly by heavily increasing the toll charges. Maintenance came to be neglected, insufficient warehouse accommodation was built in Manchester, and as a result there was much pilferage of goods stored on wharves. The accumulation of these failings, as well as increasing delays, so antagonised the merchants in and around Manchester that pressure for the building of one of the new railroads mounted. It can be said that the failings of the Trust hastened the opening of the Liverpool to Manchester railway in 1833, though as the years passed the Bridgewater Canal managed to hold its own against the growing railway traffic. The subsequent history of the Trust, which lasted until 1903, plays little or no part in this narrative, but it has been well analysed and described by F. C. Mather in his book, *After the Canal Duke* (1970).

Two months after completing his will, the duke was involved in a slight carriage accident in London which brought on a severe attack of influenza from which he did not recover, and on 8 March 1803 he died. There was no drama about his final days, and, reluctant as he always was to seek any public show, he asked to be buried quietly in the family vault at Little Gaddesden church. His memorial, designed by Westmacott, bears the inscription: 'He will be ever memorable among Those who were honoured in their generations and were the glory of their times',[25] followed by the Latin *Impulit ille rates ubi duxit aratra colonus,* that is, 'he sent barges where formerly the farmer tilled his fields'.

The death of the duke brought a widespread public appreciation of the importance of his contribution to the modernisation of England's pitifully inefficient transport system. Lord Brougham commended his career and conduct as an example to the aristocracy. It is in the nature of life that today his name is less well remembered even in the north, where his description as 'the first great Manchester man' for so long distinguished him. His kinsman, the 1st Earl of Ellesmere, writing some 50 years after his death observed: 'The Duke of Bridgewater more than any single man contributed to lay the foundations of the prosperity of Manchester, Liverpool and the surrounding districts . . . When we trace on the map of England the present artificial arterial system, some 110 lines of canal, amounting in length to 2,400 miles, when we reflect on the rapidity of the creation . . . we cannot but think that the Duke's matrimonial disappointment ranks with other cardinal passages in the lives of eminent men . . .'.[26]

On a ridge overlooking the village of Aldbury, and commanding to the south-east a long view of Ashridge, stands a tall column raised to his memory as 'The Father of Inland Navigation'. It stands as a constant reminder of a man who faced many obstacles and misfortunes but triumphed over them, and in so doing rendered his country a great service. It may also serve to remind those who today value and enjoy the 'new' Ashridge to reflect that but for the eventual success of Francis Egerton we might never have been in the position to do so.

Chapter Twelve

BROTHERLY DISCORD

THE DEATH OF FRANCIS EGERTON brought to an end the dukedom, a matter which was to be a source of everlasting irritation and regret to his cousin and heir, John William Egerton, Lieutenant-General, in the army and elder son of John Egerton, Bishop of Durham, by his first wife, the Lady Anne Sophia de Grey (daughter of Henry de Grey, Duke of Kent). He was a grandson of Henry Egerton, Bishop of Hereford, who 80 years earlier had declined to pay the relatively small fee required to vary the terms of the patent of dukedom so that his successors might have benefited from his brother Scroop's dynastic plans. That simple refusal, for whatever reason it was prompted, was to lead in the 1850s to judgement on one of the most remarkable wills that has ever challenged the legal minds of the Appeal Court, and, subsequently, of the House of Lords.

It has often been said that the only professions open to the younger sons of noblemen used to be the Church or the Army. In the case of a bishop, however wealthy or well connected, his office and precedence died with him, and his first-born could expect no hereditary title at his father's death. Thus it was with the sons of the Lord Bishop of Durham; the elder, John William, opted for the Army and his brother, Francis Henry, was educated for the Church. The 7th Earl of Bridgewater entered the Army in the conventional manner as a Cornet in 1771 at the age of 18, rising to command of the 7th Light Dragoons in 1790. He was a Major-General on the Staff of Eastern District in 1795, and was made Lieutenant-General in 1802, shortly before succeeding to the earldom. His promotion to General came in 1812.

Apart from a period in Ireland, most of his active service was spent at home and he managed to combine this with being a Tory member of parliament for Morpeth from 1777 to 1780, and for the almost traditional Egerton family seat of Brackley, Northants, from 1780 until his elevation to the House of Lords in 1803.

He was 50 years old when he inherited the vast Bridgewater estates in Buckinghamshire, Hertfordshire and Shropshire; from that date the earl seemed to have decided that the management of these would demand his whole attention and he took very little further part in the national political life. In 1781 he had married Miss Charlotte Catherine Anne Haynes, daughter of Major Samuel Haynes, a fellow officer. There were no surviving children, and, to their regret, no prospects of any further family as they entered upon their new responsibilities.

The first task was to set about rebuilding of the house. 'You would imagine upon seeing Ashridge now', he wrote to his brother, 'that there had been an earthquake, and the only things left are the white lodge, the greenhouse, the red lodge and the stables . . .'.[1] Demolition of the old house had started sometime before the death of the old duke, and was completed by about 1804. Various architects submitted designs, but James Wyatt was invited to carry out the work. It is interesting to conjecture what might have resulted had the duke lived to carry through the project. While he thought in a big and far-seeing way about his canals, his own life style was not flamboyant. He had inherited the fine Bridgewater House in London. At Worsley the Old Hall had served him for a few years, but when he built a new house there, a short distance from it, it was comparatively modest and unpretentious. Although he had at last recognised that the decaying monastic buildings of Ashridge must be rebuilt, his tastes were, if anything, classical, and it is difficult to imagine him contemplating a new mansion quite on the scale of James Wyatt's eventual design, to say nothing of the following additions by Jeffry Wyatt. The 7th Earl, on the other hand, had fewer inhibitions. Already comfortably wealthy, having inherited a number of small estates from his father, he had come into greater riches by good fortune and he felt as much that he owed it to his cousin to build in ducal style as a tribute to him, as that he wished to have a residence worthy of his illustrious ancestry and of the beautiful surroundings into which it must fit.

I should like a billiard room which should lay convenient
to the drawing, or other rooms, & would be better if lighted
by a sky light. A conservatory to open to the rooms would
be a desireable thing. & I think it might be the means
of joining the house on to the offices. The entrance if the
spot will permit should be to the north & the living rooms
to the south. — Mr Benningdon tells me that the stair
cases & passages in the Hotels at Paris are particularly
well warmed, should there be any thing particular in
the manner I shall thank you to enquire about it. I do not
mean to put you to any unnecessary trouble, but it may lay
in the way of your pursuit of curiosities to be able to
afford me some assistance. You would imagine upon
seeing Ashridge now that there had been an earthquake,
& the only things left are the white lodge the greenhouse
the red lodge & the stables. Your Legacy from the

Fig. 7. Part of a letter from the 7th Earl to his brother, 5 April 1803

His pride in his forbears never forsook him and he went to great lengths to prove that, traced far enough back, he was descended from King Edward III. The outward evidence of some of this, going back to Henry VII, may be seen in the armorial bearings which decorate the south division of the frieze in the entrance hall.[2] Those dwellings not demolished served as a pied-à-tierre for the earl and his staff during the erection of the new house. White Lodge, the original gatehouse to the monastery, had been modified and altered by converting the entrance porch to a living-room in the mid 18th century; and, linked to it by an extension was another house in the Georgian domestic style, perhaps eighty years old. The new mansion, which is described in greater detail in Chapter Fifteen, was built over the site of the northern part of the earlier monastic buildings. The entrance hall rose just to the south of the White Lodge, and the line of the southern elevation of the drawing-room and dining-room coincided with the southern boundary of the old monastic Great Hall, as is evidenced from the position of the undercroft, or so-called 'crypt', below. The western limit of the new mansion was marked by two towers, known today as the Brew House and the Laundry tower; the eastern end extended no further than the present library.

Building commenced in 1808 and it is probable that the main structure was completed by about 1810, as is shown in a family painting of that date in the possession of Mr. Geoffrey Buckingham of Wilmslow, Cheshire, a descendant of William Buckingham, the earl's steward and right-hand man. The interior fittings and furnishings took another three or four years. Shortly before the house was completed an unfortunate carriage accident in 1813 caused the death of the architect James Wyatt, and his nephew, Jeffry Wyatt, took over supervision of the work. Lord and Lady Bridgewater moved into their new mansion on 14 October 1814, an event commemorated on a brass plate in the entrance hall, though there is evidence from the *Diaries* of William Buckingham[3] that the hall at least was used for entertaining prior to this. From the arrival on the scene of Jeffry Wyatt (later Sir Jeffry Wyatville) whose primary task was to have been to complete the mansion to his uncle's design, there would appear to have been discussion of extending the original plans. Whether Jeffry had a particularly persuasive manner and played on his lordship's vanity, or whether the earl, of his own accord, felt that he had not done sufficient justice to the memory of the duke is not clear, but additional building followed. James Wyatt's chapel was completed and first used in 1817. During the previous year White Lodge was demolished. This left the way clear for an extension eastwards providing more intimate private family quarters, leading to a long orangery, which opened at its end on to an avenue of lime trees. A new and more imposing porch was added. Jeffry Wyatt also enlarged the accommodation at the western end to give additional domestic offices and stores behind a fascia wall on the north front, which linked the laundry tower to the surviving Red Lodge. A grand arched entrance was made to an area of new stables and coach-houses. Most of this work was completed by the end of 1817. The Tudor tithe barn was enlarged considerably and embellished with a large wooden lantern in the Gothic style, and a smaller cow barn was added to it. Viewed from the north, the 1814 building had received extensions which more than doubled its frontage, giving a distance between the towers at the extremities of over one thousand feet. The total cost is said to have been in excess of £300,000.[4]

At the time of the earl's inheritance, England was becoming daily more apprehensive of the threats of invasion by Napoleon's armies, and local volunteer forces were being raised to strengthen the small regular army. The earl lost very little time in making a patriotic gesture. In a letter of 1803 to the Marquis of Salisbury, Lord Lieutenant of Hertfordshire, he offered to raise a troop of yeomanry cavalry to consist of about fifty respectable gentlemen and farmers in the neighbourhood of Ashridge without any expense to the government.[5] So the Ashridge Yeomanry was born, with the general as captain of the troop, and continued in existence for a number of years. A portrait exists of William Buckingham, the earl's steward, wearing a blue uniform holding a helmet with a plume, in the rank of corporal of horse. Gold buttons adorn the tunic, embossed with a crown at the top, the word 'Ashridge' at the bottom, and across the centre the figure of a ploughman with a plough drawn by two horses.[6]

The plough was an appropriate symbol, not only of the earl's main source of income, but also of the deep interest he felt for improvements in methods of farming. No landowner of the magnitude of the Earl of Bridgewater could afford not to profess some concern for the introduction of new farming methods and inventions, and in his case he seems to have approached his new responsibilities with the same thoroughness that had characterised his military career. In 1805 he is found in correspondence with Sir Joseph Banks, the distinguished botanist and President of the Royal Society, on blight in wheat and improvements in ploughs. In another letter of the same year he is referred to by Banks as a breeder of merino sheep.[7] A letter to the Earl of Verulam gives him details of the threshing machines he had provided for his tenants in Shropshire on a rental basis of seven-and-a-half per cent. of the cost, lower by one-half to two per cent. than the prevailing rates in other parts of the country.[8] The earl was himself elected a Fellow of the Royal Society in 1809. He was very much concerned with a proper training of boys for entry into agriculture. He told a Board of Agriculture representative at a meeting in Aylesbury in 1810 that when he first went to Ashridge he was 'shocked to find the boys knew nothing of farming; nothing but the straw-plaiting and lace-making their mothers had taught them'. These were the traditional Buckinghamshire home crafts. The earl at once set himself 'to root out their effeminacy and instill into them manly principles'.[9] He set up an agricultural school in the village of Little Gaddesden, which continued for many years and which was kept going by his widow, the countess, long after his death.

For the surrounding villages the changes brought about by having the owners of Ashridge in almost permanent residence again were far-reaching. In the duke's time, although Ashridge remained the administrative centre, as it were, for his enterprises, he did not spend a great deal of his time there. His scale of living was modest, and he undertook few improvements; apart from the farms, the house and the gardens gave work for very few. At the turn of the century the number of poor and unemployed persons in the vicinity was considerable and their state of housing was generally deplorable. As the new mansion progressed and the park and grounds were being restored, more and more were employed to the point that eventually some five hundred men were working in the gardens, greenhouses and workshop. In Sir Arthur Bryant's words, 'nothing was allowed to be slovenly'. New projects were devised to provide work at a time when unemployment was at its worst. The earl is said never to have refused work to any local man, and, at times,to have increased his labour force to eight hundred.[10] A new road was built from Ashridge House to Gravel Path, making it easier for carriages to reach Berkhamsted. The earl undertook at his own expense the building of a new road from Northchurch to Ringshall to provide easier communication with Dunstable. Both he and his wife were much concerned with giving better housing conditions to the workers by building new cottages, an example to be followed by their successors, the Brownlow family, later in the century. He was a stickler for hygiene, and insisted that the cottagers' windows were to be opened for a time every day to admit the sweet fresh air, and there are, in the steward's diary for 1813, several references to the preparation of lists of inhabitants for vaccination against the smallpox, national vaccine having promoted by the government since 1809. Those poor who could not work were assisted by charitable distribution of money, fuel and food. His steward's diary entry for Sunday 4 December 1814 is typical: 'Up at 8, breakfast and shaving and cleaning. I then went on foot to Ashridge to see Lord B. in the Hall. Then over the Park to the Church. Afterwards I asked Mr. Horseman [the Rector] to dinner at Ashridge. Self, Atty, Matthews and Buckmaster in the churchyard paying the poor. On to dinner . . . Matthews came respecting list of the poor for Lady Bridgewater's gifts . . . Afterwards again on foot to Ashridge to consult with Lord and Lady B.'.[11]

It is easy in these days of state welfare and egalitarian clamour to dismiss such actions as condescending, or at most, no more than were properly called for; but set in the divisive social conditions and stratification of rural and urban life of the time, there is greater reason to attribute to them the care and consideration of an upright and devout Christian family for those for whom they felt responsible. This is not to say that the earl was a 'pushover'. He set high standards and expected honest endeavour in return. 'Mollycoddling' was not a word within his vocabulary.

The earl was actively interested in local affairs in Berkhamsted and the surrounding towns and villages. He was a magistrate and attended meetings of the local Turnpike Trust. As leader of the community it fell to him to greet King Louis XVIII of France on his way through Berkhamsted in 1814 at the start of his triumphal return to Paris following the defeat of Napoleon. The king had lived in exile in England at Hartwell House, Aylesbury, for seven years, and the way was now clear for him to return. Local preparations began in Berkhamsted the day previously, with directions being given by his lordship for making the triumphal arch and the cutting of laurels from his gardens at Frithsden. On the great day, William Buckingham recorded:

> *Weds. 20th April 1814.*
>
> Up at 6, then in the yards and gardens and in entering diary. Breakfast and then preparing ribbons for bridle. Cleaning and shaving. Atty called. On with him on horse to Ashridge to Lord B. With Atty, Wynn and Hemmings to Berkhemsted, and sworn in as special constables at Page's [*The King's Arms* inn]. Went through the town in procession with band to meet the King of France. Self on horse to attend Lord B. to meet the King and French Nobles. The King's carriage came to the town's end at ½ past 12, and was drawn through the town to Page's. Lord B. read the address of Berkhamsted to him and the King returned an answer. Stopt about ½ an hour. Set off with post horses to Watford Town's end. Then drawn by men to the Essex Arms. Atty, Wynn and self went forward to the 3 Crowns, Bushey, to take some refreshments. On to Stanmore to see the King meet the Regent's carriage with 8 cream coloured horses and 6 carriages and 6. With the Nobles to see them off. Back to Watford, Essex Arms to dinner and tea. Atty and self home to Ashridge at ½ past 10. To Lord B. and supper at Ashridge.

In May of the previous year Mrs. Haynes, the mother of Countess Bridgewater, had died. She occupied a house in Little Gaddesden for two years after being widowed, and this later gave rise to a fanciful story, based on a journey through Ashridge Park, published in *The Cornhill Magazine* of 1861[12] nearly fifty years later. In it the nameless author alleges that Lady Bridgewater longed to be able to see her mother's house 'from her own bower in Ashridge House' and that, at her desire, a broad avenue was cut in the trees in order to facilitate such a view, and 'forthwith a thousand stately trees went crashing to the earth'. Two observations on this rather absurd and implausible story seem to be appropriate. The first is that the houses which border the green at Little Gaddesden at this point were [are] all too far back from the road to be easily visible from any other point than the top of the 100-foot tower. The shrubbery of Mrs. Haynes's garden is known to have backed on to the then road to the church and so the house was even less likely to have been visible.[13] The second is that the idea of a practical and hard-headed landowner or agent agreeing to fell so many trees unless they were either fully mature or too old for useful timber seems unlikely at the least. Maybe an indulgent husband might have stretched a point for a new child-bride, but the earl and his countess had been married for 20 years before moving to Ashridge.

The even tenor of his Lordship's life might appear to have been progressing calmly as his mansion neared completion and his various projects for improvement at Ashridge came to fulfilment. Yet an undercurrent of some strength was always threatening his peace in the form of the erratic and provoking behaviour of his younger brother.

Francis Henry Egerton seems to have been something of a problem from a fairly early age, not least during his schooldays away at Eton, where he lodged at Mrs. Young's, and later as a student at Christ Church, Oxford. He carefully preserved the letters he received from his mother and father during the years 1769 and 1775, and from these can be built a picture which helps in part to explain the pattern of his future behaviour. It is clear that the biggest single influence in his life as a young man was his mother, whom he revered, and among the keepsakes he preserved was a lock of her hair and her last message to him.[14] These devotedly affectionate letters from his mother, Sophia Egerton, are charged with her concern for him and with admonitions to her younger son to bestir himself to shake off his casual and idle approach to life and moderate his conceited opinions and rebellious nature. In one, relating to a report of disaffection breaking out at Eton in 1770, there are dark references to an earlier misdemeanour:

> *9 Nov 1770.* . . . Remember, Francis, that you have been once pardoned as a child, led by a multitude. Consider now that you stand on your own legs and that having once seen the deformity and error of rebellion, if you plunge into it again *Nothing will be forgiven*—a second fault will disgrace your life . . . You must expect

no other subject from me while this is in agitation or till I have received such letters from you and such assurances from the Masters and Mrs. Young as can put my mind at rest . . .

A year later, on the occasion of his 15th birthday:

11 Nov. . . . You are coming now to an age when you must think and act for yourself, and to the dangerous age, when the passions work high and conceit makes a man think far too highly of himself. When you consult your own heart, my dear Francis, you will see that you have much conceit in it . . . if you search the *motives* on which you think and act, happiness must attend you . . .

From his father, still Bishop of Lichfield and Coventry, not yet promoted to Durham, came a warning on a theme to which he would frequently recur:

26 Feb. 1770. . . . You will find that a habit of expense is of all habits the most irksome and difficult to quit, and if indulged in your case must end in your ruin . . .'

His father's letters feature more prominently after Francis had entered Oxford.

5 Jan. 1774. . . . Tho' I am well convinced that £100 per annum is as much as you ought to spend till you have by your own ingenuity acquired more, yet to avoid any appearance of difficulty I shall allow you £30 per quarter, which with the advantages of your studentship is a large income . . . For my part I know of no infallible measure for your necessary expenses but the extent of your income, for if a man who has only £20 per annum finds it necessary to spend £30 he must of necessity go to gaol in a little. I can only judge from your past conduct, which in regard to expense, idleness and love of amusement (or rather dissipation, for anything served to amuse you that took you from study) has been most exceedingly faulty, but it is not my intention to blame for what is past, if you really mend for the future . . . At the same time if you go on in the same idle way that you did at Eton I shall remove you from Oxford and shall not suffer you to be one among the many who are daily perverting the good intentions of the benevolent founders of that noble university . . .

28 Jan. 1774. . . . You must excuse me if I again remind you to guard against that idleness which with much concern I have observed to have been so very habitual to you, that you do not seem to have an idea of what *proper study* is, at your age, and of the great number of things which you are totally ignorant of, and of which you must take pains to get a competent degree of knowledge before you can

> be qualified to make any tolerable figure in the world . . . At your age amusement is not necessary, but study is absolutely requisite . . . I cannot but reflect that any idle fool, who calls upon you to help him to do nothing may in five minutes destroy every good effect that might be expected from any attention to what I have been suggesting to you . . .
>
> *8 Nov. 1775.* . . . If I could have the satisfaction of perceiving in you a desire of improving yourself in any kind of knowledge it would not then be so difficult to give you advice and assistance . . .[15]

How many parents through the ages must have had reason at some time or other to reproach their offspring at school or college in similar vein? Yet in the case of Francis Egerton such glimpses of parental hopes disappointed by a young man's conceit, by his marked preference for the company of friends in idle amusement rather than work, by his incapacity to concentrate his mind, and by a persistent inability to manage within his allowance, all portended some of the confusions of his later life. Like most young men he had difficulty in deciding what he wanted to do, not being able to count on a sufficient allowance to avoid having to undertake some occupation. Somehow he seems to have reformed himself enough to be able to complete his course of study, at the same time acquiring a high degree of competence in and love for Latin and Greek, which he later turned to some advantage. He toyed with the idea of the Army, which his brother had recently entered, of the Navy, and the Law, and he finally settled on the Church to the approbation of his parents.

He became rector of the parishes of Whitchurch and Middle in Shropshire, and a prebendary of Durham cathedral. The former livings were presented to him by his cousin, the Duke of Bridgewater, within whose estate the two churches lay, and he held the latter preferment as a gift from his father, the Bishop of Durham. During the last few years of the duke's life Francis spent much time in the old man's company, living in his house and often accompanying him on his journeys, ostensibly with the object of gaining material for a biography of the duke. They must have made oddly-matched companions, the one a self-opinionated cleric and classical scholar, and the older man, with his mind on his business affairs, having little conversation at the best of times; both bored and boring in their respective ways. Yet Francis was able to assimilate much of the detail of the technical problems encountered by the duke in his canal construction. He carried out various investigative assignments for him and made reports. He presented a paper to the Royal Society of Arts on the Underground Inclined Plane which had formed part of the linking system for the underground canals at Worsley.[16] *His Letter . . . upon Inland Navigation,* to which reference has already been made, could not have been written without a fair understanding of what had been involved in the building of the canal. That the younger man persisted in seeking his older cousin's company in spite of this had only one true purpose. He dearly hoped to be named as his heir.

Francis Egerton's scholarly studies led him along strange paths which always seemed to be diverging. His Latin version of the *Hippolytus* of Euripides, which he had printed by the Clarendon Press, Oxford, in 1796, was well received both in England and France, and was later acknowledged to have been his best work. The success rather went to his head and led him to affirm that he had only published the work to demonstrate that he could achieve eminence by his own efforts and need not be dependent on his family connections for his advancement. He edited some poems of Sappho with distinction and later published in France a collection of literary studies, the variety of whose subjects was beginning to show the difficulty he had in concentrating for long on one particular theme. Nevertheless the publication of these works convinced him that he must now turn his mind to commemorating his illustrious ancestry. He shared with his brother an inordinately vain pride in his forbears. The trouble was, and it did not diminish with the years, that he was forever proclaiming it. He embarked on a life of Thomas Egerton, Lord Chancellor Ellesmere, but it turned out to be a shadowy account, over-full of documents from Elizabethan and Stuart sources, and of a large number of letters, not obviously relevant, which he had copied from the King's Library in Paris. The result was that the meagre text was obscured and the book sheds no real light on the man himself.[17] Convinced, however, that he had made his mark as a biographer, he announced his intention to write the biography of his cousin, the Duke of Bridgewater. When, later, he found that he had only benefited from the duke's will to the extent of £40,000 out of that huge fortune, he was filled with a sense of injustice and, in due course, in a somewhat dramatic and self-pitying manner, he refused to complete the work.

He had the misfortune to suffer from a physical deformity of the lower jaw and an affliction of speech which was disturbing to those who met him and must have been greatly embarrassing to himself and his parishioners, not that he seems to have spent much time with them. He much preferred London life or travelling abroad on his literary pursuits; and, leaving his curates in charge, he passed long periods of absence away from his parochial duties. One of these curates, James Horseman, was eventually to become the rector of Little Gaddesden in 1813. Whether Francis possessed a true vocation for the Church seems to be in question. He is said to have given way to bouts of religious ecstasy at times, from which there would have been a counter-reaction. It is not within the power of all men to remain forever balanced on a peak of purity of thought and behaviour, such as his vocation would demand, and remain completely sane. Francis could not, and in seeking relaxation from the strain he showed himself to be but a mortal man. He took a mistress, and a daughter was born to him (whom he named Sophia after his mother), to be followed later by four more. Acutely aware of the consequences of his behaviour, he decided to go abroad on the grounds of ill-health. His pride and self-esteem would not allow him to resign. He left England suddenly in 1802, and, at the age of 46, went to France. The French capital, long accustomed to the strange ways and often odd behaviour of wealthy Englishmen, was to be his home for most of the next twenty-seven years. Absentee parsons were no new phenomenon, and with England urgently preparing for war, his departure went largely unremarked.

Confident that, although he was aware that he would not supplant his elder brother as the duke's heir, he would be adequately taken care of, Francis began to spend freely. At the time of his leaving England it is probable that he had little intention of remaining abroad indefinitely, but events were to overtake him. He was in Paris when he received his brother's letter informing him that the duke had died, describing his last hours, and telling him that he had been left a legacy of

£40,000 in the duke's will. The smallness of the bequest was a bitter blow to his expensive tastes. Within weeks the uneasy peace of Amiens broke down and very soon Napoleon ordered the arrest of all British citizens in France and the confiscation of all their possessions. For the more influential or well-to-do English this amounted to little more than an inconvenient restriction of their movements. Others less fortunate were thrown into prison. Francis was only subjected to house arrest. He was, in fact, very unlucky. He had already procured passports for a return to England to consult with his brother over their joint executorship duties following the recent death of his aunt. Two days before his planned departure he was detained. Over the next two or three years he made repeated respresentations to be granted a permit to visit England, always with the same negative result. He began to suffer pangs of awareness that he was failing in his parish and prebendal duties. Moreover, if he was to continue to enjoy the emoluments derived from these appointments he needed to have dispensations for absence from the Bishops of Lichfield and Durham. Communication between England and France was now very uncertain, though not completely severed, and so his brother undertook the necessary representations to the bishops. From the large number of recently rediscovered letters passing between the two brothers between 1803 and 1821, but particularly in this early period, it is evident that, far from Francis being alienated from his family, the earl was genuinely concerned at his brother's plight. Apart from attending to the business of getting the dispensations, he undertook arrangements for looking after his brother's affairs in Whitchurch and Middle, appointing an agent, a retired farmer, to see to his house, land and animals.

As Francis became more despondent about ever being able to return he suggested resigning his livings, but the earl would not hear of this until they had a chance to discuss it together. Nowhere in the letters is there any suggestion of reproach for the unclergyman-like behaviour of Francis which led to his going away from England in the first place. Only once does Francis himself allude to it, in the first letter in which he mentions resignation: 'My object is to take off the disgrace . . . and I will set forth my reasons in a published apology or justification of my conduct . . .'.[18]

In 1806 moves to secure his release were successfully initiated by Sir Joseph Banks, President of the Royal Society, with whom both brothers were acquainted, as summarised letters show:[19]

> *24 May 1806.* Banks (in Paris) to Bernard Germaine Etienne de la ville, Comte de Lapécède, a naturalist . . . he had procured the release of the bearer, M. Rivaud, and requests in return the release of the Rev. F. H. Egerton, now on parole in Paris.
>
> *4 July 1806.* In Paris. Banks to Rivaud St. Germain (recently liberated). Mr. Egerton has been given permission to return to England, thanks to Banks's intervention, for which he is very grateful.

Shortly before receiving permission to return, Francis had appraised his brother of his thoughts of marrying 'a foreigner, a Roman Catholic, of a great family, twenty years of age, absolutely without property . . . but under the most express and sacred of all possible conditions, that our children, both boys and girls, should be brought up, solely, in the Religion of the Church of England'. He sought his brother's views, as the head of the family, and these were not long delayed. 'I never in the whole course of my life, my dear Francis, received a letter which caused me more pain and concern . . . For God's sake, reflect & consider your family, your rank, your situation & prospects of life, & then see whether the marrying a foreigner or a Roman Catholic can be possible . . .'.[20]

Francis remained in England, mostly in London, through 1807 and 1808, but very soon after that returned to resume residence in Paris. In 1808 the Clergy Residence Act had become law, and from now a dispensation for absence from his bishops was absolutely necessary. It was granted on grounds of his ill-health, though as the years passed requests for renewal had to be supported by reports from his physician.[21] Back in France, and freed from house restrictions, Francis seems to have been able to secure permission to travel about in France and to visit Italy, pursuing his searches for historical documents and autographs. He was consumed with the purpose of establishing a collection of rare manuscripts, which treasures, he was convinced, would become a lasting memorial to himself. The conceit of his youth was in no way diminished. He returned to Paris in 1814 and purchased one of the best houses in the

Rue de St. Honoré, the Hotel de Noailles, and prepared to continue his literary pursuits.

His peace was interrupted suddenly as Louis XVIII again took flight when Napoleon, lately escaped from Elba, returned to Paris. He was given three days' notice to leave his house, which was required to house a government department. Francis, for all his shortcomings, had never forgotten that he was an Englishman, and all his spirit was aroused; he told the French officials that if Napoleon wanted the house, he must take it by force. He armed his servants and barred the doors. In retrospect the situation seems ludicrous. Here was a semi-invalid English clergyman defying Napoleon, and Napoleon, not yet wholly confident, seems to have decided to leave the foreigner in peace. Similarly, after Waterloo, when various allied commanders tried to requisition the house, Francis successfully resisted all attempts to dislodge him. With the re-establishment of Louis XVIII on the throne a quieter period ensued, but among his aristocratic French neighbours Francis was hardly popular. He offended them by renaming his mansion the Hotel Egerton! He was pompous in his manner; by affecting a bizarre style of dress unsuited to his infirmities, and by parading his patriotism on every possible occasion 'the crazy Englishman' drew attention and ridicule to himself, to the despair of his friends and acquaintances. His eccentricities were becoming even more apparent. He is alleged to have had made 365 pairs of boots to avoid the necessity of wearing any pair more than once a year. If he wished to return a book borrowed from an acquaintance he would send it by his coach attended by four servants. His personal dress and the elaborate livery of his servants had long caused merriment among his friends and invoked the ridicule of his neighbours and acquaintances. The story of his dogs is better known. In the manner of the model English country nobleman that he so much strove to be, he surrounded himself with them, and their collars were embellished with his arms and crest. If he could not personally exercise them they would be sent in his carriage and four to the Bois de Boulogne to be walked by the unfortunate footman. His favourite pair were honoured at his dinner table, dressed as humans and seated with napkins round their necks, and attended by the servants as if they were honoured guests. If they misbehaved they were relegated to the servants' hall for a week or two, and two others were promoted until the favourites should be restored to grace. Unable to join in shooting-parties, he stocked the large gardens of his mansion with rabbits, pigeons and small game birds, and would there conduct shooting-parties with his friends to the utter consternation of his neighbours.

Although the correspondence between the two brothers is markedly less frequent during the four years to 1814, by reason of the difficulty of reaching Francis on his travels, signs of tension were beginning to show. Having bought his new mansion, Francis was perturbed about its disposal in the event of his death. At that time the French law, the 'droit d'Aubaine', by which at death the property of foreigners passed to the state, was still in force. A letter in 1815 from Francis earnestly besought his brother to come to Paris: 'I conceive it to be essential to your Interests and important to your Self, that you should come to Paris', to talk over matters concerning the mansion. 'It is a valuable property and will cost nearly the whole of that paltry and insufficient commutation the late Duke of Bridgewater left me by a codicil to his Will, in which he had not mentioned me'. The earl's reply was brief and pointed: 'The proposal for my coming to Paris as essential to secure my own interest has put a total stop to any idea of the journey. It is entirely for you to determine how you shall dispose of your own property . . .'[22] Some time later he compromised and sent his agent, Robert Clarke, to discuss matters in Paris.

Meantime Francis had not endeared himself to his brother by advertising to the world at large in various printed papers that his great and 'important' collection of manuscripts was to be left to Ashridge, for which purpose he was also providing in his will a sum for endowing the appointment of a librarian, who would look after the collection, and not only make it available to the public but distribute free printed copies of his own writings. His brother's reaction to this idea was very cool: 'their deposition at Ashridge with full liberty and discretion of the publick for inspection and the attendance of a librarian would make the habitation of this place insupportable to anyone . . . you have obliged me to take precautions against their admission'.[23] This refusal stung Francis's pride at just about its most sensitive spot. He found it difficult to conceive that such an opportunity to receive a collection of manuscripts and books, which would bring renown to the name of Bridgewater and to himself in particular, should be rejected.

The tragedy of Francis Egerton was that he was filled with an accumulation of self-pity at the way his life had gone. His own conduct had obliged him to go abroad; his chances of preferment in the Church had been jeopardised both by this and by his enforced detention in France. He felt let down by the duke, and he was jealous of his brother's good fortune. He had therefore set out to become, and to be seen, as a person of consequence in Paris. His conceits and his mode of living were on an expensive scale. Everything he wrote he seemed to consider worthy of printing and distributing at his own expense, and he was convinced that his collection of manuscripts would bring him fame in posterity. Accompanying all of this was a genuine history of progressive ill-health. The combination of these factors and the relative solitude of his existence brought him to a pitch of frustration and impatience amounting to an irrational hysteria, which had to be vented on his brother.

He continued to reproach him for his closeness, and made demands for loans of money, being only too well aware that the earl had no children to whom he would leave his wealth. In 1819 Francis requested a loan of £15,000, which the earl declined: he was not disposed to advance money (partly to complete the purchase of the mansion) which could only revert to the French government if Francis died. Francis also wanted his brother to guarantee certain bequests in his will. He repeated his request for a loan, but by now it had increased to £18,000 (his secretary had made a mistake, he explained). In May 1819 Francis went to Spa, Belgium, to seek a cure for his growing and debilitating ailments. He wrote his brother four letters within a week, masterpieces of scorn and sarcasm, on the now familiar lines. The earl delayed any reply until September, and sent a long and dignified refutal of his brother's complaints. Matters dragged on for a time, with Francis attempting to short-cut the question of the loan by drawing a bill on his brother's bankers for £18,000, and being aggrieved when it was not accepted. His brother offered to lend him £8,000 to assist in completing the final purchase of the Paris mansion, but not for any other purpose. This did not satisfy him and in desperation the following year Francis printed and published the four letters of May 1819, and, later, three more written in the early part of 1820, by which time the request for a loan had increased to £20,000.

In 1821 Robert Clarke, the agent, received a letter from Francis saying that he proposed to come to England at the end of April and go to the house in Little Gaddesden, which he had purchased to house his manuscripts.[24] The earl wrote to him that he would be glad to see him 'notwithstanding your conduct towards me, still more extraordinary . . . by your publication and circulation of some of my letters to you, mutilated likewise, for reasons best known to yourself . . . having determined, however, and having promised my mother (who foresaw that you was likely to give me cause) that nothing should make me quarrell with you, I shall, when you are in England, say nothing upon what has passed, or on the subjects in which I consider you have behaved improperly towards me. I shall therefore now mention that when you published to the world that I would not receive your manuscripts at Ashridge you should have added (to have been correct) upon the terms which you annexed, constituting your librarian paramount to the proprietor, and when you stated that I would not build a place for them at Ashridge, that I offered you a good house at Berkhamsted for that very purpose'.[25]

Francis did not, however, come home owing to an accident in which he was flung out of his carriage, and his head struck the pavement. He was not seriously hurt, though cut, and very severely bruised and shaken. After recovering from the shock he resumed his correspondence in the same vein: 'I am your next, your only, your full Brother and Presumptive Heir to the Title of the Family: . . . I am old, infirm in body; Palsied; Trailing after me either Leg; Unable to walk, without two persons to support me, or even to stand, alone, without falling; incapable of speaking articulately, so as to make myself understood; Blind of one eye; with a broken bone; suffering acute corporeal pain.

'You have all along declined or refused to accede to my dying requests . . . you have avoided to afford me the consolation of knowing that you will be at the small expence of burying me, decently, in the family vault, with my ancestors, when dead . . . [or] that you will comply with my last and Dying requests, as far as £20,000, conditionally alone (and what is £20,000 to you?) . . .'.[26]

His brother briefly acknowledged this letter with the assurance that 'most undoubtedly' he would bury him in the family vault, and had been making alterations there 'to render it more commodious'.[27] A few weeks later, at the limit of his patience, the earl directed a letter to M. Clarmont, his brother's banker in Paris, asking him to convey greetings to his brother on his birthday (11 November), 'but with all the regard which I still bear towards him, and ever shall, his continued determination to print & send forth to the world . . . the private correspondence between two brothers, of necessity precludes my addressing any letter to him again'. Future communications would therefore be directed to the banker with the strict injunction that they should not be put into the hands of Francis lest he should copy and print them.

On the face of it, the indifferent state of Francis's health would have suggested that in no way was he likely to outlive his brother to become the 8th Earl of Bridgewater, but events were to disprove this. The *Diary* of William Buckingham continued to record the daily round of events at Ashridge during the years 1820–1823, showing the earl following his accustomed routine of regular contact with estate matters, meeting tenants, carrying out his duties as a magistrate, making fairly regular though not prolonged visits to his London home, Grosvenor House; and receiving distinguished company, especially for shooting parties. The quarrels with his brother were no concern of his steward, even if he was aware of them, as he possibly was. As to his lordship's health, the occasional cold might intervene, but little more, until 1823.

On 16 January of that year a big shooting party assembled, consisting of the Duke of York, the Duke of Wellington, the Marquis of Salisbury, Lord Verulam and others. They dispersed on the 19th. On the following day Buckingham noted, 'Lord Bridgewater showed me a list of those to have game. I had 2 hares and 4 pheasants'. Shortly afterwards the earl took a cold, but he was about again, riding his rounds, before long.

The *Diary* continues:

> *Wednesday 12 February* . . . [William Buckingham himself being unwell] Up at 8 and breakfast. Mr. Newman of Pightstone came to sell me clover and St. Foin seed. Then on the bed in much pain. Rev. Horseman came to see me and stopt ½ an hour. Then on the bed again. Lord B. called after being round Potten End, St. Margaret's Lane with Gudgeons & Co. He desired George [William's younger son] to go to Ashridge to see time papers about Dell's team work . . .

The earl was having trouble with one foot, and current reports suggested that he had suffered frostbite as the result of too long exposure during the January shoot. There were several visits to London, accompanied by Lady Bridgewater, during March and early April, presumably for medical consultations, and from 9 April they were away in London for several weeks, during which an amputation was performed on the foot to remove some toes. On their return the earl's movements were much restricted, but things were fairly uneventful for a few weeks until 1 October, when the steward briefly recorded, 'Lord B. very unwell'. The following days showed evident concern for his state of health, such as:

> *Sunday 5th.* . . . Lord B very unwell again. He could not be seen. I remained until 4 o'clock. Sir A. Cooper and Dr. Steel came to me in the Hall . . .
>
> *Sunday 19th.* . . . Self and George to church. Lord B Prayed for . . .

On 21 October the Earl of Bridgewater died at ten minutes before six, in the presence of his wife, Sir H. Halford, Dr. Steel of Berkhamsted, Robert Clarke, his agent, and Mr. Arthur, his valet.

The funeral on 30 October was, as might be expected, a solemn affair, which William Buckingham recorded in a private family album, in a section headed 'Death of friends'.[28]

> The Earl of Bridgewater interred in Little Gaddesden Church.
> The cortege in the following order from Ashridge at 11 o'clock:
> Park Keeper and 6 Keepers on foot.
> 2 Porters on horse.
> The Valet with coronets on cushion (on horse).
> Two Porters on horse with staves.
> Plume of feathers.
> Hearse and Six horses (5 bearers own men).
> 1st mourning coach with Sir. A. Hume, Sir A. Long, Earl Brownlow, Viscount Clive (servants behind),

2nd mourning coach with General O'Loghlan, Three Chaplains, viz: Rev.'s Horseman, Jenks and Drake (servants behind).

3rd mourning coach with Mr. Clarke, Dr. Steel, Mr. Wilson (servants behind).

4th mourning coach with Mr. Ruddy, Horn, Hemming, Gossleton, Torbrah and Pointer.

5th mourning coach with Cook and house servants.

Carriages followed with servants behind, viz: The Earl of Bridgewater's, Sir A. Hume's, Sir A. Long's, Earl Brownlow's, Viscount Clive's, Earl of Verulam's, Marquis of Salisbury's, Gen. O'Loghlan's, Rev. Pechell's. Self, Atty, Adsetts, and Mr. Head, Church Warden, attended the church and yard to let in those we thought proper. George Buckingham and about 70 assistants to keep order.

So passed a wealthy nobleman to his final resting place, alongside his ancestors.

Curiously, his lordship's death seemed to attract little notice at the time. *The Times* of 22 October 1823 recorded it in a two-line entry, though since the whole newspaper of that date extended to only four pages, such brevity is understandable. *The Annual Register*[29] said of him: 'He was a man of quiet domestic turn and much esteemed in the circle of his acquaintance. He was long distinguished for his love of the fine arts, his hospitality, and the employment given to the poor on his large estates'.

Thirty years later, during the protracted law suit that followed his controversial will, an article in *The Illustrated London News* of 3 September 1853 recounted vividly the supposed events of the last hours of Lord Bridgewater as follows: 'Having just finished so glorious a palace, he (the Earl) could not believe the fatal *meni meni tekel upharsin,* and in paroxysms of disappointment exclaimed to his physicians: "No, no, it cannot be. I will give you ten, twenty,–fifty–a hundred thousand pounds, only to save and prolong my life". Alas for the vanity of human wishes! He departed within a few hours'. Bernard Falk sought to improve on this piece of journalistic extravagance in his own account; 'Warned by the physician that his last hour had come, he completely lost his nerve. "Save me," he screamed, "and I will give you £50,000." The doctor, powerless to help him, shook his head. The dying man repeated his offer and, again receiving no audible response, increased the amount to £100,000'. The story does not ring true, nor is it attributed to any witness, and it seems more likely to have been a sensational invention inspired by the proceedings of the law suit then taking place. Falk concluded his unsubstantiated obituary: 'His vanity . . . contracted to nothing, and he . . . once a General in the British Army, who on the brink of the grave, should have been steadfast and unafraid, dipped his colours and went tremblingly to his end . . . That the world might not gauge the true nature of this prince of snobs, his widow raised to his memory a monument of white marble with the fanciful inscription that "he had improved the morals of the poor" . . . from what one knew of his character, presumably it was by keeping them poor'.[30]

The earl's chaplain, the Rev. Henry Todd, whose great history of Ashridge was just about to be published in 1823 as the earl died, managed to have a final page added in tribute to his patron and friend. He had known him for well over twenty years from the days before General Egerton came into his vast inheritance. Even if due allowance is made for the rather fulsome tones that were considered appropriate to the occasion, he leaves us a picture of a man very much respected, affectionate in his domestic life, and sincere in his dealings. The inscription on his memorial[31] in Little Gaddesden church, to which Bernard Falk took such exception, was directly inspired by Todd's own words: 'From his judicious benevolence the industrious poor derived credit as well as comfort to themselves and their families: since while their industry was amply encouraged, their morals also by his means were improved . . . His time was rarely passed without benefit to others'. On the earl's final illness Todd makes an illuminating observation that he had been active from his youth and only in his last year was he confined, first to his chair and finally to his bed. 'He bore the painful disease, that overpowered him, with patience and fortitude . . .'. Bearing in mind the operation performed on his left foot, one is left with the thought that what finally caused death may well have been gangrene. And a final extract: 'In the Christian school he had learned real charity: no man sooner forgave an injury'.

The will of the 7th Earl certainly damaged his reputation. Long disappointed at having no heir, and ever regretful of his inability to have obtained the restoration of the dukedom, he devised a will deliberately designed to ensure that his ultimate successor should take steps, within five years of inheriting, to acquire the dignity of duke (or at least marquis) or else forfeit the estates to another. He regarded his brother, with whom his relations were strained, as quite unsuited to succeed; he was unstable and eccentric; he was over sixty years old, a bachelor, and his sickly state of health might even occasion his pre-decease. So Francis Egerton was to receive only the title and a life interest in part of the estates, and a sum of £18,000 a year clear. Ashridge was given to Lady Bridgewater during her lifetime, with reversion to her of the interest in such estates as was enjoyed by Francis, if he died before she did. After the death of both, then the whole of the estates and fortune were to devolve upon his great-nephew, John Hume-Cust, Viscount Alford, eldest son of the first Earl Brownlow, who had married the youngest daughter of the Lady Amelia Egerton, the 7th Earl's sister. There were, however, *certain conditions.* He was to assume the family name of Egerton, and if, within five years of inheriting the estates he failed to secure a dukedom or a marquisate, the property was to be forfeited to his younger brother, Charles, who in turn, if he failed to acquire the dignity, would forfeit the inheritance to William Tatton Egerton, of the Cheshire branch of the family, though this time without further penalty.

These conditions, when they became known, caused enormous speculation. They could not, however, be tested until after the deaths of both Francis Henry Egerton and the Countess Bridgewater, and as events transpired this would not be until 30 years later. In the controversy then occasioned by the law suit and appeal from 1851–1853 it was natural that the idea that an advancement in rank might actually be purchased for money was utterly offensive to Victorian propriety. The manner in which John Egerton, the 1st Earl, had been able to procure his title in the 17th century was certainly abhorrent now. Such an infamous notion could only succeed in blackening the earl's character and obscure his many good points.

What then is to be made of the character of John William Egerton, particularly as between the tribute paid by his chaplain and friend; the sensational and often spiteful picture drawn by Bernald Falk; and the employer revealed in the calm, matter-of-fact notes and entries of the loyal steward who served the earl, mostly in daily contact, for 20 years? The truth, as so often, lies somewhere in between, remembering that the family differences between the earl and his brother would not have concerned William Buckingham. The earl, it cannot be denied, was proud of his illustrious ancestry. Some men are born great; others have greatness thrust upon them. He came more into the latter category and it rather went to his head. He was condescending in all likelihood, but inherently kind; strait-laced, certainly, as the son of a bishop, in his attitude to moral questions in an age which did not take too seriously lapses from the paths of uprightness. He was ambitious above all to advance his rank. Since this was denied to him, then his ultimate successors must take on this task. He was excessively wealthy, but was cautious, as most Egertons had been, about how he disposed of his money. He did not consider that his brother was a good investment. As *The Annual Register* had described him, 'he was much of an economist'. The new mansion of Ashridge was pretentious, and an extravagance in conception and in cost, which he felt was a worthy tribute to his cousin, the late duke, but it was surely designed to impress his contemporaries. He was a fair and just employer, and assiduous in his care for what he had inherited and what he was creating. Both his mansion and the associated improvements around the huge estate brought badly-needed employment to hundreds in the depressed villages around Ashridge and had enabled the plight of the poor to be eased. Perhaps he might or could have done more in this direction, but he was living in his own age, whose accepted standards were different from those of today. He was an improver rather than a reformer. He pointed the way and happily his successors did not lose the trail.

* * * * *

Probably no one had more cause for astonishment than Francis Henry Egerton to find that he was now the 8th Earl of Bridgewater, nor for surprise that he had received rather more generous treatment at the hands of his elder brother than their strained relations over the past 20 years might have led him to expect. With an annual income worth about £40,000 he could now better indulge his expensive tastes. It was true that he was denied the use of Ashridge, but he had now neither the wish nor the intention to leave France. His new wealth merely served to accentuate his eccentricities.

He continued his literary studies, producing some family anecdotes in 1826, and announced that he was going to publish his memoirs, though these never appeared. So many of his writings were published not to be sold but to be given to his friends, a whim he could afford to indulge. All the time his health was slowly declining, and the paralysis of his tongue worsened to the point that he was obliged to be attended constantly by a secretary who endeavoured to interpret his wishes and communicate them to others. He died on 11 February 1829 at the age of 72, an event that passed almost unnoticed in England, and with his death the Bridgewater title was extinguished.

His will made evident that he had softened in his attitude to the old duke. Rather as if repenting for having so often maligned him, he left the design and the sum of £13,500 for the erection of an obelisk to the duke's memory. Lady Bridgewater thought that his design was 'a specimen of very bad taste', and had erected the column which now stands overlooking Ashridge and Aldbury. He made a number of curious bequests, including a sum for the repair of Isaak Walton's monument in Westminster Abbey. He is perhaps best remembered for having left £8,000 to the President of the Royal Society for the publication of a work on the Goodness of God as shown in the Creation. In fulfilment of his design eight distinguished specialists were invited to contribute separate expositions on different aspects of the subject, which have survived as the Bridgewater Treatises. He forgave his brother for refusing to provide accommodation for his fine collection of manuscripts at Ashridge and left these to the British Museum together with a legacy of £12,000 to defray the cost of looking after them and to augment the collection. As if to atone for his neglect of the parishes of Whitchurch and Middle he bequeathed to each a sum of £2,000 for the relief of the poor there. He bequeathed a quantity of his plate as heirlooms to Ashridge, some of which was thought 'not proper to be kept', and was exchanged by the executors of the 7th Earl at the firm of Grayhurst, Harvey and Denton in the Strand, London, for more suitable pieces. He left £1,000 for a memorial to himself in the church of Little Gaddesden, where his body was finally interred in the Bridgewater family vault along with his ancestors. The question of his memorial caused quite a stir at the time. Already the church at Little Gaddesden had been enlarged by Wyatville by the addition of a small chapel on the south side of the chancel to receive the lovely Westmacott memorial to the 7th Earl, the cost being borne by his widow, Lady Bridgewater. After the 8th Earl's death it was clear that he intended his own memorial to be a substantial one, and Robert Clarke, the agent, warned the executors that a new chapel might have to be built. The rector, Mr. Jenks, was opposed to any more space being provided for Bridgewater memorials at the expense of facilities for the commemoration of his parishioners. Lady Bridgewater was also strongly against the late 8th Earl having a more splendid monument than any of his ancestors had. The argument lasted until early in 1831 and was settled when Westmacott was asked to design a relief based on the flora, fauna and rocks, which were among the subjects to be studied in the Bridgewater treatises. It was finished by the end of the year and is now to be seen on the north wall of the south chapel over the entrance.[32]

In the end, Francis Henry Egerton realised many of his ambitions. He achieved the earldom, though only for six years of his life, and he had at last enjoyed some further part of his wealthy cousin's huge fortune. The worth of his early classical scholarship had been recognised, even if his many other publications failed to establish him as an author of any consequence. He is remembered as a collector of manuscripts, and by the commissioned treatises which bear his name. Above all he has provided another portrait for the great gallery of English eccentrics, whose actions have added to the variety of life through the ages.

* * * * *

The Countess of Bridgewater confidently assumed the direction of affairs after the death of her husband, displaying a competence which surprised none who knew her. She was 66 years old when her brother-in-law died, and was still enjoying vigorous good health. She was now to receive the full reversion of all the revenues that had been diverted to the advantage of the 8th Earl for his life. Relieved of all testamentary burdens, she became a very wealthy woman with an annual income only a little short of £60,000. The gossips and matchmakers lost little time in pairing her off with various members of the nobility, but she chose to remain a widow, faithful to the memory of her dearly-loved husband. She emerged as a woman of great determination and self-reliance, who knew exactly what she wanted to do, and was usually able to do it. She entertained freely and generously either at Grosvenor House or at Ashridge, and was known as a charming hostess with a capacity for setting her guests at their ease, and a sprinkling of notable political and literary figures was usually to be seen at her receptions. She commanded the absolute respect and loyalty of her tenants at Ashridge. As a devout churchwoman she gave generous support to the churches and the poor in Little Gaddesden and the villages around. The 1847 edition of *Kelly's Post Office Guide* for Buckinghamshire recorded the existence of two schools in Little Gaddesden 'patronised by the liberality of the Countess of Bridgewater'.

Few of Lady Bridgewater's account books have survived, except maybe in private hands. Those for the years 1830 to 1833 may be seen among the Hertfordshire Records, and these cover the receipts and expenditure for Home Farm, Coldharbour Farm, Little Heath Farm, and one, lately Strugnall's, at Cheddington. The expenses were analysed under the headings of The Mansion House, The House in London, Kitchen Gardens, Stables, Game Keepers and Game, the Park, Conservatories and Flower and Pleasure Gardens, as well as the Agricultural School, founded by the 7th Earl. Two miscellaneous entries illustrate incidental aspects of events at Ashridge during 1830.[33]

July 14.	To William Hingham for conveying Thomas Fountain and William Day to Berkhamsted for disorderly conduct at Ashridge on the 8th ulto...	1s. 7d.
July 31.	To Moses Simmons for his expenses at various times to lay information against poachers ..	£1 5s.

* * * * *

Her husband's friend and chaplain, the Rev. Henry Todd, had earlier been found a living at Settrington, near Malton, in

Yorkshire. His *History of the College of Bonhommes* was completed in 1823 in a sumptuous edition. He had first put forward the proposal as early as 1807[34] after he had made a careful examination of the contents of the late duke's library, removed to Bridgewater House, and after locating other relevant documents in the possession of members of the earl's family, notably the Marchioness of Stafford, later Duchess of Sutherland. A smaller edition was published in 1813, covering the monastery period and the early Bridgewaters, but it was the completion of the new mansion and the opportunity to describe and illustrate it in detail which led to the enlarged edition of 1823. Only 200 copies were produced, and most of these were presented to a carefully-selected list of recipients, including King George IV and members of the Royal Family, the King of France, leading members of the nobility, national and college libraries, and personal friends. The total cost was £3,613, making the cost of each copy over £18, which was a measure of the considerable value his lordship placed on this highly instructive piece of self-advertisement, which only benefited him posthumously. The fine illustrations were supervised by a well-known artist, F. Mackenzie, who drew most of the pictures for engraving by such experts as John and Henry Le Quex, Woolnoth, Turrell, and W. R. Smith.[35]

Mr. Todd's transition to Yorkshire was not the success he had hoped it might be, and when in 1829 Robert Clarke, agent to the countess, wrote to sound out whether he could also hold the living of Little Gaddesden if it were to be offered, Henry Todd opened his heart in reply. He could not, he wrote, hold two livings so far apart unless either of them had been a Crown living, which they were not, but he thought that he might be able to reside in Little Gaddesden and have a curate at Settrington.

'If it should be my good fortune to have the present opportunity afforded me of a removal hence, where, unlike my predecessors in the rectory, I have neither private fortune or other preferment to keep up the usual appearance and establishment of the rectors of Settrington; where we are in great measure debarred from society; where there is not a single literary friend; where I have a parish consisting mostly of Wesleyans and Ranters, the most conceited beings in the universe; where I have been robbed by some of a family whom I had greatly obliged; where we still live not with much comfort, but certainly with much fear. Can you wonder, my dear Sir, that I would be thankful for a removal? . . .'.[36] However, the offer appears not to have been made to him. Preferment eventually came when he was made archdeacon of Cleveland, and he ended his working days in a position admirably suited to his scholarly achievements as the Librarian at Lambeth Palace.

Without the solace of a husband's companionship or the comfort of children to cheer her old age, the Countess of Bridgewater devoted her remaining active years to her estates and to the welfare of her tenants, whom she ruled with an almost despotic benevolence. As she approached the age of 80, however, she found it more difficult to get around, and some neglect of the estate was apparent. Speculation about the outcome of her late husband's will took on a new interest as two of the original trustees died, leaving as the sole trustee Earl Brownlow, whose son and heir apparent, Viscount Alford, was due to benefit. As the earl was now approaching 70 new trustees were appointed in the persons of the Earl of Powis and Mr. Wilbraham Egerton. The testing time was still to be delayed, however, as the old lady lived on to the ripe age of 85 before she died quietly and suddenly, seated in her chair, on 11 February 1849, having outlived her husband by more than twenty-five years.

* * * * *

Viscount Alford, succeeding to the Bridgewater estates, subject to the stipulations enjoined, assumed the family name of Egerton by royal licence. Although he was only 38 years of age he had not enjoyed good health for some years, and in 1849 he was advised to pass the winter in a warmer climate. Accompanied by his wife, Lady Marian, he departed for Egypt, but returned the following summer having derived no benefit from the change. The burning question was whether he would be able to achieve the stipulated rank of marquis or duke within the five-year period alloted. It was a question unfortunately not destined to be answered, for within a year he died. He was buried at Little Gaddesden, though six months later, as a result of a re-reading of the wishes expressed in his will, a faculty was obtained for his body to be removed, and it was reinterred at Belton.[37]

There were suddenly two claimants to the Bridgewater estates: John William Spencer Cust Egerton, Lord Alford's eldest boy, and his uncle, Charles Henry Cust, the second son of Lord Brownlow, who challenged his nephew's claim on the grounds that the vital condition imposed had not been complied with. Rarely had litigation of the kind that ensued excited so much public interest, for what was at stake was not only a huge fortune, but the whole question of whether the condition imposed could possibly be upheld without grossly transgressing public policy.

The very lengthy case was heard before Lord Cranworth, the Vice-Chancellor, who declared that the legal question to be decided was whether the obtaining of the rank of marquis or duke by Lord Alford was a condition precedent or subsequent to vesting the estate in his son as heir male: if it were precedent, then it was immaterial to consider whether the condition was impossible to fulfil or contrary to public policy. His lordship finally gave his judgement on 20 August 1851, expressing the opinion that it was a condition precedent, which had not been fulfilled, and he therefore found in favour of the uncle.[38] The effect of his judgement was to deprive the male heirs of Lord Alford of their rights to the Bridgewater estate, by now valued at £70,000 per annum.

The representatives of the young Lord Alford took their case to the House of Lords. The ensuing delay in the process of petition seemed unbearable. Lady Marian Alford, left as the only acting guardian because of the absence from England of Mr. Perry Cust, was concerned not only about her son's health but about the continuing neglect of the Ashridge estate. She sought the help of any influential friend who might be able to persuade the Lord Chancellor's office to advance the date of the hearing. Among those she approached were Lord Salisbury, and the prime minister, Lord Derby, who gracefully declined to intervene on the grounds that his office of state required that he should remain neutral. A letter to Lord Redesdale, dated 1 June 1852 reveals her worries:

> . . . If the petition for an early hearing is allowed and we could get through the business in the next session, it would be of most important benefit to everyone concerned. You may imagine the condition of any large landed property which beyond the park gates has been entirely neglected for the past twenty years. We were doing our best for the wretched population and setting on past plans for their improvement, never doubting, though everyone else was aware of it, that we could never carry any of them out. Now the estate is in Chancery, everything is standing still—or rather falling back again—and the discontent and misery are very great, leading to incendiaries, poachers, &c, to flourish and increase. It is not through entirely selfish family grounds that I am so anxious that the possessorship of the estate should be ascertained as speedily as possible . . . Your assistance, if you will give it, towards the calling of the petition for an early hearing will be a charity to thousands . . .[39]

By the time that the petition reached the Lords in 1853, however, Lord Cranworth had become Lord Chancellor. He was supported at the hearing by four eminent law lords, Lyndhurst, Brougham, Truro and St. Leonards. The Lord Chancellor held to his previous judgement, but each of his four colleagues took the view that the main issue was the general principle of the public interest. They contended that the notorious stipulation as to advancement of rank was a 'condition subsequent' and was not properly applicable to the limitations or contingent use of an estate. The condition was contrary to the public good, and as such must be held to be null and void. Lord Cranworth bowed to the majority opinion and the decree of 1851 was reversed.[40]

Public opinion and the press were strongly in support of the verdict, condemning the late 7th Earl for presuming to imagine that he could use the power of his money after his death to procure an honour that had not been merited.

The decision of the law lords was given on 19 August 1853. Less than one month later Earl Brownlow died at Belton, and his grandson, John William Spencer Cust Egerton, so recently confirmed in his right to inherit the Bridgewater estates, suddenly found himself to be the second Earl Brownlow, heir to the very substantial Cust estates in Lincolnshire; and, at the age of 12, probably the wealthiest young boy in the country.

Chapter Thirteen

GRACE ABOUNDING

AS LADY MARIAN ALFORD contemplated the reality of this new development in her family's fortune she might have been excused for finding it at once exciting and daunting. Only two years had passed since her husband had died, leaving her to bring up their two boys, but the elder daughter of the 2nd Marquis of Northampton was well endowed with a strength of character and intellect to meet such a challenge. She managed the establishments and estates at Ashridge, Belton, and in Shropshire with determination, resolved on preserving the heritage intact until her elder son should come of age and be able to shoulder his own responsibilities. Her principal concern, and an increasing one as he reached and passed through adolescence, was whether his health would permit him to do so, because the signs were evident that tuberculosis had already begun its grim assault on him. Advised that he ought to pass his winters in a drier, sunnier climate, Lady Marian devotedly made the annual pilgrimage with him to Madeira, and later to Mentone, Italy, sparing no expense. Although possessed of many shining virtues she had never been able to number thrift among them, an instance of which was that when she learnt that good mutton was not to be obtained in Madeira, she imported a flock of 50 Southdowns with a shepherd to look after them.[1]

Benjamin Disraeli, that star of the political firmament, enjoyed the friendship of the family, and in his newly-found role of country gentleman, lately established at Hughenden Manor, Buckinghamshire, he was almost a neighbour. One of his greatest enjoyments was visiting country houses: he regarded it, as he confided to his friend, Mrs. Sarah Willyams, as one of the duties of his position. Visiting Ashridge with his wife in 1865, he afterwards noted in his diary impressions of his hosts:

> Lord Brownlow [then 22 years old], a great deal beyond six feet high, slender, rather bent, with one lung already lost . . . intellectual, highly educated, with a complete sense of duty, and of a soft and amiable disposition: living, as it were on sufferance, but struggling to perform his part . . . A devoted mother watches every glance and every word, shares his annual exile, where she actually has not a single companion . . .
>
> Adelbert Cust, Brownlow's only brother, has both his lungs, is as tall, well-formed, and one of the handsomest fellows in England. . . . The brothers were always devotedly attached to one another —naturally affectionate, their mother has studiously developed their mutual love.

Disraeli's admiration for their mother was no less sincere. He described her as 'a woman of commanding ability. Above the common height, a fine figure, but a countenance of animation and intelligence, marred by a red and rough complexion . . . very pretty hands, which tell particularly in a large woman; well shaped and small and plump and white . . .'.[2] The blemish in her complexion was as the result of an earlier carriage accident.

Lord Brownlow attained his majority in 1863 and began to take as active an interest in his estates as his state of health would allow. His coming-of-age was celebrated with great feelings of warmth and goodwill at a grand party at Ashridge, attended by relations, friends and representatives of the tenantry of all the estates, many travelling from Lincolnshire and Shropshire. So large was the number of guests that a large marquee had to be erected in front of the house to provide extra bedrooms. A masque was performed in his honour. The Ashridge and Thame Rifle Corps Bands were among those providing musical entertainment in the gardens. During the afternoon addresses of loyalty were presented, gifts were made, and over five hundred were entertained to dinner in the early evening in a large pavilion erected in front of the conservatory. Fireworks and dancing to Coote and Finney's band carried the celebrations forward until past three o'clock in the morning. An entry in the accounts reveals that blankets and comforts were given to the poor on all the estates to mark the occasion, at a cost of £1,087 7s. 1d.

In his unhappily short life the 2nd Earl is chiefly remembered for the furore created by an attempt to restrict by enclosure rights of way over part of Berkhamsted Common. The manor of Berkhamsted had been leased to the Duke of Bridgewater by the Duchy of Cornwall in 1761, but as recently as 1860 Lord Brownlow's trustees had been able to purchase the manor for Ashridge for a little under £150,000. With a view to making new roadways across the central part of the Common, as well as to try to preserve its natural beauties against the depredations caused by indiscriminate gorse-cutting and the damage to walks by cartwheels, the advisers of Lord Brownlow proposed to restrict access to that part by fencing it under the General Enclosure Act. By way of compensation the commoners of Berkhamsted were offered land for a central recreation ground in the town. The majority readily assented to the proposal and more than four hundred persons signed a deed of release, which was not, however, completed.[3] A small number, on the other hand, were opposed to the loss of rights to cutting gorse and grazing sheep on the heath. Opposition began to be stirred up by articles in newspapers,[4] and grew rapidly, coming seemingly more from the articulate urban townsfolk than the poorer villagers. One of the objectors who took up and led the cause was an influential man, Augustus Smith, M.P. for Truro, 'lord' of the Isles of Scilly, and the largely-absentee owner of Ashlyn's Hall, Berkhamsted, which his father had purchased in 1801. As a wealthy young man recently out of Oxford, and seeking a purpose in life, as well as an outlet for his undoubted energy, he had been moved deeply by the poverty among the labouring classes he had seen around him in the countryside adjacent to Berkhamsted. He opposed the sloth and the *laissez-faire* attitude of the parish elders in their responsibilities towards the poor of the parish, and embarked upon a struggle to improve their lot and reduce the awful burden of the rates by more effective management. At the same time he sought to find ways of teaching the poor to help themselves. Convinced that the surest way lay through education, he proposed to establish schools for children of every denomination in which the learning of a useful industry would form an essential part of the curriculum. At first he received support and some acclaim, until local ministers of the Established Church denounced the idea, asserting that they could not work alongside Dissenters in such a venture. At least this forced them into founding a school of their own, but the effect was to divert promised funds, including the support of Lady Bridgewater, away from Augustus Smith's schools, and he was obliged to bear the entire cost of their upkeep until the British and Foreign Schools Society, an undenominational body, helped him with a grant. He continued to support the schools generously, as they developed with no small success, right up to the time of the Education Act of 1870 when they were taken over as Board Schools.

It was not, therefore, as a person disinterested in the affairs of Berkhamsted that he took up the cause of the commoners. He had roots in the town, though he no longer lived there, and the cause appealed to his sense of justice and his reforming zeal. Augustus Smith had already built up a reputation for himself in the House of Commons as a champion of the rights of the public against the claims of the Crown and the Duchy of Cornwall to ownership of the foreshore of the coasts of Cornwall. Early in 1866 Lord Brownlow went ahead with the enclosure, and over a mile of iron railings was erected. Mr. Smith, learning of it, discussed the situation with a member of the Commons, Open Spaces and Footpaths Preservation Society,[5] and they resolved to take quick action to abate the enclosure by the forcible removal of the fences as a demonstration and 'an assertion of right, not less conspicuous than their erection' had been. A contractor was engaged for the demolition who hired a small force of 120 navvies in London. These men, taken at night by a special train from Euston to Tring, arrived in the small hours of the morning of 6 March 1866. From Tring they were marched up to the common and in the moonlight they uprooted all the railings. Lord Brownlow instituted legal proceedings for trespass, though later he expressed a willingness to settle the matter amicably outside the courts. Mr. Smith, however, declined to do so, seeking to extract the maximum publicity and effect from long litigation. As it happened the trespass action was never heard, owing to the untimely death of Lord Brownlow in Mentone in the following February. This sad occurrence probably served to allay some of the discord caused between Ashridge and Berkhamsted, and good relations were fairly quickly restored.

Augustus Smith brought a counter-action, not heard until late in 1869, which he eventually won on a judgement given by the Master of the Rolls that insufficient lands had been left unenclosed to meet the rights of the commoners. In 1878 Lady Marian Alford, who, as the principal guardian of her son, may have recognised some responsibility for the unwise advice which had provoked the whole affair, published privately a fair defence of her elder son's actions. It was a belated protest against the lingering criticisms of him and refutation of a pamphlet printed and distributed by Augustus Smith in 1866. In a well-documented narrative[6] she described their good intentions to preserve and improve a part of the common, and incidentally, to make it a safer place to walk in. She recollected her first visit in 1841 to the Countess of Bridgewater, who maintained a large number of keepers to warn people off the common for fear of brigands. On another occasion she wrote that Lady Bridgewater 'took us to a ball at Berkhamsted, and we were guarded by outriders with loaded pistols in their holsters for fear of our being attacked as we rode across the Common'.

A perplexing irony of the court's judgement given in favour of Augustus Smith was that while the commoners would continue to enjoy a right of access to the common for the purpose of taking furze and firewood and to graze their sheep, no legal right of access existed for recreation. The public might not in law enjoy it, nor had the lord of the manor any right to protect it. Local jubilation at the outcome was predictably enthusiastic. Costs were given against Lord Brownlow, but Augustus Smith's expenditure over a prolonged case had been very heavy and his victory probably cost him at least £3,000.[7] Lady Marian Alford, who was seen to be, and undoubtedly was, the power behind her ailing son, having managed the affairs of Ashridge for many years, lost the contest against a formidable and very determined opponent and deserved to do so. Her error of judgement in this instance, however, should not be allowed to detract from her manifold good qualities and achievements. 'Her generosity was unbounded, she loaded her many friends with gifts, which apart from their intrinsic value, were chosen with unerring comprehension of what would best please the recipient. Her public liberalities exceeded the measure of what her resources allowed . . .'.[8] So wrote her nephew, Sir George

Leveson Gower, who had been brought up as a small boy in her family after the death of his mother in giving birth to him. Her care and sympathetic consideration for the poor and distressed came from the heart. She instituted repairs to farms, cottages, reading rooms and churches which had been neglected in the later years of Lady Bridgewater's long life, and she built new schools and almshouses. As much as for anything she deserves to be remembered for having given Little Gaddesden and Ringshall a piped water supply in 1857.

Lady Marian continued to live at Ashridge until her other son Adelbert, who succeeded as 3rd Earl, married in 1868. Then she moved to her London residence, Alford House in Kensington, which she had designed for herself. There she welcomed and entertained royalty, statesmen, artists and men of letters. She was herself a skilful artist in water-colours. She travelled widely, especially in Italy, where she had been born, and whose cultural and artistic influences greatly coloured her tastes. The internal restyling of the interior of Ashridge is ample evidence of this. She was the leading founder of the Royal School of Needlework, and her *History of Needlework* has survived as a standard work on the subject. Her warm personality made her a person very much loved by all, rich or poor, who knew her. She died at Ashridge on 8 February 1888; and at the park entrance in Little Gaddesden a simple but elegant memorial in the form of the Iona Cross[9] commemorates the life of a great lady.

* * * * *

The 3rd Earl, Adelbert Wellington Hume Cust, was 22 years old when he inherited the vast combined estates in 1867. After leaving Eton he had entered the Army and served for three years as a lieutenant in the Grenadier Guards until 1866. He sat in the Commons as M.P. for North Salop, but only briefly, as within a year he stepped up into the House of Lords. In that same year he was made Lord Lieutenant of the County of Lincoln, surely one of the youngest men to have received such an appointment, which he held until his death over fifty years later. His marriage in 1868 was a great social event. His bride, whom he had first met in Rome when she was only 16, was the Lady Adelaide Talbot, the youngest of three daughters of

Henry John Talbot, 18th Earl of Shrewsbury. All three sisters were girls of great beauty, but Adelaide was acknowledged to be the prettiest of them. The eldest, Lady Gertrude, became the Countess of Pembroke. Her husband died rather young and she spent much of her widowhood at Ashridge. She has a small place in this history because the curious stone Bible, to be found amid a circle of incense cedars at the end of one of the long walks in the garden, was placed there by Lady Adelaide in her memory. The middle sister, Lady Constance Talbot, became the Marchioness of Lothian. She, too, was widowed early, but continued to live for the next 30 years in her home at Blickling Hall, Norfolk, where she was able to give reign to her rather advanced artistic tastes, which included acquaintance with the so-called Holland House group of artists such as Van Prinsep, Spencer and G. F. Watts.

The very great happiness with which the marriage of Lady Adelaide and Earl Brownlow was blessed was to sustain them through nearly fifty years. It was an ideal union—a strikingly handsome nobleman and a beautiful girl: the very stuff on which fairy tales thrive had come true. In a curious way something of the subtle aura emanating from this happy state still pervades Ashridge, and at no time more than on those very rare occasions when the house is completely closed and one can wander quietly on a summer evening through the Great Hall, the public rooms, the chapel, and out into the gardens, reflecting on the serenity of life there in those calmer and more gracious days during the 50 years which preceded the First World War. Under the influence of Lady Alford the house had undergone much interior change, notably in the drawing room, with its fine marble, the painted ceiling and walls hung with green silk brocade. To adorn these some of the fine paintings collected by Lord Brownlow's maternal great-grandfather, Sir Abraham Hume, were brought in. These included Albert Cuyp's masterpiece 'The Mass at Dordrecht', Bellini's 'Adoration of the Shepherds' (both were sold in 1923 as part of the estate); and a study of the 'Mona Lisa', which the collector had purchased for 90 guineas at a sale of the effects of Sir Joshua Reynolds. This, the third version of Leonardo's famous work (the others being in the Louvre, Paris, and in the Prado, Madrid) was carefully locked away each night. It is now at Belton

House. Such elegant surroundings served to heighten the warmth of welcome given to the many distinguished visitors, royalty, relatives and friends, who were to be the guests of Lord and Lady Brownlow over the next four decades.

The prominence of Lady Adelaide as a society hostess owed much to her good looks, her simple dignity and personal charm. In the 'sixties and 'seventies she was acknowledged as the supreme beauty of her day, and later, in the company of her lifelong friend the Princess of Wales (later Queen Alexandra) it was commonly held that there were not two more beautiful women in London. As Lady Battersea wrote in a tribute after her death in 1919, 'with her commanding height, her well-poised head, her delicate features, dark hair and deep blue eyes, it would have been impossible for her to pass unnoticed in a crowd'. Bishop Samuel Wilberforce, a frequent visitor, recorded in his diary: 'Ashridge, 10 December 1872. This is always a charming house–*he* so good, so true and kind and *she* quite bright in her beauty and loveliness'.

Adelaide Brownlow possessed with it a shy gentleness and humility, and was entirely unaffected in her manner. She found it quite hard to undertake public duties such as sitting upon committees or speaking at meetings, yet her sense of duty was strong and she supported her dear husband, 'Addy', devotedly in the many causes and functions they were called upon to sponsor or undertake. Lady Brownlow set out to know all the cottagers on her husband's estates at Ashridge and Belton, and they trusted and adored her. She was a woman who was deeply sensitive of the worries and problems of others, and, especially towards the end of her life, the distress brought about by war affected her profoundly. Her readiness to listen involved her in all the cares of her many relations.The house seemed ever full of such visitors, drawn by the bountiful hospitality and elegant comfort and the warmth of welcome they received. George Leveson Gower was moved to confide to a friend: 'Dear Adelaide Brownlow is too anxious about many things . . . she is more weighed down by brothers and sisters than many women by a large family of their own . . . I sometimes feel as though I should like to shut her up in a nice comfortable, well-furnished, gardened prison, strongly bolted and barred to the world, and there set to work to *teach* her [to free herself of "useless cares"]

. . . I believe that, if there were no chance of seeing any Talbots for a month she would settle down and develop amazingly'.[10] In the eyes of some of her friends she was nevertheless maturing, as Lady Waterford wrote to a friend: 'I hear of Adelaide dining at the Gladstone's in red velvet up to her chin, and a row of pearls, looking beautiful—a beautiful woman, the girl gone'.[11]

Visitors were not confined to relations, however, for the Brownlow circle was a large one. Queen Victoria was a visitor to their London residence, remembering no doubt a very early visit to Ashridge in 1823 when as a small girl of four she was taken by her mother, the Duchess of Kent, to see Lady Bridgewater and planted the fine oak tree which stands proudly on the south lawn. On this occasion the young princess held her first 'drawing room' in the present Hoskins Room, when all the maids passed before her, and she greeted them graciously with such words as, 'Mrs. Cranfield, I shall not forget you . . .'.[12]

For Queen Mary, who came both as Princess of Wales and as queen, it was in a special sense a return to one of her childhood temporary homes. In 1866 her parents had spent their honeymoon at Ashridge, which had been loaned to them by Lady Marian Alford, and it was one of the houses at which she had stayed with her mother, the Duchess of Teck, during those periods of financial stress which often affected the life of Mary Adelaide. The princess was also a guest at a house-party in December 1886. Her later visits, usually to luncheon in the summer, were marked by a predilection for red currants from the garden. Coffee after lunch was always taken in the conservatory, where the royal visitor would sometimes smoke a cigarette, which was thought to be rather advanced. On one occasion, when accompanied by her children, the little Princess Mary fell into the boating pond (now a rose garden)—an occurrence, it was always believed, of which her brother, the future Prince of Wales, was not wholly innocent.[13] Then there was King Alfonso of Spain, who came to lunch and in whose honour the dining-room received new chairs in gold and red, and for whom the vases on the table were filled with flowers in the same national colours. On such occasions as this, wrote Constance Sitwell, 'the gold plate was massed on the table, and the gold jugs, given by Queen Adelaide to both these god-children of hers, who were later to meet and marry each other . . .'.[14]

Accustomed as she had been from her youth to meeting prominent people in her father's house, Adelaide Brownlow entertained a wide range of friends including Carlyle; Disraeli; the Gladstones; John Ruskin; Edward Clifford, the painter, whose portrait of her hangs at Belton next to one of her husband by that other friend, G. F. Watts; Oscar Wilde; E. F. Benson; and the young H. G. Wells, who owed his start in the literary world to the encouragement of Harry Cust, M.P., Lord Brownlaw's heir-presumptive, and the brilliant editor of *The Pall Mall Gazette*. All these and many more were received at Ashridge or at No. 8 Carlton House Terrace, where art, music, literature, politics and ideas were seriously discussed and where conversation was never mere gossip. Mrs. Gladstone noted in her diary in December 1885, when she was a guest at Ashridge (Disraeli also being of the party): 'To dinner with Mr. Compton. All in small tables'.[15] The innovation of small tables, rather than the formality of a long table, was designed to promote easier conversation.

The highlight of the year 1889 was the visit to Ashridge of the Shah of Persia, in the course of a state visit to Britain. Though the event lasted some three weeks and was generously reported in the national press little is known of the details of this private visit, except for a photograph showing His Majesty and entourage with their hosts and distinguished guests assembled on the lawn. It has to be presumed, however, that Nasir-ad-Din was by now better acquainted with Western customs than had seemed to be so on the occasion of his earlier visit in 1873. With reference to this event George Leveson Gower described how the Shah visited certain great country houses, 'but owing to his disregard of European moral conventions and to the uncleanly habits of his suite, these were not a success. Amongst other places he went to Ashridge, and at the end of his visit presented Brownlow with a huge and appallingly bad marble bust of himself, which was relegated to a dark and remote corner'.[16] It is sad, nevertheless, to recall that he met his death by assassination in 1896 after a reign of 48 years.

At a house-party in the summer of 1890 the future Viceroy of India was to meet his bride-to-be. A beautiful and charming American, Mary Leiter, had recently arrived in London and had been invited to Ashridge by Lady Brownlow. It was her first

Mansion Ho.

Nicholson, Household expenses		2800 - 0 - 0
Ice house, filling & Carting &c.		13 - 9 - 6
Insurance	Mansion 96 . 5 - 0 Pictures 21 . 0 - 0	117 - 5 - 0
Waitingroom Berk^d Station	Gas & Coke	8 - 11 - 0
	Cleaning do.	5 - 4 - 0
Carriage of Iron for Stove [?] Smith		3 - 3 - 0
Coal for — do.		7 . 12 - 0
Burning charcoal, Grubbing roots & splitting do.		126 - 2 - 11
Postman; Harness Rep^g		2 - 9 - 7
Cow yard	Straw for thatching Farm Stack	10 - 5 - 0
	Mowing do.	13 . 9 - 4
	Carting Hay for do.	2 - 12 . 5
Food for Poultry.		50 - 11 . 4
attendance on do.		32 . 16 . 4
Cleaning Chancel Gaddesden Church		2 - 12 - 0
Potatoes		28 - 7 . 0
Letter Bags (Making up)		10 - 0 - 0
Poultry troughs, cutting oak bells [?]		0 . 16 . 5
Beef at Xmas		106 . 11 . 4
Wages & Salaries.		
Revd C. G. Lane		50 - 0 - 0
Etheridge	attendance	109 . 4 - 0
	Lodgings.	26 . 0 . 0
Watchmen		86 . 8 - 0
Sunday do.		3 - 19 . 6
Postman		43 . 4 - 0
Artificers		125 . 13 - 0
		3799 - 7 . 7

R^d for Stocking [?] £28 . 15 . 4.

Fig. 8. Extract from Estate accounts, 1869

introduction to an English country house and to that singularly English gathering, the house-party, and she was quite captivated:

> We were about thirty in the house which is gorgeous beyond description . . . black iron, brass and stone stairways, the ballroom Italian marble and Van Dycks and Rubens, the dining room panelled in gorgeous oak and brocade. Lady Brownlow is one of the most noble women. I can only compare her position with Mrs. J. J. Astor's in New York. She has the beauty of an Empress . . .[17]

One of the guests was George Curzon, later the 1st Marquess Curzon of Kedleston, 11 years older than Mary and already marked out for high office by his unrivalled experience of foreign countries, especially those of the East, and by his parliamentary gifts. Not for the first time did the Ashridge rose-garden give its silent blessing to budding romance. The friendship blossomed: they became engaged three years later and were married in 1895. Four years later came Lord Curzon's appointment to India, and this self-assured young American, who had made such an impression on London, proudly arrived with her husband in Delhi as Vicereine of the vast empire of India.

It would be a mistake to assume from such a list of prominent and interesting visitors that life at Ashridge was no more than a great and continuous social whirl. Nothing could be more wrong. These were occasional and pleasurable interludes over a long period in the lives of two people who took life very seriously, both concerned more with what they could do for others rather than for themselves. Relatives were very frequently of the company, such as Harry and Nina Cust, Lady Gertrude Pembroke, Alfred Talbot and his brother Sir Reginald Talbot, governor of Victoria, Australia, with his wife Margaret, a very talented pianist, and these were as much at home at Ashridge as anywhere. Life was lived generally on a high plane. Morning prayers, read in the chapel by Lord Brownlow after breakfast, would begin the day. Conversation, discussion of literature or politics, music, the reading aloud of poetry, walking—whatever was engaged in was done with a zest that was unforced, yet the house was large enough for contemplation and privacy if the mood called for it. A small army of servants kept the wheels turning smoothly, the domestic staff being presided over in Edwardian times by an enormous old housekeeper, Mrs. Potter, who bred King Charles spaniels. Private theatricals were a popular form of entertainment for which a well-equipped little theatre existed at the end of the orangery. On special occasions a visiting company would perform in the open air, such as when Mr. Ben Greet and his company performed *As You Like It* in the summer of 1896. The real highlight of the summer programme, however, was the annual village flower show, an event eagerly anticipated by everyone, because it brought all together in a common enjoyment. The relationship of the Brownlows to Little Gaddesden and the other villages of the estate was essentially a paternalistic one, the style of which is unlikely to be seen again. It is not possible, nor is it within the scope of this book, to dwell on aspects of life in the villages. For this the reader could not do better than turn to the writings of Vicars Bell, especially *Little Gaddesden: the story of an English village,*[18] though regrettably this is now out of print.

Looking back over Lord Brownlow's long and useful life, one sees that his public duties kept him well occupied in the House of Lords or in county affairs in Lincolnshire, and to a much lesser extent in Hertfordshire. He had already been made an Ecclesiastical Commissioner in 1882. From 1885 he began to be more involved in the national scene, becoming Parliamentary Secretary to the Local Government Board. He was made a privy councillor in 1887 when he became Paymaster General in Lord Salisbury's Conservative government. Two years later he was appointed Under Secretary of State for War, and remained so until Mr. Gladstone's Liberals regained power in 1892, but after the Conservatives came back in 1895 Lord Brownlow did not again hold any office in government. He had long been active in the Volunteer Forces, which had been revived in the 1860s, and he remained closely associated with the movement all his life, commanding the Home Counties Brigade and later the Bedfordshire Volunteer Infantry Brigade for 14 years, and serving as Volunteer A.D.C. to three monarchs. As a keen shot he was President of the National Rifle Association for many years.

On the sporting side the shooting parties at Ashridge were famous, drawing prominent guests over the years including King Edward VII and King George V, and most of the royal dukes, though in their later years both Lord and Lady Brownlow came to regard such parties as social obligations rather than intrinsic pleasures. About fifty keepers, wearing a green livery with silver buttons bearing the earl's crest, were employed on the various parts of the estate in Little Gaddesden, Ringshall, Aldbury, Dagnall and Studham, under a head keeper and a deputy. The beaters were mostly workers on the estate, and these were dressed in white overall coats and wore red caps. A glance at the earl's game book for 1912 shows that over a three-day shoot it was not uncommon for a party to claim up to 1,500 pheasants alone.

Lord Brownlow's artistic inclinations and considerable knowledge, most surely derived from his mother, led to his appointment in 1897 as a Trustee of the National Gallery. His personal talents lay in the direction of wood carving, marquetry and painting on glass, and as he became older he preferred the quiet of his studio. His other great interest was ornithology, and with his long stride he would cover many miles in the ideal country around Ashridge in search of some particular species of bird life.

It became obvious to him that the control of two such large estates as Ashridge and Belton, and of extensive lands in Shropshire, was a consuming task which could not be combined with a serious political career, which is why he did not seek further office. In a national valuation return in 1883 his holdings were shown as being in excess of 58,000 acres, bringing an annual income of £86,426. These lands were spread through the counties of Shropshire, Lincoln, Buckingham, Bedford and Hertford; and, in the north, Durham, the North Riding, Berwick and also in Flint. He would spend as much time as possible at Belton, for the greater ease of carrying out his duties as Lord Lieutenant, but it was the proximity of Ashridge to London that made this and his London home in Carlton House Terrace his principal residences. If there was any conflict of attachment it was that Lord Brownlow's heart was more in Belton, the original family home, whereas Lady Brownlow's lay undeniably in Ashridge.

In the opening years of the new century rising German militarism and the growth of her naval power led to a total review of Britain's military preparedness. Reforms of the Army included the amalgamation of the County Yeomanry and Volunteer units into a new Territorial Association. As a stalwart supporter of the Volunteers, and as a past Under Secretary of State for War, Lord Brownlow fully understood the need for change and gave the movement all his practical support; and Ashridge and Belton parks were made available as training areas for the new T.A. units. The experience of the Boer Wars had also shown a need to co-ordinate the work of the various county nursing societies, and in 1905 the British Red Cross Society was formed primarily to provide a better organisation of the back-up medical services that the Army at home would need, especially in the event of an invasion. Although she was never keen to accept public office Lady Brownlow was persuaded to become President of the Lincolnshire branch. It was not surprising that when war came accommodation at Ashridge was given over for a Ministry of Health hospital and convalescent home, under the control of the St. Albans hospital, and that the unit was staffed mostly by members of the British Red Cross. A small plaque on the wall of the Brownlow Hall commemorates this event. One of the notable visitors to Ashridge in 1914 was Field Marshal Lord Kitchener who was staying nearby at Champneys, Tring, and who drove over with his sister for the day to call on his friends. During tea on the loggia outside the library a telegram was handed to him. He read it in silence and put it in his pocket, and then rising, said to his hostess, 'Lady Brownlow, I am sorry but I must leave at once. Do not worry, I will take care of you'. He gave no explanation, merely adding, 'You will know why tomorrow'.[19] He had been summoned back urgently to the War Office. The date was 3 August and on the following morning war with Germany was declared. The Bedfordshire Volunteers at once moved out of Ashridge park, where they were encamped under the command of Colonel Wheatley, but it was not very long before more camps were established and the park and common and the villages around were echoing to the bustle of the Inns of Court O.T.C. on their exercises. Belton park also became a training centre for the 11th (Northern) and 30th Divisions, and as many as eighteen thousand men were in camp there at one period.

As the war proceeded with its appalling casualties in France and Belgium, the pressure of Lady Brownlow's welfare work for the men encamped at Belton, coupled with her vivid imagination and extreme sensitivity to the sufferings of war, told on her health. The strain became too much, and after a long period of illness she died at her London home on 16 March 1917, and was buried at Belton on 21 March. A long life of unceasing usefulness and care for others had come to an end, and the sadness of the event was not confined to her personal circle, for there was hardly an inhabitant of the villages of the great estates who did not feel the loss of a friend. After a totally happy marriage lasting 49 years Lord Brownlow's grief was profound. Adelaide had been in the truest sense 'the very light of his dwelling'. He was already mourning the death only a few weeks earlier of his cousin and heir-presumptive, Harry Cust, and it was said by his friends that he was never quite the same man again. As soon as peace was declared he began to take stock of his affairs. He set in hand the sale of most of his Shropshire lands and other smaller holdings, making it relatively easy for his tenants to acquire their freeholds by private treaty. Early in March 1921 he attended the first peace-time investiture of King George V, when he was invested as a Knight Grand Cross of the Royal Victorian Order for his services during the war. He returned to Belton, apparently well, but suffered a heart attack; after an illness of only a few days he died on 17 March and was buried beside his wife. He was in his 77th year.

Adelbert Brownlow was a man of considerable stature, not only physically, but in all ways, yet there was nothing flamboyant about him. His upright figure was admirably caught in a cartoon portrait of him when *Vanity Fair* featured him in is 'Man of the Day' series in 1913. In himself he was modest, rather retiring and good-humoured; he never sought the headlines, shunning superficial contacts, but never shirking duties. In many ways he had not fully moved out of the Victorian age in which he had lived the most active part of his life. He was certainly no great innovator, no spectacular pioneer. Such an obvious improvement as the installation of electricity was denied to Ashridge because he had never been convinced that it was not dangerous. As a result two men had to be employed constantly on trimming and cleaning the 46 oil lamps that were needed around the house; and guests, with or without tiaras, lighted themselves up the great staircase and along the dark corridors to their bedrooms with a candle. There a can of water and a hip bath in front of the fire had to suffice for most people, as even at the time of his death there were only two proper bathrooms in this vast home. Similarly in agricultural matters and practices he was content to rely on the good sense of his tenant farmers, as he was entitled to do, and it was his agent, Colonel William Wheatley, who introduced deep ploughing by steam engine to the Ashridge farms. Through all of this, however, comes the picture of a man whose life had been of great worth, upholding standards of personal living and public service that should stand as a model. His death brought to an end an era of family life at Ashridge which had spanned over three hundred years. No previous occupants had enriched Ashridge more with grace and elegance or furnished a better example of two lives of service to others founded upon deeply rooted spiritual values. Old Thomas Egerton could not have predicted the course of events during the three centuries after his death, but he would have approved wholeheartedly of the last private owners of the estate which he had had the good sense to acquire in 1604.

* * * * *

When Earl Brownlow's will was proved, showing a personal fortune of about one and a half million pounds, the main provisions directed that the Ashridge estates and all lands and premises in the counties of Hertford, Buckingham and Bedford were to be sold to pay off any mortgages and expenses. Belton and the estate in Lincolnshire, and any remaining in Salop and Flint, together with the jewels, plate, pictures, furniture and the residue were left to his successor. Since there were no children of the marriage the earldom was extinguished and the successor to the baronetcy was Lord Brownlow's second cousin, Major Aldelbert Salusbury Cockayne Cust, a descendant of the second son of the 1st Baron Brownlow, and younger brother of Harry Cust, who died in 1917. He entered the Army from Eton and served in the Somerset Light Infantry. Later he was organising secretary of the Royal National Lifeboat Institution, but in 1914 he rejoined the Army in the Provost Marshal's Branch. After the war he was a director of Flax Production at the Board of Agriculture and Fisheries. To him and his fellow trustees fell the task of carrying out the earl's directions for the sale of Ashridge, a process that had started but was not completed at the date of of his death on 19 April 1927. He was succeeded as 6th Baron by his only son, Peregrine Francis Adelbert Cust, who had followed family tradition and entered the Army after Eton and Sandhurst, joining the Grenadier Guards. His brief period of active service in France was, he once claimed, the shortest on record. Aged only 19 he arrived at the front line on the evening of 10 November 1918 and hostilities ceased the next morning at 11 a.m. After leaving the Army he built up large business interests in the West Indies. He was a close personal friend of the Prince of Wales and became a personal Lord-in-Waiting to him as King Edward VIII during his brief reign. He was one of the few confidants who shared the king's inner anxieties during the abdication crisis, and escorted the then Mrs. Wallis Simpson (later Duchess of Windsor) when she left England for France. When war came in 1939 Lord Brownlow offered his services to the Royal Air Force and was for a time Parliamentary Private Secretary to Lord Beaverbrook at the Ministry of Aircraft Production: he also held various staff appointments. Afterwards he resumed his business interests in Jamaica and Grenada, and again became Lord Lieutenant of Lincolnshire, completing in all 14 years in that office. He died in 1978 and was succeeded by his son by his first wife, Edward John Peregrine Cust, the present 7th Baron Brownlow.

Chapter Fourteen

A CHANGE OF GUARDIANSHIP

AS MAY EASILY BE APPRECIATED the sale of Ashridge was not accomplished quickly. The first announcement was that Christie's would sell the important decorative pieces and furniture, and also the pictures, in May 1923. Among the lots was one consisting of relics of Princess Elizabeth—embroideries, a small table cover, a white satin cap, shoes, a pair of brushes covered in red velvet, and 18 pieces, 'some of ye child bed things made when Queen Mary was thought to be with child'. These did not reach the reserve price of 380 guineas and were withdrawn. The furniture, porcelain and objets d'art, including two Louis XV vases of Chinese mazarin blue porcelain fetched £22,472. Of the pictures, Cuyp's 'The Mass at Dordrecht' was bought by Lord Duveen for £18,375, and Bellini's 'Adoration of the Shepherds' brought £4,410.

The sale of the house and estate was announced on 5 October 1925. National interest and local emotions were immediately aroused. What was going to be the fate of one of the finest estates in the country? During the years following the war a huge demand had grown for more dwelling houses, together with a desire and a determination on the part of those who could afford to do so to leave the centre and crowded suburbs of London and settle themselves in the more attractive Home Counties. Good schools existed in and within reach of Berkhamsted. Train services were tolerable and would hopefully get better. Roads were beginning to improve as the mass-produced cars of Henry Ford, William Morris and Herbert Austin brought a new and independent means of travel within reach of thousands. The stark realisation that acre upon acre of magnificent trees might be felled for timber, that woodlands which for years had provided a haven of popular recreation for town dwellers and local residents alike might be about to be sacrificed to the whims of speculative builders bore heavily on the minds of those most closely affected. If any action were possible it had to be taken quickly, as the Trustees were due to meet to consider an offer for outright purchase of the estate and mansion by a syndicate. At the same time an anonymous offer of £20,000 had been received to enable part of the land to be bought for the National Trust.

The action started with a letter to *The Times* on Friday, 9 October from Mrs. Constance Sitwell, herself a Talbot, deploring the threat to Ashridge. Later, in her charmingly evocative book, *Bounteous Days,*[1] she described the events of the following week-end, which she was spending with Miss Bridget Talbot at Little Gaddesden House. Together, worrying about the possible outcome of the sale, they decided that an attempt must be made at a high level to save Ashridge, and with the aid of a neighbour, Mr. Jim Crauford, they drafted a letter appealing for funds, which they hoped might be signed by the prime minister. Miss Talbot, a cousin of the late Countess Brownlow, was a young woman of great determination and drive with many useful political connections. She undertook to present the letter. On the Monday morning, taking an early train and pausing only at Euston to acquaint her brother, Humphrey Talbot, one of the trustees, with the details of their plan, she hurried off to Downing Street and later in the day was able to meet Mr. Baldwin, who promised his support. The prime minister consulted senior colleagues and friends, and the subject even figured on the Cabinet agenda during that week. Meanwhile, other letters were appearing in *The Times,* but on 20 October there was printed one over the signature of Stanley Baldwin, James Ramsay Macdonald, Lord Grey of Fallodon (Vice President of the National Trust) and Lord Asquith, expressing strong sympathy for proposals to try to acquire Ashridge park for the National Trust, and appealing urgently for funds as only three weeks were left in which to raise the money. Lord Brownlow was invited to call at Downing Street, and as a result the trustees agreed to defer for a short time their decision on the offer received in order to see if the appeal would succeed in raising sufficient funds.

Scarcely a day passed during the next month without *The Times* carrying either editorial comments, letters or photographs about Ashridge. As the response to the appeal mounted, frequent lists of subscribers were published. By the middle of November the total was standing at over £40,000, and the National Trust was able to announce that negotiations had been successfully completed to reserve a considerable part of the land for purchase for the nation. Three months afterwards it was confirmed that the Trust would purchase 1,700 acres, and *The Times* expressed enthusiasm for and satisfaction at this outcome. A further 165 acres, including Frithsden Beeches, were acquired about a year later. The very small match applied by the little action group had been sufficient to start a national fire of enthusiasm and practical support, and Miss Bridget Talbot and her friends deserve to be remembered for it with gratitude.

In November 1927 it was reported that Ashridge had been sold to a Mr. E. C. Fairweather and would be immediately offered for resale in small and large blocks. In the following May the house and 1,200 acres were bought by Mr. Thomas Place, and were immediately put on the market again by John D. Wood & Co. of Mount Street, London. At about the same time Hampton & Sons, who had negotiated the sale to Mr. Fairweather, announced that in associated sales 8,700 acres had already changed hands in transactions involving about a quarter of a million pounds. There still remained to be sold one other important asset. The 11 windows of the chapel were of stained glass of 16th-century German origin. For a long time they had been acknowledged by experts to be both rare and beautiful. The glass was purchased by the 7th Earl of Bridgewater *c.* 1811 and was fitted into place over the next 20 years. Most of it had come originally from the Abbey of Steinfeld in the Eiffel district of Germany, and had been imported into Norwich by an antiquarian bookseller named Stevenson acting in collaboration with a German merchant named Christian Hamp.[2] The windows were removed and offered for sale by Sotheby's in July 1928, where they brought £27,000 in a matter of minutes. The report of the sale was followed a few days later by a statement from the Victoria and Albert Museum that they had received a munificent gift of the glass from a donor who wished to remain anonymous.

By far the most significant news about the future of Ashridge came on 14 June 1928 when it was disclosed that the house and 80 acres had been purchased to be presented to the Conservative Party for an educational and political training centre, thus ensuring the preservation of the mansion and the beautiful gardens.[3] Further land was acquired later. For the background to this development it is necessary to look behind the scenes at the activities and influence of the then M.P. for Hemel Hemstead, in whose constituency Ashridge lay. In 1917 J. C. C. Davidson (later Viscount Davidson) was Private Secretary to Andrew Bonar Law at the Exchequer, and a warm friendship developed between the two men. Bonar Law had entered parliament in 1900 at the age of 45 with a considerable reputation as a businessman in the iron trade in Glasgow. He became leader of the Conservatives in 1911, in succession to A. J. Balfour, during the long period of Liberal government before the 1914–1918 war. He joined Lloyd George's war cabinet and was also in the following Coalition Government of 1918–1921. In 1921 failing health obliged him to resign the leadership, but on the fall of the Coalition in 1922 Law was persuaded to resume the leadership, and he became prime minister, albeit with some reluctance on account of his health. In the following year the throat cancer from which he was suffering brought about his death. Although opinions may have varied about his qualities as a statesman and parliamentarian, his reputation as a skilled debater, and his mastery of detail, his memory for facts, and ability to present a clear case was considerable, and his personal integrity and modesty have never been disputed.[4]

When Bonar Law resigned the leadership in 1921, J. C. C. Davidson became Parliamentary Private Secretary to Stanley Baldwin at the Board of Trade. He remained his P.P.S. when Baldwin became prime minster, but was later given the post of Chancellor of the Duchy of Lancaster. His esteem in the eyes of the Party hierarchy was rising rapidly. His respect for Bonar Law made him enthusiastic to see a suitable memorable created for him, and an opportunity was to arise before very long. In his *Memoirs*[5] Lord Davidson related how he learnt of the intention to sell Ashridge in 1924 (the sale was not announced until October 1925), and he decided that since it was in his constituency some effort should be made to save at least a part of the park. He stated that it was he who persuaded Baldwin, Macdonald, and the Lords Grey and Asquith to sign the appeal letter to *The Times,* adding, 'I did not appear very much in the publicity but preferred to work in the background'.

Throughout a distinguished career this preference for working behind the scenes was characteristic. He was a skilful negotiator with a clever sense of appropriate timing. In 1927 Davidson became Chairman of the Conservative Party and set himself the primary task of raising funds without blatant recourse to the sale of political honours, and of developing a system of political education in every constituency. At this time the party had a training centre at the Philip Stott College, near Northampton, but this was not entirely satisfactory as it was too small. The fact that Ashridge was now to go on the market was a challenge and an opportunity which he took up with vigour. He gained the generous support of Mr. Urban Broughton, and as a result Ashridge House was purchased and presented to the party. The gift of a fine house and grounds nearer to London was one thing, but it needed altering, equipping, staffing and a sufficient endowment for it to be run. John Davidson arranged for an immediate loan to start the work, and in the period from 1927–9 he worked very hard to persuade a small number of wealthy men, including Lord Inchcape and Sir Edward (later Lord) Brotherton to make generous contributions. He managed to raise more than £200,000 for an Ashridge endowment fund, and in the same period such was his success that he raised over one million pounds for his party.

The identity of the donor of Ashridge was disclosed in *The Times* of 14 August 1928 as Mr. Urban Hanlon Broughton, formerly M.P. for Preston. The objects of the gift as then stated were 'to preserve for the nation a historic site and beautiful building, and to establish a centre where all grades of Conservatives can find a curriculum suited to their requirements, and to give enjoyment to the public by admitting it to the gardens once a week'. Urban Broughton's career as a civil engineer had taken him to the United States in 1887 at the age of 30, where he worked in mining and railways and eventually in financial management. He became President of the National Copper Bank of New York, and President and

Director of the Utah Consolidated Mining Company. He came back to England in 1912, entered parliament in 1915 under the leadership of Bonar Law, and represented Preston until 1918. Had he lived he would have been granted a baronetcy for his public services, but his death on 30 January 1929 prevented this. The circumstances at the opening of the year 1929 were unusual on account of the serious illness of King George V, and the New Year's Honours List was not published until 1 March. In that list the honour to have been conferred on the donor of Ashridge was conferred on his son, Urban Huttleston Rogers Broughton, 'in consideration of the public, political and philanthropic services of his father, Urban Hanlon Broughton, whose elevation to the Peerage would have been recommended to His Majesty but for his death on 30 January 1929'. The new baron took the title of Baron Fairhaven of Lode, Cambridgeshire, and his mother was granted the style and title of a baron's widow.

In December 1929 a memorial to Urban Broughton was unveiled in the Ashridge chapel by Mr. Baldwin. It is a mural tablet, placed above the entrance doors, bearing the coat of arms of the Fairhaven family and a figure of the Madonna and Child. Amber glass in the window opposite illuminates it with a rich warm glow. The remaining windows of pale green glass were presented by the family, and replaced the plain glass installed after the stained glass had been removed. A noted art collector and the owner of a racing stud, Lord Fairhaven became a founder governor of the college and he made many generous gifts to Ashridge. When he died his home at Anglesey Abbey, near Cambridge, together with his fine art collection, was bequeathed to the National Trust. In 1961, when it was realised that the title would die out because Lord Fairhaven was a bachelor, the baronetcy was granted to him again, but this time with remainder to his brother, Major Henry Rogers Broughton, who succeeded him as 2nd Baron in 1966.

A Bonar Law Memorial Trust was established with the object of bringing the new college into existence. Mr. Stanley Baldwin became the first chairman, and the college was formally opened on 1 July 1929 in the presence of over one thousand people. Mr. Davidson presided and the title deeds were handed over to Mr. Baldwin by Lord Fairhaven. The scene was thus set for the new college to embark on its task, the course of which has been narrated in the opening chapter.

As for the remaining land of the Ashridge estate, much of this lay on the fringe of the park and was sold mainly for building sites. Land was reserved for a golf course, which enjoys a setting as fine as could be desired anywhere. The total effect of the breaking up of the estate was to change the character of the village of Little Gaddesden quite markedly. As estate cottages were sold they were purchased mostly for improvement or enlargement by 'incomers'. The sizes of the new houses erected on the outer fringes were governed by the terms of the sale, and thus new owners tended to be either persons retired from business carried on far outside the village, or those whose occupations took them daily to London or the nearer large centres. One consequence of this was that new council cottages had to be built for village people, thereby extending along the ridge a village already over-long. Time has worked its compromises, however, and if the village has acquired new characteristics its capacity to survive change is undiminished because its roots are deep, dating back to a church founded here—though not the present building—probably in the 12th century, many years before the Bonhommes came to Ashridge.

Chapter Fifteen

THE MANSION AND GARDENS

The Old House

A DISADVANTAGE to a full appreciation of Ashridge's remoter past is the absence of a ground plan of the monastic buildings. The earliest located plan is contained in a survey map of the estate, made for the 3rd Duke of Bridgewater by George Grey in 1762,[1] which shows the outline of the buildings of that date on a scale too small for accurate identification (Pl. 5). Measurements of some parts of the monastery were included in the report of an inquisition into the value of Ashridge in 1575, shortly before Queen Elizabeth parted with it.[2] Early in the 18th century the antiquarian, Brown Willis, visited the house and recorded the dimensions of many of the ruins, which he conveyed to Scroop, 1st Duke, in a letter dated 23 September 1723.[3] More recently some plans have come to light, submitted to the 3rd Duke and the 7th Earl between 1800 and 1806 as designs for a new mansion, which indicate the positions of some remains (mainly the Great Hall and the Porter's Lodge) close to the proposed new building. Taken together with other evidences approximate positions can be deduced or guessed, but much more work is required before any degree of accuracy can be claimed.

The only features remaining are the **Undercroft**, loosely known as the crypt, with its octagonal pillars and ribbed, vaulted roof. This was under the Great Hall of the monastery, which formed part of the 17th-century buildings. It extends in today's terms beneath the conference room and the common room, the former drawing and dining rooms, from mid-point to mid-point. The **Well**, formerly enclosed within an 'engine house', is situated beneath the chancel of the chapel. The original **Monks' Barn** forms the eastern end of the enlarged

Wyatville barn of 1821, and is identified by the fine roof timbers inside. A small length of stone, flint and clunch wall is preserved behind the Brownlow Hall.

The 1575 report makes it evident that the conventual church was a large building 132ft. in length, excluding the steeple tower. It is likely to have appeared in plan as suggested in Fig. 9, and probably stood just south of the present chapel. The **Dorter House** was 108ft. long and 34ft. in breadth.

A **Porter's Lodge**, which stood a little to the north of the present main entrance, survived with alterations, and was occupied until it was pulled down in 1816 to make way for Wyatville's east wing.[4] The **Great Hall** was 64ft. long by 24ft. across.[5] The **Library** measured 33ft. by 23ft., and since it was above the chapter house it may be assumed that the latter was of the same dimensions. The values assigned to the buildings by the assessors in 1575, as if they were to be sold as materials only, are of interest, as shown by the following selection:

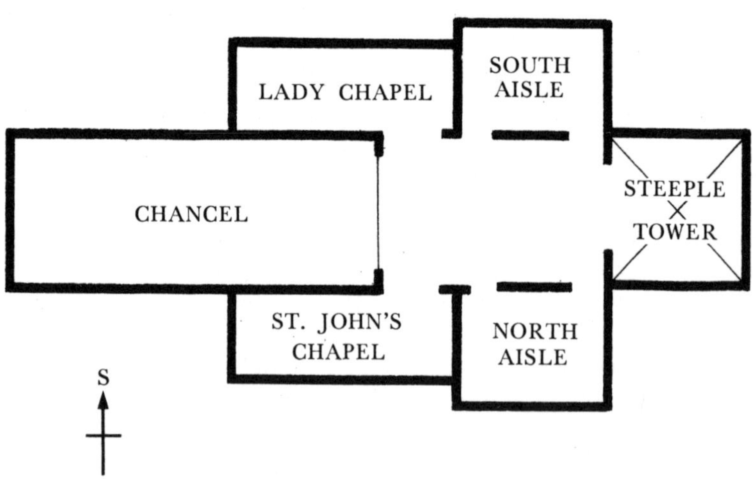

Scale: 1in. = 40ft.

Fig. 9. Notional plan of the conventual church of St. Mary the Virgin

	£	s.	d.
The Church	151	0	0
The Dorter House	50	0	0
The Great Hall	30	0	0
The Porter's Lodge	8	6	8
The Boiling House and Fish House	6	8	4
The Dry Larder	1	10	0
The Kitchen	3	6	8
The Barn	20	0	0
The Well House	7	0	0

In one of the several woods, Southwood, 100 acres of thinly-planted beech about seventy years old was valued at 11s. per acre. The total acreage of the estate was then about six hundred, including about three hundred acres of 'common woods', and was valued at £166 16s. 0d.

The report also shows that the tenants of Gaddesden Manor owed service to Ashridge amounting to:

18 men for one day in Autumn
1 man for ½ day in Autumn
3 chickens at Christmas.

and from Frithsden:

25 men for one day in Autumn
1 man for ½ day in Autumn
20 hens at Christmas
100 eggs at Easter.

The quarry at Totternhoe, which supplied most of the stone from which the monastery was built, and which at the beginning of the 19th century was to provide stone facing for the new mansion, was assessed as having little or no value.

An early glimpse of part of the house is given us by Thomas Baskerville, to whose visit in 1681 reference has already been made. He described the hall as 'a noble room in which some good horses which my lord hath been owner of, are drawn in full proportion'. 'From hence', he continues, 'at the lower end you descend into the buttery or pantry, being a fair room vaulted over and adorned with many heads and horns of stags or red deer which hath been killed out of my lord's park'. What appears to have made an even greater impression, however, were the beer cellars. '. . . In that for beer was a range of vessels bound with iron hoops, each vessel containing the quantity of two pipes; and in some peculiar rooms made on purpose for them, for here was but one great vessel in a room, were some which might vie with the Prince Heidelburg's tun, they look so big upon you. They told me that to brew one of these vessels of liquor they put in about six pounds' worth of hops, when hops were at 1s. 6d. and 2s. or 2s. 6d. a pound'. He also makes a passing reference to the 'fine cloister, remarkable for this, because my lord will not have it blurred out, for having in paint upon the walls some scripture and monkish stories'.[6]

It is not until 1790 that a fairly full account of the old house is found in *The Topographer*,[7] with some description of the buildings, some of which had already been pulled down on the orders of the 3rd Duke:

> The front of this ancient building is still enclosed within a Court, to which the entrance was thro' a handsome old gateway formerly the Porter's Lodge, but large enough to contain several comfortable apartments . . . As soon as we are in the Court we have a full view of the principal Front . . . Along the middle part run the seven high Gothic windows of the hall. On each side are wings, which project a little, and have each a large embattled window; and beyond these extend other wings, evidently of a later erection, having each the zig-zag ends of Q. Elizabeth's or James I's reign.
>
> We enter through a porch into the passage, called in a college the *Screens* [i.e. at the West end] . . . on the one side [West] is the Buttery-hatch; on the other, the two doors into the Hall, which was part of the Abbey itself. It is a noble-sized room, very lofty, with a wooden coved fret-work roof. It is crowded with stags horns, and a large gallery over the Screens . . . Returning to the Screens we pass through into the Cloisters, a wonderful curiosity, which were also a part of the Abbey itself. These form a quadrangle . . . round the sides was beautifully painted in water colours the history of our Saviour in 40 compartments, of which the greater part are now defaced[8] . . . The damp, probably occasioned by the reservoir of water, which the Cloisters surround, has done much damage. The Church stood in the garden ranging with the Cloisters.

Although this account fixes the position of the Cloisters, over two sides of which ran a gallery containing portraits, and over the other two sides of which were suites of rooms, the author[9] forbears to give any orientation and leaves the reader guessing as to how to interpret the word 'ranging'. He describes most of the rooms as being much injured by the damp and uninhabitable, and continues: 'The House is entirely surrounded by walls, within is the old garden, much neglected and growing wild. Here are large laurels and yew trees grown to an unusual size'. The writer adds a note at this point that several stone coffins had been dug up in the garden in the past, which indicates fairly certainly that the old burial ground was in the vicinity of those yew trees which survive on the south lawn today, probably between these and the eastern boundary (the line of Lime Walk).

The Porter's Lodge was fitted up 'as a temporary habitation for the Duke, at the time the house was intended to be rebuilt, which intention was so near being put into execution that many of the materials were prepared and are still lying at the back of the house . . . Here the Duke lives, when he is at Ashridge'.

The New Mansion

The demolition of most of the old buildings followed two sales of materials and some of the contents in 1800 and 1802,[10] and it was completed about 1804. Among the architects who submitted designs for the new house were William Wilkins, who had built Downing College; James Lewis, who had worked on Cleveland House for the duke; James Cundy, of Pimlico; and also James Wyatt, who had succeeded in 1796 to the office of Surveyor General and Comptroller of the Office of Works. Wyatt's first design suggests that he proposed to incorporate, and presumably restore, the old Great Hall, which would have formed part of the south side of a central court 130ft. square. On the west and north sides were to be the domestic offices and servants' quarters, and on the east, a suite of rooms, a library and a conservatory. The principal rooms and a chapel were planned adjacent to the Great Hall, on its south side. The three sides of the court were to be served by an enclosed covered walk in the style of cloisters. It was an interesting and compact plan, but lacked the boldness and imagination of his second design eventually adopted.

Work on the new building started in 1808, the foundation stone being laid on 25 October by the Countess of Bridgewater.

The original part of the house is symmetrical, with two large bay windows on the south flanking the small loggia with its three arches and oriel window over. The solid square tower over the great staircase at one end and the stepped-back tower and tall spire of the chapel at the other end give the building an impressive outline. The sudden death of James Wyatt in 1813 led to his nephew Jeffry (later Sir Jeffry Wyatville) completing the work to his uncle's design. Ashridge owes its rather sprawling characteristics to the additions made by Wyatville between 1814 and 1821, much on account of the site, one assumes, and a possible reluctance to build more compactly over some of the former monastic remains. Few would deny that his new main porch gave greater importance to the building. The slightly offset east wing, with orangery beyond, provided private quarters for the 7th Earl, following the general trend towards greater privacy which the owners of great houses were beginning to prefer. It enabled the bedrooms of the original building to accommodate house-parties from 30 to 40 guests that were to become such an established feature of 19th-century life. Wyatville completed his uncle's chapel, designing the fine oak woodwork of the screen, the stalls and the organ casing.[11] He added to the administrative offices at the west end, and on the north front he balanced the main porch with a proud arched entrance to the stables area. He enlarged the Monk's Barn, giving it dormer windows and a lantern turret, setting back the south wall to form a covered walk, and using old oak timbers from the building for the supporting pillars. Leaving aside the notable modern additions by Andrew Carden and his associates, the original house is thus a blending of two men's work, which Pevsner describes as 'wholly admirable'.[12]

The new composition, however, did not seem to arouse enthusiasm in that indefatigable traveller and letter-writer, the Prince von Puckler-Muskau,[13] during his tour of some of the great houses of England in 1828–9. 'I must confess', he wrote, after visiting Ashridge, 'that this modern Gothic (castellated) style, which looks so fairy-like on paper, in reality often strikes one as not only tasteless, but even absurd, from its overloaded and incongruous air'. Yet he had to admit that 'the interior of this house certainly has the most striking effect, and may truly be called princely'. Time and the atmosphere have greatly mellowed the glaring white of the new stone, in the same way that erosion has robbed the building of some of its pinnacles and disuse has enabled some chimneys to be removed, so that today it presents a somewhat simpler, softer outline.

The names of some of the craftsmen employed by the Wyatts at Ashridge are known and include Francis Bernasconi, of Buckingham, a plasterer skilled in scagliola work, who was often employed by James Wyatt and later worked for Wyatville at Windsor. He was paid £879 between 1813 and 1815. William Adron, a mason and stone carver, was paid £318 between 1810 and 1813 for chimney pieces. Roger Bradley, a master mason from Hertford, worked at Ashridge from 1815–1817 and received over £2,000. William Pistell, a decorative carver was paid £180, and Edward Wyatt, not a member of the architect's family, received £200 for stone carving.[14]

Controversy has long endured about James Wyatt, the principal architect. In addition to his position as Surveyor General he built up a large private practice, mostly by the neglect of his official duties. He was difficult to contact in his office, being the more likely to be away travelling and visiting his various commissions. If he was not working for the king at Windsor Castle (most of which work his nephew was later to efface), then it might have been Fonthill, Belvoir Castle or Ashridge. He was notoriously a very inefficient manager, particularly of the finances attending his projects, over-spending in an often irresponsible way. He was obviously capable of responding to pressure, but the frequent delays caused by his bouts of laziness and his fondness for a bottle of wine (or something else) were only too well known. Lord Liverpool described him thus: 'Though a man of the most considerable talents as an architect, he was certainly one of the worst Public Servants I can recollect in any office, not I am persuaded from dishonesty, or want of zeal, but from carelessness and from his always choosing to engage in a great deal more business that he was capable of performing'.[15] He could have had a very successful practice, but he died heavily in debt. He met his death in a sad and unfortunate accident. On 4 September 1813 he was travelling back from Wiltshire in the company and carriage of his patron and friend,

Christopher Codrington, on whose house at Dodington he was working. While they were driving at a fast rate, a rider on horseback met the carriage at a place where another carriage or cart stood, which made the passage between the carriages so narrow that the horse and rider were thrown, and their carriage passed over the rump of the horse and was overturned. Wyatt at the time was reading a newspaper and had his hat off. The top of his head struck the roof of the carriage with great violence, and the concussion caused his immediate death.[16]

James Wyatt nevertheless achieved much to his everlasting credit in the revival of the Gothic style. By the application of Gothic features to the Elizabethan style of building he arrived at an elegance of design which established him as the leading exponent of this form, which his nephew was also to follow with great ability. His talent was nowhere better displayed than in his most careful attention to detail, especially in his interiors. This is very marked in the chapel, which derives much from the influence of his restoration of Henry VII's chapel at Westminster, and in the great staircase hall, almost a hundred feet high, in which the fine Westmacott statues[17] perfectly complement the setting. Pugin was later to brand him as 'Wyatt the destroyer' for having removed a good deal of clutter from some of the cathedrals on which he worked, though as at Lichfield,[18] this was often done on the instructions of the Dean and Chapter for quite practical reasons. It seems a pity that so many people are unable to remember anything else about him. In his original work, rather than in his restorations, he demonstrated that Regency Gothic was not governed by absolute or established rules. Those which were to prevail 'were based on the purposes for which buildings were needed and on the constructional problems involved'.[19] At Ashridge he designed a monastic-style house adapted for domestic use, and it remains the most complete of his surviving works.

The reputation of Wyatville rests much less on his work at Ashridge than on his restoration of Windsor Castle for George IV. When the queen moved into the castle from Queen's Lodge she complained that she had moved into 'the coldest house, rooms and passages that ever existed'. Wyatville succeeded in transforming it. 'He found a workhouse, and he left a palace . . . a warm, dry, comfortable and well-appointed house'.[20] He was by one account a 'busy, bustling, vain little man'. When the foundation stone of a new archway was being laid by the king, he asked leave to change his name from Wyatt to Wyatville, to avoid confusion with other members of his family. 'Ville or mutton, call yourself what you like', the king is said to have replied amiably, and the change of name occasioned the following quip in a newspaper:

> Let George, whose restlessness leaves nothing quiet,
> Change, if he must, the good old name of Wyatt;
> But let us hope that their united skill
> Will not make Windsor Castle, 'Wyatt-ville'.[21]

The king signified his approval of Wyatville's endeavour by knighting him in 1829. Jeffry's desire for a distinguishing appellation was perhaps understandable since no less than nine members of the Wyatt family were engaged in architecture, sculpture and associated crafts, and Benjamin, son of James, was one who worked at Ashridge.

A later relative who was shortly to arrive on the scene was Sir Matthew Digby Wyatt (1820–1877), who by comparison with his predecessors must have seemed the embodiment of Victorian respectability. Secretary of the Great Exhibition of 1851 and author of a number of books, Digby Wyatt was responsible between about 1857 and 1863 for extensive remodelling of the interior principal rooms in the Italian style so much beloved by Lady Marian Alford. To the drawing room he gave the two huge marble fireplaces, based on those by Scamozzi (*c.* 1590) in the Doge's Palace, Venice. The supporting figures were modelled and carved by Mark Rogers, junior, who employed some of the estate workers as models. Tall marble columns support the two entrance doors. The painted ceiling, elaborately decorated, has as its centre panel a copy of Guido Reni's 'Aurora' (*c.* 1600), reckoned his finest piece, from the Palazzo Respiglioso in Rome, in which the Goddess of Dawn is depicted preceding the chariot of Apollo. In the dining room he introduced panelling of Austrian walnut, and the ceiling moulding, an intricate design of fruits, was based on that of the Scala d'Oro (Golden Staircase) in the Doge's Palace. In the morning room[22] (later the billiards room, now the Hoskins room) he set a beautiful Italian fireplace, with an inset marble head of a woman, bearing the inscription, *G. Pandiani fece in Milano 1353*; and delicate mouldings ornament the pillars and ceiling. The library was given a new ceiling, while in the garden he built a fernery (now a conservatory). The building now known as Brownlow Hall was erected partly as stables and partly to house carriages. The frescoes now decorating the interior north wall of the hall are almost certainly the work of Dora Carrington, friend of Lytton Strachey, about 1913.[23]

In 1928–9, prior to the opening of the College, Sir Clough Williams-Ellis carried out various alterations, the most prominent being the conversion of the conservatory between the former dining-room and the chapel, in order to create a new dining-room for the College. He enclosed the arcade on the south side with brick (since faced with stone) and set smaller mullioned windows in the arches. The glass roof was removed and replaced with a floor of bedrooms over. In the past 20 years very extensive fabric renovations have been carried out under the direction of Mr. Andrew Carden, the College architect, aided by generous assistance from the Historic Buildings Commission for England. These have included the main tower, the chapel, especially the tower and spire,[24] and repairs to the curtain wall of the orangery. Andrew Carden has also been responsible for major alterations to the Monks' Barn, for the new Lazell Building (1972), and, with his associates, for the new blocks of bedrooms (1977–9) at the west end on either side of the Coronation Walk.

Two special features, not conveniently fitting into the foregoing account, remain to be considered. The chapel organ, a two-manual instrument set in Wyatville's lovely oak casing, was built and installed in 1818 by Thomas Elliott, of Tottenham Court, London, probably with the assistance of William Hill. Apart from maintenance the organ has remained relatively unchanged since it was made, and so it provides a quite rare example of the work of this period. At the time that Ashridge was purchased in 1928 it was in fairly poor condition, and money could not then be made available for more than sufficient repairs to make it serviceable. It suffered some deprivation by the removal of some of its pipes in the course of an overhaul in 1939, but it continued in regular use for the weekly morning services. Interest in the organ was greatly reawakened in 1971 by Eric Pask, organist of Enfield parish church, who appreciated its historic importance; and he has given recitals, made recordings, and written knowledgeably about it.[25] A happy outcome of his interest was brought about two years later when the Bank of England, which has sent a number of its staff to attend courses here, generously made a gift of £200 towards the restoration of the missing ranks of pipes, and additional work has been carried out since. Various well-known organists have given recitals arranged by Alan Johnson, the present college organist, and these have helped to direct attention to this undoubted treasure.

The second feature is not in the chapel, but is situated beneath it. The very deep well, sunk in monastic days through solid chalk, continued to provide Ashridge with water until about 1857. Records indicate that Henry VIII, who visited the monks in 1530, was shown the dogs that were used in the lifting of water (p. 65 ante). By the 17th century horses had replaced the dogs, and Thomas Baskerville described the process:

> The water comes first from a deep well, drawn by a horse in a great wheel, in two barrels or large buckets, a man always standing by as soon as the bucket comes above the collar of the well to empty it into a leaden cistern; and here the ingenuity of the horse must not be forgotten, for as soon as the man lays hold on the bucket to empty it, the horse turns himself in the wheel without forcing or bidding and travels the other way to draw up the next bucket. And so the water, after it hath served all the offices of the house, runs into the pond [i.e., in the old cloisters] where do live some hungry carp, and this is all the fish pools I saw about the house . . .'.[26]

In 1748 Per Kalm, a Swedish naturalist interested in English agricultural methods, visited William Ellis in Little Gaddesden and was brought to see the great wheel of the well, driven by a horse 'which caused the buckets to be lifted up and down'.[27] At the time that James Wyatt concealed the well under his new chapel, new lifting gear was installed, possibly derived from experience of getting water away from the mine at Worsley. This incorporated a three-stage pumping system, with the motive force provided by donkeys or ponies, operating a cast-iron wheel. By 1855 it was apparent that the villagers of Little Gaddesden, Hudnall and Ringshall were sorely distressed by a lack of water, particularly after two successive years of bad drought. Vicars Bell has related how the cottagers were reduced to collecting water from the muddy ponds, which had to be allowed to stand until the mud settled before it was pronounced fit to drink.[28] Lady Marian Alford and her co-guardian of the 2nd Earl Brownlow decided that a new form of water supply was urgent. The Ashridge Water Company was formed, and water from a new covered reservoir, constructed at Ringshall, was brought to a pumping station in Little Gaddesden, from where it was carried in pipes to all the cottages in these villages and to Ashridge House. The accounts show that over £15,000 was spent on the project. The contract was signed in September 1856 and the new supply was working by the end of the following year. From about that time the well appears to have fallen into disuse; gradually the pipework collapsed from lack of maintenance. The well had every appearance of having gone dry, and by the late 1960s the heavy donkey wheel was canted at a dangerous angle because the supporting timbers underneath had rotted. During the winter of 1970–1 the college sponsored an exploration of the well by members of the Watford Underwater Club, led by the late Mr. Len Cook. The pumps and all the damaged pipes were lifted out and several tons of accumulated debris were removed. It was found that this was being supported by a heavy oak platform covering the water surface, and when the platform was lifted water to a depth of 30ft. was revealed and found fit to drink. The measured depth of the shaft is 224ft. Although the lifting mechanism was too badly damaged to be reinstated the donkey wheel was remounted, and the essential parts and pumps have been preserved in a small museum relating to bygones of Ashridge, which has been formed in the Well House.

An unusual aspect of Ashridge was that it used to lie within two counties, the boundary line passing right through the house, with 'that portion of which comprises the principal apartments, together with the chapel and conservatories, being in Buckinghamshire; and the inferior domestic offices and stables, with their accompaniments westward of this line, in Hertfordshire'.[29] Such a division could have curious consequences.

On one occasion, a maintenance worker named Jones died suddenly at work on the Hertfordshire side, and his body was brought into the house, but before the inquest could be held the remains had to be carried back into the county in which the tragedy had occurred.[30] Under a revision of the county boundaries in 1895 the whole of Ashridge was subsequently placed in Hertfordshire.

The Gardens and Grounds

The original Ashridge Park of over four thousand acres comprised land better known today as Berkhamsted Common, Northchurch Common, and the golf course, and land stretching out beyond Ringshall towards Aldbury and Ivinghoe Beacon, much of it now forming the National Trust Ashridge Estate. Some part of it was landscaped by 'Capability' Brown, *c.* 1760, but very little trace of his work remains. The present grounds surrounding the house, mostly to the south of it, extend to about two hundred and thirty-five acres. These are owned by the College and are entirely independent of the National Trust. About forty acres of arable land are let for farming, and the remainder comprises about ninety acres of garden proper, with the rest woodland.

The beautiful gardens present a continuing memorial to the work and ideas of many persons through the years, though pride of place ought to be given perhaps to the first designer, Humphry Repton (1752–1818). A disciple of 'Capability' and already well known for his work at Brighton Pavilion and Russell Square, London, he was invited by the 7th Earl of Bridgewater in 1813 to advise on the layout of the 'pleasure garden' near to the house. 'Of all the subjects on which I have been consulted', he wrote,[31] 'few have excited so much interest in my mind as the Plan for the Gardens'. He admitted that the locality had not much natural beauty, other than a good view of the park away to the south. Its drawbacks were the flatness of the ground and the absence of any water. He therefore decided to exclude the distant landscape and break up the flatness by making new plantations nearer to the house, and by forming a series of small gardens each differing from the other in size and in the nature of the planting. Along with the striking seasonal colour masses provided by the rhododendrons, the roses and the formal bedding, these small gardens remain one of the chief delights for the visitor today.

Repton's plans included a rosarium, the present circular rose garden in front of the dining-room, though without its surrounding hedge; a monks' garden, by restoration of the former monastic garden just a few yards to the south-west of the chapel, and a holy well or conduit to be positioned directly between the present dining-room and the rosarium. The one garden he found that was still being maintained was in front of the early 18th-century house which stood until 1816 where the east wing now is. His plan for this was to extend the garden with a lawn stretching westwards across the broad front of the new mansion, with a parterre in front of the terrace. He was much impressed with the new plants then being imported from America, and one of his ideas was to have a small garden of magnolias and other American plants. Although this did not materialise, magnolias were planted against the south wall of the house and grew to a great height, until the severe frosts of the winter of 1962–3 so badly damaged them that they had to be cut to the ground, from which setback they are only now properly recovering. At the time that Repton made his proposals for Ashridge, Wyatville had not begun the extensions to the house that he was to make between 1814 and 1821. Although work on the new plantings started in 1814 under the earl's head gardener, Hemmings, there was no supervision of the work by Repton, and after his death in 1818 many of his plans were considerably varied as Todd says, 'by the directions of the Earl and Countess of Bridgewater'. The enlargement of the Monks' Barn by Wyatville, with its new covered walk, was combined with a relocation of the **Monks' Garden** in the corner formed by the barn and the line of the old stone wall of the monastery. A new flint wall was built to screen the garden from the dairy yard (later a gardener's yard). In 1972 arches were pierced in this wall to afford a view through to Malcolm Lingard's new rock and water garden for the Lazell Building. Wyatville retained Repton's idea of a holy well and conduit in the Gothic style, but he designed a new one, which he made the centre-piece of the monks' garden. The cast-iron cross or fountain was made by Mr. Parker of Argyle Street,

London, in 1821.[32] When it was overhauled in 1968 it was found to consist of over two hundred separate pieces. Most old photographs of this garden and barn show it to have been heavily planted with herbaceous and climbing plants, in strong contrast with the formal simplicity of today. The design of the four clipped box beds represents arms of the Egerton and Brownlow families, although the patterns are now badly defaced.

The **Italian Garden**, in front of the east wing, though now somewhat altered, is contemporary with the interior alterations in the Italian style made for Lady Alford (*c.* 1857–63), and is depicted in its original detail in a plan of the gardens made by J. Wright in 1871. The **Mount Garden** was designed by Repton to provide a desirable relief in the level site, and much of it is constructed with Hertfordshire pudding-stone brought from Water End.[33] At its west end it looks down on a grotto and small pool, beside which, in a flint-lined tomb lies 'Duke', a favourite horse, which died on 10 December 1857. An underground passage, also lined with local flints hung from an iron frame, leads from here back into the mount garden, on the north side of which is a small rock garden.

The **Sunken Rose Garden** below the south-east corner of the main lawn was constructed by Malcolm Lingard, Ashridge's garden superintendent in 1974–5, and occupies the site of an artificial water feature made in the mid 1870s.[34] This was variously described on old plans as a boating lake or skating pond, and was doubtless the former when it was constructed and later, when it had ceased to retain water satisfactorily, perforce it made a very good skating area in winter. The absence of water had long been a remarkable feature of Ashridge, though there was an old moat at the southern extremity of the garden separating it from the rhododendrons and the arboretum. In about 1873 the architect, George Gilbert Scott (1837–97), submitted a plan[35] for an elegant stone terrace along the entire 700ft. of moat, which would have involved deepening the moat and building new basins at the east and west ends. While no estimate of the cost has been preserved, it must be assumed that it was so high that the more modest compromise of one large square pond had to suffice.

An interesting relic of bygone living is the old **Ice House** on the western boundary, now firmly closed off for safety. It consists of a cavern dug into a bank, with three doors to insulate it against heat, giving on to a pit about thirty-five feet deep, in which ice cut from the local ponds in winter was placed between layers of straw and kept for summer use. In the arched roof of the well was fixed a pulley, and when ice was required for the house a man would be let down in a form of bosun's chair to dig it out and pass it up by bucket.

One of the principal attractions of the grounds is the wealth of evergreen planting, so that at any season of the year there is something of interest for the eye to behold. This is not only a feature of the plantations near the house, but it extends into the **Arboretum**, with its formal avenue of Wellingtonias flanked by high banks of rhododendrons, richly varied in colour. The systematic clearing of unsightly undergrowth in recent years has brought into prominence a wide variety of beech, chestnut, both sweet and wild, oak, lime, sycamore, holm or evergreen oak, Corsican pine, and many other species, while in the spring great drifts of daffodils and snowdrops never fail to gladden the heart.[36]

Every age develops its special fashions in garden planning and ornament, which reflect the social tastes of the times and the ambitions of the owners. The 7th Earl of Bridgewater, who had a soldierly passion for tidiness, maintained a huge force of men to care for his gardens. The 3rd Earl Brownlow employed 36 gardeners before the 1914–18 War, excluding the kitchen gardens at Frithsden. Today, with the aid of modern machinery, Ashridge manages with nine or ten. The gardens are certainly less fussy than in Victorian or Edwardian times. Gone are the statues from their pedestals; gone, too, regretfully, most of the elegant stone vases of classical design. The huge tubs of plants brought from the conservatory on to the terraces for the summer season used to stand like sentries, watching the family and their guests at tea, or playing croquet. These lent to the scene an air of dignity, matching the formality of an age in which to hurry over anything seemed to be rather bad form. If today we have managed to adapt to the faster, more brittle pattern of living, it is reassuring that gardens such as this can still offer an ambience for spiritual refreshment amid natural beauty, and a sense of order and sequence, without which our perspectives might so easily remain in danger of becoming distorted.

There could be a few conclusions more appropriate than the words of old John Skelton:

> 'A pleasanter place than Ashridge is, hard were to find.'

APPENDIX ONE

Election of a Rector of the College of Bonhommes of Ashridge (1529)

To John, Bishop of Lincoln, or his Commissary:

Thomas Hill, co-rector of the College of Bon-hommes ot Asheruge, dioc. Linc. of the Order of St. Augustine, and Nicholas Edington, Helias Bernard, Michael Draper, Robert Ewar, John Hatfield, Robert Hychyn, Richard Gardyner, Thomas Waterhouse, Wm. Knighton, Richard Bedford, Richard Canan, George Stepneth, Roger Bircheley, William Yong, presbyters, fellows of the college, and professed canons of the Order of St. Augustine, and forming the entire Chapter:—

Whereas our College lately became vacant by the death of John Malden our last Rector, whose body we honorably and decently committed to the sepulcre, We, the aforesaid co-rector and president and fellows of the said College unanimously determined to proceed with the election of a Rector on 20 July 1529, in the 2nd Indiction, 6 Pope Clement VII, whereof we gave formal notice to all concerned in the following terms, *Universis sancte Matris Ecclesie filiis* etc., dated in our Chapter house under our Common Seal, 7 July 1529. On which day, 20 July, the Mass of the Holy Ghost having been celebrated at the altar in the Chapel of St. Mary the Virgin in our conventual church, and the bell being rung to summon the chapter, we entered the Chapter house and chanted the Hymn, *Veni, Creator Spiritus* and having invoked the grace of the Holy Spirit, and the statutes of the college having been read, whereby no licence from any patron was required for election, Mr. Henry Morgan, Ll.D. read the chapter *Quia propter,* and declared the various modes of election. We then unanimously chose him as our Director and John Franckishe, not. pub. as actuary and secretary, and Masters Thomas Jakeman, Ll.B. commissary and official of the Archdeaconry of Bucks, Henry White M.A. and Richard Franckishe *utriusque juris Bac.* as witnesses: and after Thomas Hill, as co-rector and president had made protestation that all who had no right to concern in the election should withdraw, we confessed among ourselves, and decided to proceed by way of compromise, and chose Thomas Hill, our co-rector, Nicholas Edington, Helias Bernard, Michael Draper and Robert Ewar as Compromissaries, promising to accept whomsoever they, or the majority of them should elect before 6 o'cl. of that day. Subsequently, at 4 p.m. they announced that they had decided to leave the choice of a Rector to yourself, John, Bishop of Lincoln, our ordinary, and we unanimously agreed to accept whomsoever you should appoint. And we appointed Mr. Henry Morgan, Ll.D. as our proctor and special messenger to act for us in this matter of election and to supplicate that you would grant our request, and nominate and appoint a Rector of our College.

Sealed under our Common Seal, 21 July 1529.

Certified by John Franckishe, lit. notary public, by authority of the Apostolic See, as actuary and clerk.

* * * * *

The messengers delivered this request, but the Bishop refused to act and instructed the College to observe the provisions of their Constitution. They accordingly met in Chapter and elected Thomas Waterhouse, as the following document shows. Both parchments, in Latin, are preserved in the Lincolnshire Archives, and each bears the seal of the College.

Election of the Rector of the College of Bonhommes, Ashridge, 25 July 1529

To the Rt. Revd. Father, John Bishop of Lincoln, or to your Vicar-general or Commissary, We, Thomas Hill, co-rector and president of the Chapter of the house of Bonhommes of Ashridge, of the Order of St. Augustine, Nicholas Edington,

Helias Bernard, Michael Draper, Robert Ewar, John Hatfield, Robert Hychyn, Richard Gardyner, Thomas Waterhouse, William Knighton, Richard Bedford, Richard Canan, Joseph Stepneth, Roger Bircheley, and William Yong, presbyters and fellows of the said College, professed in the Order of St. Augustine, hereby notify and declare that on Friday 23 July inst. A.D. 1529, in the 2nd Indiction, in the 6th year of Pope Clement VII:

We being assembled chapter-wise in our Chapter-house, and forming a complete Chapter, your letter having been received to the effect that it did not please you to undertake the office of electing our future Rector by way of compromise which we had made to you, we withdraw that compromise; and wishing to proceed in the matter of the election lest our College should suffer grievous harm through longer vacancy, we appointed Master Henry Morgan, Ll.D. as Director, John Franckishe, not. pub. as Actuary, and 'dominus' William Ventres, rector of Aldebury, and John Fox, secular chaplain of our College as Witnesses, and for greater expedition we resolved to proceed by way of compromise according to the retracted form; and we nominated the said Henry Morgan, Ll.D. with Helias Bernard and John Hatfield as our compromissaries, giving them powers to chose any member of our College as Rector, providing only that such election be made before mid-day on Saturday, and promising to accept gratefully and unanimously whomsoever they, or the majority of them, should choose.

Subsequently the afore-named Compromissaries with the Actuary and Witnesses betook themselves to a certain chamber adjoining our Chapter-house, and within its outer door, commonly called the *S . . . chamber. There they conferred with one another, and chose 'dominus' Thomas Waterhouse, a professed brother or our order, in priests's orders, of full age and legitimate birth, a man of good morals and virtuous actions, circumspect both in spiritual and temporal matters, and nominated him as Rector of our College. Straightway they returned to the Chapter-house in which the rest of us were assembled, and Master Henry Morgan, in the name of the others, read as follows:—

*not clear.

In Dei Nomine, Amen. Whereas the College of Ashridge, of the Order of St. Augustine was vacant by the death of John Malden late Rector, and it pleased its members to proceed by way of compromise in the matter of the election, and to appoint myself and the two others, named as compromissaries, We therefore, after long consideration of many persons, with the help of Divine grace, gave our votes for Thomas Waterhouse, which I therefore the said Henry Morgan in the name of the two other compromissaries declare elected Rector of the said College.

In this election all the convent, except the said Thomas Waterhouse, concurred, gratefully accepting and confirming it, and gave authority to Henry Morgan, our director, to proclaim it openly; and going apart, with the exception of our Elect and our brothers Michael Draper and Robert Hychyn, we appointed the two last-named as our proctors with full power to act for us in the matter of this election, and we promise to ratify anything done by them.

Leaving then our Chapter-house and entering the Church chanting *Te Deum Laudamus, 'partim per organa partim per humanorum vocum modulamina'*, we placed our Elect prostrate in the Chancel, and the psalm being ended and certain prayers said, Henry Morgan, our director made public announcement of the election of the said Thomas Waterhouse, and John Franckishe, not. pub. certified, and William Ventres, rector of Aldebury, and John Fox, chaplain of our college, testified as witnesses. On the morrow Thomas Waterhouse made his formal assent and acceptance of the office, and the record of it was drawn out in due form by the Notary, under date 25 July 1529.

Seal of the College.

Note.—These transcriptions are reproduced by kind permission of the Lincolnshire Archives Office and the Bishop of Lincoln.

THE OWNERS OF ASHRIDGE, 1604–1921

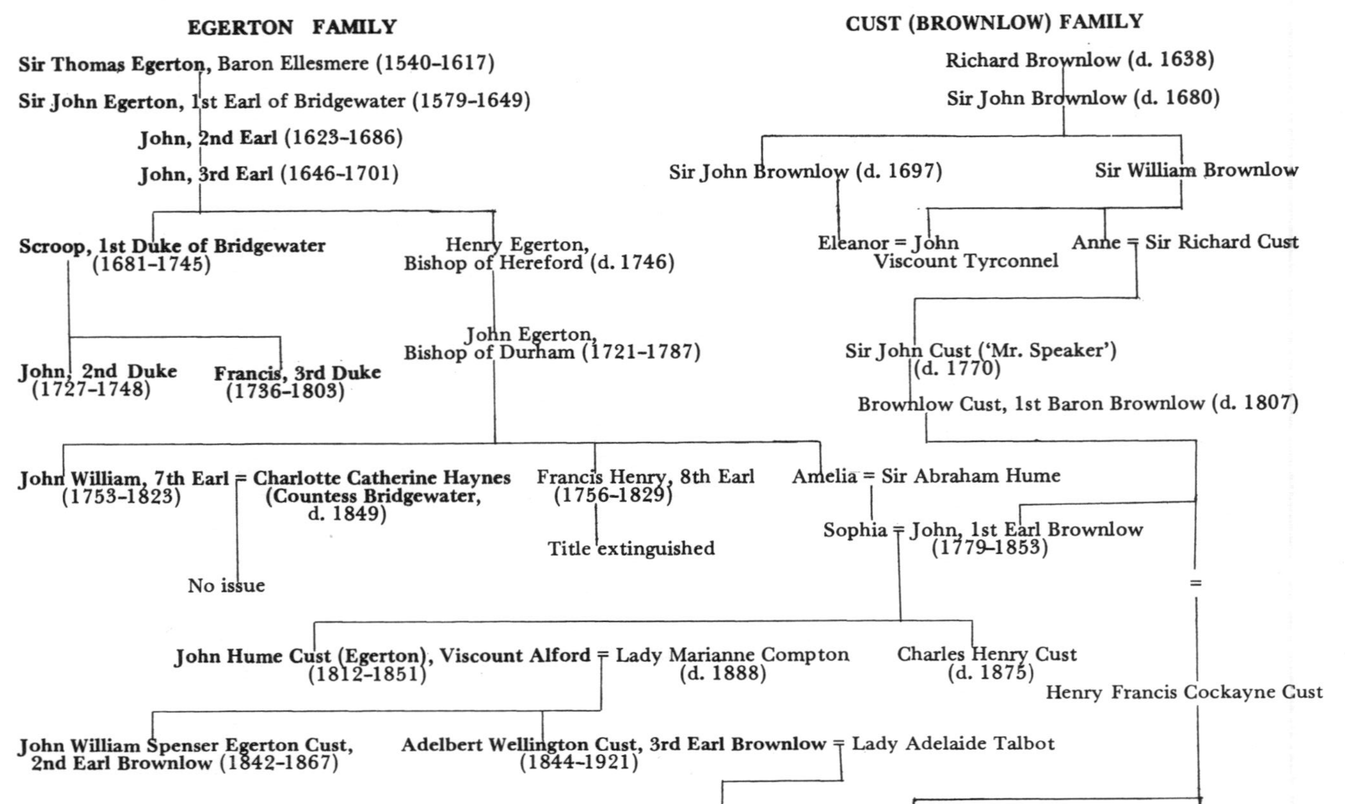

APPENDIX THREE

A NOTE ON CRESTS

The College of Bonhommes

Crest: Gules, on an Altar-Tomb, a Lamb passant guardant Argent, carrying a banner of the last charged with a cross of the first, the dexter fore-foot resting on a Mount Or.

Bridgewater

Crest: On a chapeau Gules, turned up ermine, a lion rampant, also Gules, supporting an arrow, erect Or, headed and feathered Argent.

Motto: 'Sic Donec' (thus until).

Brownlow

Crest: A lion's head erased Sable, gorged with a Collar Paly, wavy of six Argent and Azure.

Motto: 'Esse quam videri' (to be, rather than to seem to be).

NOTES AND REFERENCES

Abbreviations Used in the References

Chauncy: Chauncy, Sir Henry, *Historical antiquities of Hertfordshire* (1826).
Dugdale: Dugdale, Sir William, *Monasticon Anglicanum* (1830).
Falk: Falk, Bernard, *The Bridgewater Millions* (1942).
Kennet: Kennet, White, *Parochial Antiquities* (1818), 2 vols.
Knowles: Knowles, David, *The Religious orders in England*, 3 vols. Cambridge University Press (1948).
Knowles and Hadcock: Knowles, D. and Hadcock, R. N., *Medieval Religious Houses: England and Wales* (1971).
Lipscomb: Lipscomb, G., *History and antiquities of the County of Buckingham*, 3 vols. (1847).
Newcome: Newcome, P., *The history of the Abbey of St. Alban* (1795).
Todd: Todd, H. J., *The history of the College of Bonhommes at Ashridge* (1823).

BM: British Museum
CR: Calendar of Charter Rolls
CRO: County Record Office
DNB: Dictionary of National Biography
EGB: Egerton archives, Belton House
HMC: Historical Manuscripts Commission
LP: Calendar of State Letters and Papers
LRS: Lincoln Record Society
Pap. Reg.: Calendar of Papal Registers—Papal Letters
PR: Calendar of Patent Rolls
PRO: Public Record Office
SP Dom.: State Papers: Domestic series
VCH: Victoria County History

* An asterisk against a reference indicates that the quotation in the text to which it refers is reprinted by courtesy of the publishers or agents.

Chapter 1. A Modern College

1. 'The hutments were then leased again for use by the Public Record Office as a Repository, and have so remained since, although their vacation is now in prospect'.

2. *Ashridge Journal* (Jan. 1947), vol. 135, 2.
3. Street, Pamela, *Arthur Bryant: portrait of a historian* (1979), 128-134.
4. The Ashridge (Bonar Law Memorial) Trust Act (1954).

Chapter 2. The College of Bonhommes

1. Fowler, Sir James, *History of Beaulieu Abbey* (1911), 175. A mark was worth one third of a pound.
2. Holinshed, R., *Chronicle of England* (1577).
3. I am obliged to Mr. F. S. Green, of Dagnall, Herts, for this account, which he copied from a skin parchment found at Ashridge before 1920, but not now identified. A similar version is found as a note in an Ashridge scrapbook at Belton House.
4. This story is ascribed to the historian, William of Malmesbury, *c.* 1135.
5. Todd, 4.
6. Chaucer, Geoffrey, *The Pardoner's Tale*.
7. Todd, 4(r).
8. Bryant, Sir A. *The Medieval Foundation*, Collins, 88-9.*
9. In 1953 a series of medieval wall paintings was discovered in a room in some old cottages at 68, Piccotts End, Hemel Hempstead. The pictures, dated as being about the year 1500, are of religious subjects and suggest that originally there was a hostel for pilgrims here. The location is roughly half-way between the shrine of the martyr at St. Albans and the College of Bonhommes at Ashridge, within whose lands the cottage was situated. See *Hertfordshire Archaeology* (1973), vol. 3, 78-89.
10. Knowles, D., *op. cit.*, vol. 1, 7.*
11. Thompson, A. H., *Visitations in the Diocese of Lincoln, 1517-1531*, LRS vol. 33, xxii(n).
12. Bryce, J., *The Holy Roman Empire* (1864, 1966), 209.
13. Roche, T. W. E., *The King of Almayne* (1966).
14. Midgeley, L. M., *Ministers' Accounts of the Earldom of Cornwall, 1296-1297* (1942-5), vol. 1, 184, 199, 251.
15. Todd, H. J., *op. cit.*, 9, gives the date of death as 1 Oct. 1300.
16. Smith, L. J., (ed.) *Leland's Itinerary in England and Wales* (1964), vol. i, 104.
17. Newcome, P., *op. cit.*, 301
18. VCH Bucks., vol. 1, 386.
19. *Ibid.*, 386.
20. CR, II, 324-5.
21. Todd, 15.
22. VCH Bucks, vol. 1, 386.
23. *The Register of Bishop Sutton, 1280-1289*, LRS, vol. 48, 160.
24. Newcome, *op. cit.*, 302.

25. Chettle, H. F., *Downside Review* (1949), vol. LXII, 44.
26. Todd, 58-9.
27. Mullinger, J. Bass, *Encyclopaedia of Religion and Ethics*, ed. by J. Hardinge, vol. IX.
28. Romier, Lucien, *A History of France* (1962), 88-9.
29. Leland, J., *op. cit.*, vol. II, 23-4.
30. Knowles, D., *op. cit.*, vol. II, 23-4.
31. Todd, 10. *Fraxinei dorsi per eum novus ordo virescit.* 'On account of him the new order of Ashridge grows green'. From an epitaph on Edmund of Cornwall by a monk of Ashridge or Hailes.

Chapter 3. The Foundation of a College

1. Yaxlee, Susan (ed.), *History of Hemel Hempstead* (1973), 3-4.
2. CR, vol. II, 325.
3. Dugdale, Sir W., *op. cit.*, vol. VI, pt. 1, 515-517.
4. Fuller, Thomas, *Worthies of England* (ed. by J. Freeman, 1952), 233.
5. CR, vol. II, 324. This is marked as a vacated charter, but see Chap. 2, p. 32, ante.
6. CRO Herts., AH 918, 919.
7. CR, vol. II, 324.
8. *Ibid.*, 384, 385.
9. *Ibid.*, 463, 464.
10. *Cal. of Close Rolls* (18 Edw. I), 9 Jul. 1290.
11. PR (19 Edw. I).
12. Cal. Inquisitions (Chancery) Misc., vol. I, 1366.
13. PR (14 Edw. I).
14. Cobb, F. H., *History and Antiquities of Berkhamsted* (1893), 18.
15. Bryant, Sir A., *The Age of Chivalry*, Collins (1963), 18.*
16. PR (19 Edw. I).
17. Chauncy, Sir H., *op. cit.*, 479.
18. Lipscomb, G., *op. cit.*, 440-1.
19. Kennet, W., *op. cit.*, vol. I, 440.
20. Pap. Reg., vol. I (1198-1304), 573.
21. *Ibid.*, vol. II (1305-1342), 43.
22. *Ibid.*, vol. V, 432.

Chapter 4. The Cloistered Life

1. *New Catholic Encyclopaedia* (1967), vol. I.
2. Todd, 13(iv), *Tunicas griseas.*
3. *Ibid.*, 14. Todd relates that the body of one so wrapped, with lead over his dress, was discovered in digging for the foundation of a building at Ashridge 'a few years since'.
4. *Black Prince's Register*, Part IV (1351-1365), 105.
5. *Ibid.*, 105 (folio 60d).
6. *Ibid.*, folio 116.

7. *Ibid.*, 21 Feb. 1359.
8. Thompson, E. R. (ed.), *Chronicon Anglias (1328-1388)* (1874), 20.
9. Leland, J. *op. cit.*, vol. II, 23-4.
10. *Ibid.* II, 104.
11. *Ibid.* I, 304.
12. Dugdale, Sir W., *op. cit.*, vol. VI, 1345.

Chapter 5. Change and Achievement

1. Todd, 21, 23d.
2. Kennet, W., Vol. I, 426.
3. *Memoirs of the Verney family* (1907), 2 vols., vol. I, 40.
4. Todd, 22.
5. Riley, H. T. (ed.), *Chron. rerum gestarum in Mon. S. Albani* (1871), vol. I, 34.
6. Myers, A. R. (ed.), *English Historical Documents*, vol. V, 621.
7. Knowles, D., *op. cit.*, vol. I, 280-3.
8. Riley, H. T. (ed.), *Gesta Abbatum Mon. S. Albani* (1867-9), 3 vols., vol. III, 262-6, 433.
9. McKisack, M., *The Fourteenth Century, 1307-1399* (1959), 308.
10. Todd, 58-9 gives a list of these.
11. Translation by Vicars Bell.
12. British Library, Royal Mss., 3DVI.
13. *Ibid.*, 7FXI.
14. *Ibid.*, 15CXVI.
15. Todd, 21, 23d.
16. In John Rylands Library, Manchester.
17. *Athenae Oxon* (1813), vol. I, 269-73, and DNB.

Chapter 6. Decline and Fall

1. Knowles and Haddock, *op. cit.*, 254.
2. Pap. Reg. vol. II, 73.
3. *Ibid.*, vol. VII, 305-6.
4. *Ibid.*, vol. IX, 267.
5. *Ibid.*, vol. IX, 638.
6. *Ibid.*, vol. IX, 544.
7. Hill, R. M. T. (ed.), *Ordination lists of Bishop Sutton, 1290-1299*, LRS (69), 1, 9, 14, 35, 48.
8. VCH Bucks, vol. I, 389.
9. Knowles, D., *op. cit.*, vol. III, 4.
10. *Visitations of religious houses in the Diocese of Lincoln*, LRS (7), vol. I, xxx.
11. Lincs Archives, 2/7.
12. LRS (35), 73.
13. *Ashridge Quarterly*, vol. I(5) (1948), 231.
14. *The Court Book of Bishop William Attwater*, LRS (61), 16-17.

15. *Ibid.*, 59; and VCH Bucks, vol. IV, 244, 580.
16. LRS (35), 71.
17. Skelton, John, *A Garland of Laurel* (1523).
18. Lincs Archives 2/17.
19. LRS (35), 73.
20. LP Foreign and Domestic, vol. II (1531-2), 20-23 Hen. VIII.
21. This could have been sent before his arrival.
22. A reference to the very deep well.
23. Hackett, F., *Henry VIII* (1946), 27.
24. *Ibid.*, 294.
25. Myers, A. R. (ed.), *English Historical Documents*, vol. V, 621.
26. Raleigh, Sir W., *History of the World* (1614).
27. Newcome, P., *op. cit.*, 305; and Todd, 26-7.
28. PRO, Deputy Keeper's Report, vol. VIII, Appx. 9; and Chauncy, *op. cit.*, 479-480.
29. Newcome, P., *op. cit.*, 304; and Todd, 27 (vi).
30. Todd, 25.
31. DNB.
32. DNB.
33. Hodgett, G. A. J. (ed.), *The state of the ex-religious and former chantry priests in the Diocese of Lincoln, 1547-74* (1959), LRS (53), 89, 96, 138.
34. Roche, T. W. E., *The King of Almayne* (1966), 197.

Chapter 7. The Young Tudors and Ashridge

Background reading

The following are the main sources consulted:

Hackett, Francis, *Henry the Eighth* (1946).
Jenkins, Elizabeth, *Elizabeth the Great* (1958).
Luke, Mary, *A Crown for Elizabeth* (1971).
Mumby, Frank, *The Girlhood of Queen Elizabeth* (1909).
Neale, J. E., *Queen Elizabeth* (1934).
Strickland, Agnes, *Lives of the Queens of England* (1868) vol. 3.
Williams, Neville, *Elizabeth, Queen of England* (1967).

References

1. Knowles, D., *op. cit.*, vol. III, 260.
2. Baskerville, G., *English monks and the suppression of the monasteries* (1937).
3. Todd, 83.
4. *Ibid.*, 82-6, q. Exchequer Augmentations, 34 Hen. VIII.
5. *Hatfield Papers*, HMC, vol. II, 108.
6. Written from Hunsdon, May 1536.
7. Froude, J. A., *History of England*, vol. IV, 126.
8. Todd suggests that the naming of the western avenue in the park, Prince's Riding, may have been connected with this event.
9. Cussens, J. E., *History of Hertfordshire* (1879-81), vol. III, 138; Luke, M., *op. cit.*, 129.

10. SP Hen. VIII, vol. IX, DCCCI.
11. From St. James's, 31 July 1544. In Italian, Bodleian Library, the earliest surviving letter of Elizabeth, aged 11.
12. Dated 8 September 1544. Cottonian MSS.
13. LP Dom. Hen. VIII, vol. XIX(2), 726.
14. MS Cherry 36, Bodleian Library.
15. Swain, Margaret H., 'A New Year's gift from the Princess Elizabeth', *The Connoisseur* (1973, Aug.), 259.*
16. Jenkins, E., *op. cit.*, 26.
17. Harleian MSS 6986, 83 (British Library).
18. Neale, J. E., *op. cit.*, 26.
    The Ashridge and Hatfield household at this time was nominally under the control of Sir Walter Buckler, but was largely run by Thomas Parry (Williams, N., *op. cit.*, 23).
19. Ascham, Roger, *The Scholemaster* (1570).
20. PR Edw. VI, vol. III, 238.
21. *Ibid.*, vol. IV, 88-9. Todd's account (p. 31) differs slightly.
22. Harleian MSS 6986.
23. HMC 13th Report, Appx. Pt, 2,(1893). (Portman MSS II)
24. SP Dom. Mary (SP11) 3, no. 21; Strickland, A., *op. cit.*, III, 53; Mumby, F. A., *op. cit.*, 102-3.
25. Ashridge Library (original lease).

Chapter 8. The Lord Chancellor

Background reading

For the background to Chapters 8 to 11, *The Bridgewater Millions* by Bernard Falk (1942, out of print) is the only full length account of the Egerton family. It is a valuable source of fact and anecdote. It is not, however, free from bias and some of his judgements have been rendered unsound by the emergence of new archive material.

References

1. Todd, 32-3. The total of £1,189 19s. 10d. ignores a confusing discrepancy in Todd's record, suggesting an error in copying or printing. A further Inquisition into the value of Ashridge, made on 20 Oct. 1575 implies dissatisfaction with the earlier report. Carried out by a Commission under two of the Surveyors of the Queen's possessions, it shows a much lower assessment of some of the values, e.g.: the buildings, £363 13s. 4d.; the woods, £151 8s. 0d. Their report (Todd, 60-4) is in greater detail, and is referred to in Chap. 15 *ante*.
2. PR (14 Eliz. I) pt. VI, 2679.
3. Chauncy, Sir H. *op. cit.*, 480.
4. Falk, B. *op. cit.*, 31.
5. F. H. Egerton explained the motto by reference to a deed of 5 April 1603, in which the King signified that he wanted Sir Thomas Egerton to exercise the duties of Lord Keeper *until*

the royal wishes were better known. On 3 May 1603 at Broxbourne the King confirmed his wishes in person. Thomas Egerton was created Baron Ellesmere on 19 July, and a few days later was made Lord Chancellor.

6. Egerton, F. H., *Life of Thomas Egerton* (1801), 98.
7. Todd, H. J., 35-6.
8. CRO Herts., Priv. Coll., Ashridge, II, 3.
9. Todd, H. J., 38-9.
10. *Ibid.*, 64-5.
11. *Ibid.*, 39.
12. *Hatfield Papers*, vol. 21, 130. From a letter to his neighbour at Hatfield, the Earl of Salisbury, dated 11 Oct. 1609.

Chapter 9. The Earls of Bridgewater (1617-1701)

1. The Lady Frances Stanley was descended on her mother's side from Henry VII, who married Elizabeth Plantagenet of York.
2. Some purists have held that in spelling the title of Bridgewater, the first 'e' should be omitted. Examination of MS letters of the 2nd and 7th Earls show that the 'e' was more often used. Todd, in one letter uses both forms. For simplicity I have followed the conventional spelling.
3. *The Topographer* (March 1790), 139-140.
   The DNB (Milton) suggests that the location was more likely to have been Harewood, in Middlesex, close to their mother's home.
4. CRO Herts, AH 996, 1007.
5. HMC 5th Report (1876), Pt. I, 90.
6. Kingston, A., *Hertfordshire during the Great Civil War* (1894).
7. EGB, Belton. There are other letters in CRO Herts.
8. SP Dom. (1651), 155.
9. Todd, H. J., 47-56.
10. *Regulations for the Household of Sir Thomas Egerton*, *c.* 1603. In the Huntington Library, San Marino, Cal. Ellesmere MSS, EL 1179, 1180. Not seen by the author but quoted by Mark Girouard in his valuable study, *Life in the English Country House* (1978).
11. Todd, 45.
12. CRO Herts, AH 1060.
13. Pepys, Samuel, *Diary*, 30 Dec. 1667.
14. Portman MSS, vol. II, 388.
15. Chauncy, Sir H., *op. cit.*, 484.
16. Churchill, Sir W., *Marlborough: his life and times*, Harrap (1947), vol. I, 202-3.*
17. *Verney Memoirs*,(1907), vol. II, 388.
18. Luttrell's Diary, 1678-1714 (1857), vol. II, 399.
19. EGB, Belton.
20. Todd, 67.

Chapter 10. The Dukes of Bridgewater (1701-1748)

1. Green, D., *Sarah, Duchess of Marlborough* (1967), 196.*
2. *Ibid.*, 238.*
3. *Ibid.*, 239.*
4. *Ibid.*, 259.*
5. Dobree, B., *Sarah Churchill* (1927), 86.
6. Sloane MSS, 260, 263. British Library.
7. *Ibid.*, 261.
8. Falk, B., *op. cit.*, 86.
9. Malet, H., *Bridgewater: the Canal Duke, 1736-1803* (1977), 32.

Chapter 11. The Canal Duke (1748-1803)

Background reading

The most complete study of the 3rd Duke is *Bridgewater: the Canal Duke, 1736-1803*, by Hugh Malet, Manchester Univ. Press, 1977, which is a development of his earlier biography *The Canal Duke* (1961), reinforced with much additional archive material and new evidence. A good short guide is to be found in *The Duke of Bridgewater's Canals*, by Frank Mullineux, published by the Eccles and District History Soc. (1959, reprinted 1975).

References

1. Malet, H., *op. cit.*, 4.
2. Horace Walpole to Sir Horace Mann, 14 May 1761.
3. Egerton MSS, Tatton Park, Cheshire. Quoted by F. Mullineux, *op. cit.*, 9.
4. Malet, H., *The Canal Duke* (1961), 32.
5. Espinasse, F., *Lancashire Worthies* (1874), 254-293.
6. Young, Arthur, *A Tour through the North of England* (1770).
7. Yarranton, A., *England's improvement by sea and land* (1669), vol. I, 64.
8. Rees, Abraham, *Cyclopaedia of Arts, Sciences and Literature* (1919), vol. 16.
9. CRO Northants. Ellesmere Brackley MSS, EB 1459.
10. CRO Northants. General Accounts of the Duke of Bridgewater. Book 'D', 1760-1790. EB 1460.
11. Malet, H., *op. cit.*, 1977, 56.
12. CRO Northants. EB 1460.
13. CRO Northants. EB 1459.
14. Egerton, F. H., *A Letter . . . upon Inland Navigation* (1820), 72.
15. Rees, A., *op. cit.*, vol. 16.
16. CRO Northants. EB 1461.
17. Gower, Lord Granville Leveson, *Private Correspondence, 1781-1821*, vol. I, 71.
18. Cust, Lionel, *The Bridgewater House Collection of Pictures* (1903).
19. CRO Herts. AH 1834.
20. British Library. Additional MSS, 34568, 345.

21. EGB. Catalogues, annotated with prices realised.
22. D'Israeli, Isaac, *Curiosities of Literature* (1893), 344.
23. Grieg, J. (ed.), *The Farington Diaries* (1922-28), vol. II, 72-3.
24. EGB. 'Account of the debts, funeral expenses and legacies of Francis, Duke of Bridgewater, deceased . . .'.
25. Ecclesiasticus, 44, v. 7.
26. Lord Ellesmere, *Essays* (1858).

Chapter 12. Brotherly Discord

1. EGB. John William Egerton (JWE) to Francis Henry Egerton (FHE), 5 April, 1803.
2. Todd, 93 and Appx. III.
3. CRO Herts. *Diaries of William Buckingham*, D/EX 230/Z.
4. *Annual Register, 1824*, 81.
5. Home Office, Mil. Corres. (HO 50), 73, 336.
6. In the possession of Mr. Geoffrey Buckingham, his great-great-grandson.
7. *The Banks Letters*, ed. by W. H. Dobson, BM (1958), 822.
8. *MSS of the Earl of Verulam*, HMC (1906), 179.
9. Davis, R. W., *Political change and continuity, 1760-1885: a Buckinghamshire study* (1972), 16.
10. Bryant, Sir A. *Protestant Island* (1966), 138, 158.
11. Buckingham Diaries, *op. cit.*
12. *Cornhill Magazine, 1861*, 348-9.
13. Buckingham Diaries, 24 May 1813.
14. In his will he left directions and the sum of £3,000 for the care of his mother's hair and her last letter to him. These are now in the possession of Lord Brownlow at Belton.
15. EGB. F. H. Egerton, MSS Letters, vol. 1.
16. R.S.A. *Transactions*, vol. XVIII.
17. Egerton, F. H., *Life of Thomas Egerton* (1801).
18. EGB. FHE to JWE, 23 June, 1806.
19. *The Banks Letters, op. cit.*, 515.
20. EGB. FHE to JWE. 23 June 1806.
21. A contrasting case is of interest. The Rev. Thomas Gilbert, son of John Gilbert, had been presented by the Duke of Bridgewater with the living of Little Gaddesden, Herts, but was removed from it by his Bishop in 1812 for failing to reside there and carry out his duties.
22. EGB. FHE to JWE, 21 Aug. 1815, and JWE's reply, 4 Sept. 1815.
23. EGB. JWE to FHE, 19 April 1818.
24. Francis Egerton purchased a house in Little Gaddesden, belonging formerly to a Miss Maberley, but later decided that it was too damp for his manuscripts. He conveniently omitted to refer to his brother's offer of a house in Berkhamsted for the same purpose.
25. EGB. JWE to FHE, 26 March 1821.

26. EGB. FHE to JWE, 11 August 1821.
27. EGB. JWE to FHE, 28 August 1821.
28. This extract is reproduced by kind permission of Mr. Geoffrey Buckingham.
29. *Annual Register*, Jan. 1824, 81.
30. Falk, B. *op. cit.*, 182.*
31. The memorial was designed and sculpted by Sir Richard Westmacott; called 'The Mid-day Rest', it is regarded as one of the sculptor's best pieces.
32. CRO Herts. AH 2495, 2568, 2578, 2589, 2600, 2641, 2642, 2648, 2656, 2668.
33. CRO Herts. AH 2477-8.
34. British Library. Stowe MSS 163, fol. 226-9.
35. CRO Herts. AH 2442-2550.
36. CRO Herts. AH 2528.
37. I am indebted to the Rev. Canon H. Senar, Rector of Little Gaddesden, for this note about re-interment.
38. *Annual Register, 1851*, 388-392.
39. Lady M. Alford MSS Letters, Belton.
40. *Annual Register, 1853*, 296-308.

Chapter 13. Grace Abounding

1. Leveson Gower, Sir G., *Years of Content*, John Murray (1940), 15.*
2. Moneypenny, W. J., and Buckle, G. E., *Life of Benjamin Disraeli* (1910-20), vol. IV, 420.
3. Preserved at Belton House.
4. *The Times* (1866), 10, 16, 17, 22 Feb. and 10 March.
5. Lord Eversley, whose book, *Commons, Forests and Footpaths* (1910) is quoted by P. C. Birtchnell in *A short history of Berkhamsted* (1972), 96. See also Whybrow, G. H., *History of Berkhamsted Common* (1934).
6. Alford, Lady M., *Berkhamsted Frith or Common and Ashridge*, privately printed, 1878.
7. Inglis-Jones, E., *Augustus Smith of Scilly* 1969, chap. 11.
8. Leveson Gower, G., *op. cit.*, 14.*
9. *Little Gaddesden Parish Magazine*, Mar. 1888; Aug. 1891.
10. Leveson Gower, G., *Years of Endeavour*, John Murray (1942), 84.*
11. *Complete Peerage* (1912), vol. II, 350c. Letter dated 10 Mar. 1876.
12. From an Ashridge scrapbook at Belton.
13. Remembered by Miss Pearl Wheatley.
14. Sitwell, Constance, *Bright Morning*, Jonathan Cape (1942), 37.*
15. Masterman (ed.), *Mary Gladstone, her diaries and letters* (1904), 100.
16. Leveson Gower, G., *op. cit.*, 60.*
17. Nicolson, N., *Mary Curzon*, Weidenfeld and Nicolson (1977), 39.*
18. Bell, Vicars, *Little Gaddesden: the story of an English village* (1949).

19. I am indebted to Miss P. Wheatley for this recollection of an event at which she was present.

Chapter 14. A Change of Guardianship

1. Sitwell, Constance, *Bounteous Days* (1976), 69-71.
2. Yarrington, W., *The history of Stained Glass* (1848), 69; Rackham, B., 'The Ashridge Stained Glass', *Old Furniture*, Sept. 1928, 33-36; *Jnl. of Brit. Soc. of Stained Glass-painters*, 1928, 210-11; James, M. R., *Notes of Glass in Ashridge Chapel*, (1906).
3. *The Times*, 1928, 14, 15 June; 14 Aug.
4. Ramsden, J., *The age of Balfour and Baldwin, 1902-1940* (1978), 65-6, 174. See also Blake, R. H. W., *The Unknown Prime Minister* (1955).
5. Rhodes James, R. (ed.), *Memoirs of a Conservative: J. C. C. Davidson's memoirs and letters* (1969), 290.

Chapter 15. The Mansion and Gardens

1. CRO Herts. AH 2770.
2. Todd, 60-4 (in Latin).
3. Todd, 59. Willis's letter has not been traced, but Todd gives some details.
4. Derek Linstrum, in his book, *Sir Jeffry Wyatville: architect to the King* (1972), states that Wyatville remodelled the lodge in 1803-4.
5. *The Topographer* II (3), Mar. 1790, 143, gives the measurements as 44ft. by 22ft., quoting an Addendum by Richard Gough to Camden's *Britannia*, vol. I, 519,i in which the writer says, 'they appeared to us to be larger'. Lyson's *Magna Brit.*, vol. I, Pt. 3, 492, gives the same dimensions. I prefer to follow the more complete report of the Inquisition of 1575 (see note 2 above), which accords more closely with the dimensions of the Undercroft still remaining.
6. Portman MSS, vol. II, 306.
7. *The Topographer*, *op. cit.*, 132-154.
8. Todd, 58-9, gives a list of the paintings that could be identified.
9. Todd, 66d, suggests that the author, who is un-named, was the Rev. Stebbing Shaw, a historian of Staffordshire.
10. The first sale, held on 26, 27 June and 9-11 July 1800, yielded £1,481; the second, from 12-14 August 1802 brought in £1,439. (Catalogues, Belton)
11. The first sermon was preached in the Chapel in November 1817 by the Rev. H. J. Todd.
12. Pevsner, N., *Hertfordshire* (rev. ed. 1977), 238.
13. Puckler-Muskau, Prince von, *Tour in England, Ireland and France, 1828-29* (1832), 199.
14. Gunnis, R. (ed.), *Dictionary of British Sculptors* (1951).

15. Crook, J. M., and Port, M. H., *History of the King's Works*, vol. VI, 1782-1851, chap. 3.
16. Grieg, J. (ed.), *The Farington Diary* (1922-28), vol. VIII, 178.
17. Sir Richard Westmacott (1775-1856) designed and executed, between 1815 and 1823, the eight figures of founders and benefactors of the monastery, which are set at first floor level. His statue of Edward VI was completed when the house was first occupied in 1814. Another figure, of Elizabeth I, completed in 1815, was set outside in a niche on the south-east terrace beyond the library. It was removed in the 1920s, when Ashridge was being sold, and its present location has not been traced.
18. Staffordshire Archaeol. and Hist. Soc. *Transactions*, XIX (1977-8), 33.
19. Boase, T. S. R., *English Art, 1800-1870* (1959), 67-8.
20. Morshead, Sir Owen, *Windsor Castle* (1957).
21. Hibbert, C., *The Court at Windsor* (1964), 163.
22. The first payment to Digby Wyatt is found in a Summary of Accounts for 1857. 'To Mr. Wyatt for work at Billiard Room, £178 1s. 9d.'.
23. *Dora Carrington: her letters and diaries* (1961), 163.
24. The original spire was taken down in 1922 as being in a dangerous condition. It was restored in 1969, when an exact replica, constructed of fibre-glass, was lifted into position by helicopter on 6 June.
25. Pask, Eric, 'The Organ at Ashridge', *The Organ*, LI (202), Oct. 1971, 58-65.
26. Portman MSS, II, 306.
27. Kalm, P., *Visit to England, 1748* (1892), 228.
28. Bell, Vicars, *Little Gaddesden* (1949), 117-9.
29. Lipscomb, G., *op. cit.*, vol. III, 447.
30. Related to me by Mrs. Ella Storer, of St. Albans. Mr. Jones was an uncle of her mother.
31. Repton, Humphry, *Fragments on the theory and practice of Landscape Gardening* (1816). Fragment XXVIII.
    For further reading, a reliable short account is *Humphry Repton*, by Kay N. Sanecki (1974).
32. Linstrum, D., *op. cit.*, 229.
33. Buckingham Diaries.
34. *Cornhill Magazine*, 9 Sep. 1876. 'There is now a sheet of water in the park, but the place is undoubtedly *sine flumine vivo*.'
35. Belton Library.
36. A more complete description of the present garden is contained in an illustrated booklet, *The Gardens at Ashridge* by Kay N. Sanecki, published by the College, 1975.

Appendix I

Lincs Archives, 4/12 Box 92.

Short Guides

Bryant, Arthur, *The Story of Ashridge* (1929). Out of Print.
Gordon, Henry, *This is Ashridge* (1949). Out of print.
Langridge, Derek, *A Guide to Ashridge past and present* (1960). O.P.
Coult, Douglas, *Ashridge: a short guide* (1971, 2nd ed. revised, 1979).

General articles (periodicals)

Country Life (1898), 5 and 12 Nov.; (1921) 6 and 13 Aug.

INDEX